Moral Complexities in Turn of the Millennium British Literature

Moral Complexities in Turn of the Millennium British Literature

Mara E. Reisman

LEXINGTON BOOKS
Lanham • Boulder • New York • London

Published by Lexington Books
An imprint of The Rowman & Littlefield Publishing Group, Inc.
4501 Forbes Boulevard, Suite 200, Lanham, Maryland 20706
www.rowman.com

86-90 Paul Street, London EC2A 4NE

Copyright © 2023 by The Rowman & Littlefield Publishing Group, Inc.

All rights reserved. No part of this book may be reproduced in any form or by any electronic or mechanical means, including information storage and retrieval systems, without written permission from the publisher, except by a reviewer who may quote passages in a review.

British Library Cataloguing in Publication Information Available

Library of Congress Cataloging-in-Publication Data

Names: Reisman, Mara E., author.
Title: Moral complexities in turn of the millennium British literature / Mara E. Reisman.
Description: Lanham : Lexington Books, [2023] | Includes bibliographical references and index. | Summary: "This book offers a critical analysis of morally complex social, political, and cultural issues in novels by Kazuo Ishiguro, Patrick McGrath, Graham Swift, Andrea Levy, and Jeanette Winterson. It examines how the work illuminates intricacies of human experience, encourages political engagement, fosters communication, and facilitates social change"—Provided by publisher.
Identifiers: LCCN 2022036886 (print) | LCCN 2022036887 (ebook) | ISBN 9781793648464 (cloth) | ISBN 9781793648471 (epub)
Subjects: LCSH: English fiction—20th century—History and criticism. | English fiction—21st century—History and criticism. | Literature and morals—Great Britain—History. | English literature—Social aspects—History. | Ethics in literature.
Classification: LCC PR830.M67 R45 2023 (print) | LCC PR830.M67 (ebook) | DDC 823./9209353—dc23/eng/20220922
LC record available at https://lccn.loc.gov/2022036886
LC ebook record available at https://lccn.loc.gov/2022036887

∞^{TM} The paper used in this publication meets the minimum requirements of American National Standard for Information Sciences—Permanence of Paper for Printed Library Materials, ANSI/NISO Z39.48-1992.

To my wonderful family and friends

Contents

Credits		ix
Introduction		1
1	History, Morality, and Social Responsibility in Kazuo Ishiguro's *The Remains of the Day*	11
2	Destabilizing Institutional and Social Power in Patrick McGrath's *Asylum*	45
3	The Language of Transgression and Empathy in Graham Swift's *The Light of Day*	73
4	Negotiating Identity and Building Community in Andrea Levy's *Small Island*	95
5	Subverting Cultural and Political Power in Jeanette Winterson's *The Daylight Gate*	129
Conclusion		151
Bibliography		157
Index		167
About the Author		175

Credits

Excerpt(s) from ASYLUM by Patrick McGrath, copyright © 1997 by Patrick McGrath. Used by permission of Random House, an imprint and division of Penguin Random House LLC. All rights reserved.

Excerpts from *Asylum* by Patrick McGrath, copyright © 1997 by Patrick McGrath. Reprinted by permission of ICM Partners.

Chapter 2 is derived in part from an article published in *Critique: Studies in Contemporary Fiction* 58.2 (2017) copyright Taylor & Francis, available online: http:tandfonline.com/10.1080/00111619.2016.1178099.

This work was funded by the Northern Arizona University Research Investment Fund.

Introduction

Two important trends in recent British literature are an attention to social justice and an interest in morally complex issues. *Moral Complexities in Turn of the Millennium British Literature* examines this dual focus in books by five British writers whose work consistently addresses complex social and moral issues: Kazuo Ishiguro, Patrick McGrath, Graham Swift, Andrea Levy, and Jeanette Winterson. A common concern in their books is the relationship between language, power, and moral judgments. What further connects these authors is their belief that literature has a moral function in relation to social change and social responsibility. Reflecting their shared interest in social justice, these authors consciously situate their fiction in talks and in interviews in terms of the social and political power that literature can have.

In this book, I address moral issues in two different ways: how novels by Ishiguro, McGrath, Swift, Levy, and Winterson engage with morally complex social, political, and cultural issues and how these novels serve a moral function by challenging readers to be socially engaged and to understand their world and other people in new and empathetic ways. The books in this study—Ishiguro's *The Remains of the Day* (1989), McGrath's *Asylum* (1996), Swift's *The Light of Day* (2003), Levy's *Small Island* (2004), and Winterson's *The Daylight Gate* (2012)—exemplify this focus on moral complexity and social change. They also offer a valuable lens through which to examine issues of morality and social responsibility in the context of twentieth- and twenty-first-century British politics and culture. In choosing these texts, I have picked books that address a diverse range of complex issues often associated with moral judgments: war, racism, adultery, maternal neglect, mental illness, murder, suicide, professional misconduct, witchcraft, and religion. Although these books cover a wide variety of topics and their settings range from the seventeenth century to the late twentieth century, they include similar arguments about how empathy, personal responsibility, and civic engagement can create more productive social relations.

The 1980s, where this study begins, were characterized by a conservative political and economic agenda, cuts to welfare programs, increasingly restrictive immigration policies, personal self-interest, and social apathy. The ideological, economic, cultural, and political divisions created by these policies and attitudes continued to develop in 1990s and in the twenty-first century. In a 1997 interview with Eleanor Wachtel, Winterson addressed the social and economic inequalities and feelings of helplessness that people were experiencing at the turn of the millennium. "We have to fight against the disintegration of society," she urged, "which is happening not just here but in many places in the world, and unless we fight against it, it will certainly happen, and then all the forces of reaction and of money and of power will take over."[1] Winterson contends that literature and art can play an important role in improving this cultural climate. As she tells Wachtel:

> I think that art can make a difference because it pulls people up short. It says, don't accept things for their face value; you don't have to go along with any of this; you can think for yourself. It gives you a kind of self-reliance. We all feel powerless and we can't really manage to do anything because there's just so much. I want to try and cut through those feelings of apathy and powerlessness and be a kind of rallying point, offer a rallying cry, to people who would otherwise feel dispossessed.[2]

Winterson's call to action continues to resonate in the twenty-first century.

The same issues of inequality, social breakdown, powerlessness, and dispossession that Winterson described in this interview became an important part of the 2016 EU referendum discussions. The UK's vote to leave the EU and the subsequent Brexit negotiations revealed a deeply divided society and a profound lack of consensus about the UK's national identity, its relationship with Europe, and its place in the world. The vote may have been a decisive and pivotal event, but as Winterson's words suggest, the problems it represented were not new. Kristian Shaw makes a similar point when he argues that the referendum "marked a critical moment at which the politicized narratives surrounding devolution, immigration, Englishness, austerity and Euroscepticism reached breaking point, bringing to the surface tensions which had been bubbling under the surface of British society for decades."[3]

Since the 1980s and 1990s, Ishiguro, McGrath, Swift, Levy, and Winterson have been addressing these pervasive and deep-seated cultural divisions in their work by showing how narratives that shape people's lives and social expectations are constructed and legitimized and by presenting alternative models for personal, social, and political relationships. Reflecting their concerns about power, inequality, and social divisions, they use their writing to reveal and upset literary, cultural, and political fictions and to promote social engagement. In these ways, they challenge readers to question what seem to be entrenched beliefs and fixed power structures.

An important part of their literary strategy is to encourage readers' thoughtful skepticism, but these authors share the view that their role is not to tell their readers what to think or how to act. Swift articulates these points when he argues:

> I don't think novels are there to provide an authority on things, in the sense of giving clear answers to questions about what people should do and how they should live and what the world should be like. I think novels are saying, over and over again, none of us really knows those things; none of us has clear answers to so many questions. I think I raise doubts and I raise questions all the time, but I'm not in the business of giving authoritative answers.[4]

Instead of being prescriptive, the authors in this study hope their work initiates productive, empathetic, and engaged conversations about complex issues; facilitates readers' better understanding of their world and of others; helps them consider alternative ways of looking at the world; and encourages them to come to their own conclusions about important personal, political, and moral issues.[5]

Swift links the development of empathy and understanding to the imagination, which he sees as integral to the moral function of literature. In an interview with Catherine Bernard, Swift argues: "I think that whatever else novels do . . . they do fulfill a highly moral function. . . . [A]ll real morality, rests on doing what a novelist makes a specialty of—that is, attempting to get inside the experience of others. . . . Imagination is the basis of morality."[6] Related to the moral potential of the imagination, curiosity is another way of encouraging readers to learn more about themselves, about others, and about their place in the world in relation to others. Echoing Swift's ideas about the moral role of fiction, author Angela Carter maintains that the moral function of the novel should not be "horatory in any way—telling people how to behave."[7] Instead, she contends: "I would see it as a moral compunction to explicate and to find out about such things. I suppose I would regard curiosity as a moral function."[8]

Curiosity is precisely what Ishiguro advocates as an ethical strategy in *The Remains of the Day*. He conveys this idea through the character of Reginald Cardinal, who understands that curiosity is not just about gathering information but, more importantly, about being engaged with and caring for others and that these qualities are the key to being a politically, morally, and socially responsible individual. Swift's novel *Waterland* also connects social consciousness and personal engagement to curiosity. History teacher Tom Crick, the narrator of *Waterland*, articulates the importance of an engaged relationship with the world when he implores his students to "be curious." He then explains that "[n]othing is worse (I know it) than when curiosity stops. Nothing is more repressive than the repression of curiosity. Curiosity begets love. It weds us to the world. It's part of our perverse, madcap love for this impossible planet we inhabit. . . . How can there be any true revolution till we know what we're made of?"[9] Curiosity, Crick suggests, is an essential element for creating social change and for positively shaping the future.

Recognizing the enervating effects of apathy and the revolutionary potential of engagement, Ishiguro, McGrath, Swift, Levy, and Winterson understand the crucial role that literature can play in getting readers to consider new ideas and to become socially aware. Contemporary readers, argues Levy, are especially attuned to how literature can help to create personal, social, and political change, and one of the things that they want from literature is for it to function in this pedagogical way. In particular, she points to the increasing popularity of books that are "telling you about how other people live" and which offer "insight into understanding how people think and feel in another culture or another country."[10] Levy believes that this experiential learning can result in improved relationships between people. Addressing the particular discrimination, hostility, and intolerance experienced by the Muslim community in England but also considering the idea of cultural and national prejudices more broadly, Levy contends that "people who are decent minded want to understand. There are a lot of people who really, really don't want to be prejudiced, and one of the ways not to be is to get some sort of understanding of what it feels like to be someone else, or from somewhere else. I think that fiction, novels and memoir can really help people with that."[11] As Levy suggests, part of readers' attraction to and "hunger for" books that teach them more about the lives of other people is their desire to become more socially responsible human beings.[12] The starting point for this personal, social, and national transformation is communication and an openness to new ways of thinking.

One of the biggest impediments to change and to productive communication is guilt. However, as Levy points out, finding a solution to this problem is particularly important, because a large part of "the history of the Caribbean and the British Empire is about . . . guilt and not engaging," and this lack of engagement between individuals and nations has resulted in divisive and dysfunctional social and political relationships.[13] Levy believes that "truth and reconciliation" is the way to move forward from this problematic history and the means to change the future.[14] Applying these ideas to her fiction, Levy provides a truthful look in her novels at Britain's colonial history and its social and economic effects. She also offers models for reconciliation based on empathy and engagement, and she represents the personal and community benefits of people trying to understand a perspective beyond the one they have been taught. The larger goal of Levy's literary approach is to encourage readers to see that their lives are intimately connected to the lives of other people. She hopes that, ultimately, this awareness will allow people "to live in a country free from racism and social divisiveness."[15]

Like Levy, McGrath and Winterson recognize the importance of coming to a new understanding of human behavior as a way to facilitate social and political change. In his work, McGrath makes even his morally suspect characters understandable by laying bare the social structures and hierarchies that shape their lives and that influence how others judge them. He also uses the unreliable narrator to upset readers' preconceived ideas about moral authority. Through both of these strategies and through his attention to language, McGrath disrupts the conventional connection between moral authority and power. Winterson disrupts this connection in her novels as well. By revealing how power is naturalized and how it can be used to perpetuate social injustices, she shows (like Levy) that real moral authority comes from seeing one's life as connected to rather than in competition with others.

In the following chapters, I address the complex moral and social concerns depicted in Ishiguro's, McGrath's, Swift's, Levy's, and Winterson's books and the related issues about language, power, community, politics, and social justice. Despite their diverse characters, settings, and plots, the moral and social issues depicted in their books are in dialogue with one another. This ideological and narrative engagement offers more intricate and nuanced understandings of the moral issues that each author addresses individually and provides additional ways of thinking about complicated social problems.

Chapter 1, "History, Morality, and Social Responsibility in Kazuo Ishiguro's *The Remains of the Day*," examines how the moral issues of personal and social responsibility in regard to war and fascism are addressed in Ishiguro's book and in the 1993 Merchant-Ivory film adaptation. In an interview with Gregory Mason, Ishiguro explains that he is particularly interested in "people who, in all sincerity, work very hard and perhaps courageously in their lifetimes toward something, fully believing that they're contributing to something good, only to find that the social climate has done a topsy-turvy on them by the time they've reached the ends of their lives. The very things they thought they could be proud of have now become things they have to be ashamed of."[16] In *The Remains of the Day*, Ishiguro's point about how a society's changing values affects individuals applies both to Lord Darlington and to his butler, Stevens, the latter of whom is trying to figure out his place in the world in light of evidence that Lord Darlington was a Nazi sympathizer. Both the book and the film show the characters' closely held beliefs being tested, and the depictions of the past and present show the instability of these belief systems over time. Rather than providing a definitive judgment about Stevens's and Lord Darlington's moral characters, the book and the film provide a range of responses to difficult ethical questions that encourage audiences to think critically about their own beliefs. What Ishiguro proposes as a solution to the question about how to contribute to the creation of a better world in times of conflict and instability is not a specific perspective or answer but instead a responsible engagement with the world. He does not expect individuals to get everything right, because "the values of society are always in flux."[17] However, he does believe it is important for people to make an effort to be aware of the world around them and to understand that, because the world is constantly changing, they need to remain engaged with and responsive to these changes. This view is exemplified by Lord Darlington's godson, Reginald Cardinal, who argues that curiosity (which symbolizes an engagement with the world), concern for others, and a willingness to act on one's own beliefs are all necessary in order to be a socially responsible individual.

Chapter 2, "Destabilizing Institutional and Social Power in Patrick McGrath's *Asylum*," addresses how institutional and social power structures are established, maintained, and perpetuated in 1950s British society. Like *The Remains of the Day*, *Asylum* focuses on social values being in flux in post–World War II Britain. McGrath then shows how these values are constructed and naturalized. In *Asylum*, McGrath chronicles the relationship and aftermath of an illicit love affair between Stella, the wife of a forensic psychiatrist and deputy superintendent at a hospital for the criminally insane, and Edgar, a patient who has been convicted of murdering, decapitating, and enucleating his wife. This relationship and McGrath's fictional depiction of Broadmoor Lunatic Asylum provide the lens for his commentary on the politics of mental illness, marriage, and motherhood in late 1950s Britain. Through explicit comparisons between mental health patients and women, mental health professionals and husbands, and mental health institutions and the institution of marriage, McGrath highlights the problems with women's lives, marriage, and motherhood within a system that mirrors the hierarchies of the asylum. *Asylum* also offers a critical examination of how deviant behavior, ranging from unconventional to criminal, is defined and judged based on traditional ideas about gender and power. In this chapter, I argue that McGrath emphasizes the parallels between mental institutions and marriage in order to expose the social and gender inequalities of both institutions that often are masked by a philosophy of benevolent paternalism and by naturalized power relations. I further argue that McGrath's use of an unreliable and pathological narrator is crucial to his argument about power and gender. The shift in the reader's perception about psychiatrist narrator, Dr. Peter Cleave, from a wise and kind father figure to a deluded and dangerous individual emphasizes McGrath's indictment of Peter and his misused power as well as his indictment of the society that unquestionably grants authority to people in Peter's social and professional position. More importantly, McGrath's unreliable narrator is meant to unsettle readers' entrenched social beliefs and to make them rethink their moral judgments about paternalism, mental illness, criminal insanity, and deviant women.

Chapter 3, "The Language of Transgression and Empathy in Graham Swift's *The Light of Day*," offers a critical analysis of the relationship between language, morality, and empathy in Swift's novel *The Light of Day*. As Swift explains in an interview, these issues are connected in terms of their personal and social impact. He argues that "empathy is the beginning of sympathy, sympathy is the beginning of compassion, and compassion is where morality really accrues. . . . To get out of yourself is empathy. It might lead on to better and greater things."[18] In *The Light of Day*, Swift's detective narrator, George Webb, is committed both professionally and personally to this empathetic philosophy of imaginatively understanding the experiences of others. Through George's narrative perspective, Swift depicts multiple stories of transgression related to adultery, murder, and professional misconduct. Each of these transgressive acts carries with it a set of moral assumptions about good and bad behavior and good and bad people. Swift problematizes this binary view of the world, because it has a divisive effect on people and relies on what Winterson describes as "false choices."[19] Among his narrative strategies to disrupt this type of worldview, Swift offers multiple ways of looking at transgressive acts that unsettle simple moral judgments about them. Swift also shows the role that language plays in perpetuating conventional moral views about transgression. I argue that Swift's careful attention to language upsets a prescriptive way of thinking about morality that effectively encourages readers to empathize with other perspectives and people. In contrast to the personal and social divisions that moral judgments perpetuate, Swift's writing encourages connections between people and helps to create a less divided world. A world free from harmful cultural divisions is precisely what Andrea Levy tries to facilitate through her fiction as well.

Chapter 4, "Negotiating Identity and Building Community in Andrea Levy's *Small Island*," addresses how Levy uses food and domestic space as a way to engage with important issues of national identity, race, and class in early to mid-twentieth-century Britain. With its present day setting of 1948, *Small Island* documents the complex relationship between Britain and its colonies in this postwar period and in the decades leading up to the war. *Small*

Island also engages with issues of immigration and racism as Levy depicts the mixed reception received by the Windrush generation who came to England after World War II seeking social and economic opportunities. Levy's approach to these political and social issues is to complicate them rather than to present a single point of view. By revealing the historical, cultural, and class factors that have shaped each of the main characters—the Jamaican born Gilbert and Hortense and the English born Queenie and Bernard—and by giving each character the chance to narrate his or her story, Levy treats with understanding her characters' flaws and prejudices and portrays the complexities of their worldviews. Levy's representations of food and domestic space also reveal the characters' views about race, class, and national identity; how they understand their place in a changing society; and how the socially ingrained power structures to which they have been committed can be disrupted and dismantled. In *Small Island*, food acts as a method of communication and mediation between individuals that allows for the renegotiation of personal relationships and the reformation of divisive institutional, social, and political structures. Like all of the authors discussed in this book, Levy uses her writing to encourage readers' empathy in order to build a better, more cohesive community.

Chapter 5, "Subverting Cultural and Political Power in Jeanette Winterson's *The Daylight Gate*," examines the connections between language, power, and morality in Winterson's novel *The Daylight Gate*. Like Levy does in *Small Island*, Winterson reveals the historical, cultural, and class factors that have shaped each of the characters in order to help readers better understand the characters' beliefs about the world. One of the central concerns in all of Winterson's work is how power is institutionalized and legitimized through social conventions and through cultural and historical narratives. *The Daylight Gate* continues her project of destabilizing social, political, and gender conventions. In this book, Winterson uses the seventeenth-century Pendle Hill witch trials as a lens to investigate questions of power and to examine the complex relationship between power and morality. I argue that Winterson's depiction of the historical, social, and political issues surrounding these witch trials reveals the arbitrary nature of power and subverts a moral authority based on traditional power structures. Through her representation of the social and political hierarchies in seventeenth-century Lancashire, Winterson illuminates the problems of institutionalized power inequalities. She also challenges a binary way of thinking about power and morality and suggests that moral power is not linked to one's place in the social or economic structure but instead is correlated with one's beliefs and actions. In *The Daylight Gate*, moral authority is represented by the characters who make conscious decisions not to cause harm to others, even in order to save themselves. This form of selflessness is predicated on seeing oneself as connected to rather than divided from other people, and this relational identity is crucial to creating a socially responsible world.

At their most basic level, stories are a form of communication between individuals and an effective way to convey new ideas. The ability of stories to make people engage intellectually and emotionally is also what makes stories so powerful. In the contemporary cultural climate, the transformative capacity of art is critical. "The arts," argues Winterson, "aren't a leisure industry—the arts have always been an imaginative and emotional wrestle with reality—a series of inventions and creations. A capacity to think differently, a willingness to change our understanding of ourselves. To help us to be wiser, more reflective, less frightened people. . . . [I]magining alternatives is what we [artists] do."[20] In their books, Ishiguro, McGrath, Swift, Levy, and Winterson articulate different stories about the world, but their shared goal is to facilitate connections and communication between people and to offer new ways of thinking about personal, social, and political relationships. They do so through the stories they tell, their decisions about narrative, and their empathetic approach to their characters. Their literary interventions that engage with morally complex issues continue to make an important contribution to discussions of morality, ethics, identity, and social responsibility in the present moment as individuals attempt to address social and political divisions in order to secure a better future for everyone.

NOTES

1. Jeanette Winterson, interview by Eleanor Wachtel, *Malahat Review* 18 (1997): 71. Winterson has also addressed these ideas about social disintegration and dispossession in relation to the 2016 EU referendum. The vote to leave the EU, she argues, was the result of "the absolute failure of the neoliberal Project Few, whereby capitalism has been hijacked to serve the rich, where investing for the long term has been replaced by short-term profiteering and where globalisation has been allowed to wreck local economies in the name of free trade. Too many people in Britain face no future at all—no security at work, no certainty of a home, diminishing access to education and resources" (Winterson, "We Need to Build a New Left"). To address this socio-economic divide, Winterson proposes a joint political and literary solution: a "new left alliance for the 21st century" that unites people rather than divides them and "better stories" that imagine and articulate alternative ways to achieve this change.

2. Winterson, interview by Wachtel, 71.

3. Kristian Shaw, *Brexlit: British Literature and the European Project* (New York: Bloomsbury Publishing, 2021), 23. For more on post-Brexit literature that addresses the social, national, and political divisions that Shaw describes, see Shaw, Eaglestone, and Everitt.

4. Graham Swift, quoted in Fiona Tolan, "Graham Swift," in *Writers Talk: Conversations with Contemporary British Novelists*, ed. Philip Tew, Fiona Tolan, and Leigh Wilson (London: Continuum, 2008), 127.

5. This position accords with the ideas of Fay Weldon, another British writer interested in issues of justice, morality, and ethics, whose "objective is not to write a morality tale—despite the moral questions presented [in her work]—but rather to keep the moral ground in flux so that readers continually rethink their belief systems" (Reisman, "Shifting Moral Ground," 647).

6. Graham Swift, interview by Catherine Bernard, *Contemporary Literature* 38, no. 2 (1997): 224.

7. Angela Carter, quoted in John Haffenden, "Angela Carter," in *Novelists in Interview* (New York: Methuen, 1985), 96.

8. Ibid.

9. Graham Swift, *Waterland* (New York: Vintage Books, 1992), 206.

10. Andrea Levy, interview by Blake Morrison, *Women: A Cultural Review* 20, no. 3 (2009): 333.

11. Ibid. The prejudices against the Muslim community that Levy describes in this 2009 interview only intensified in the following decade. Kristian Shaw argues that the denigration of Muslims became an entrenched part of the referendum narrative: "British political and public discourses during the referendum involved a disproportionate and irrational concentration on two main groups: Eastern Europeans and Muslims. While economic anxieties were attached to Eastern Europeans (particularly after the 2008 economic crisis), security concerns were associated with Muslim immigrants. The more general public demagoguery of Muslim communities within Britain became increasingly ethnically coded and such discursive prejudice was driven home by the right-wing press during the referendum campaign" (Shaw, *Brexlit*, 32).

12. Levy, interview by Morrison, 333.

13. Andrea Levy, interview by Charles Henry Rowell, *Callaloo* 38, no. 2 (2015): 270.

14. Ibid.

15. Andrea Levy, "This Is My England," *The Guardian*, February 19, 2000.

16. Kazuo Ishiguro, interview by Gregory Mason, *Contemporary Literature* 30, no. 3 (1989): 339.

17. Ibid., 344.

18. Swift, interview by Bernard, 224–25.

19. Jeanette Winterson, quoted in *Bill Moyers on Faith and Reason: Jeanette Winterson* (Films Media Group, 2006).

20. Jeanette Winterson, *12 Bytes: How We Got Here, Where We Might Go Next* (New York: Grove Press, 2021), 279.

Chapter One

History, Morality, and Social Responsibility in Kazuo Ishiguro's *The Remains of the Day*

In contrast to the enterprise culture encouraged by Thatcherism, many British authors in the 1980s emphasized the importance of social responsibility in their texts. Kazuo Ishiguro's Booker Prize–winning novel, *The Remains of the Day* (1989), is part of this literary trend and addresses what it means to be a socially and morally responsible individual in the twentieth century. In *The Remains of the Day*, Ishiguro uses pre– and post–World War II settings as a way to explore how moral beliefs shift and how the definition of social responsibility can change over time.

The prewar 1920s and 1930s past of the novel includes discussions about the efficacy and fairness of the Versailles Treaty, the rise of fascism, the British government's policy of appeasement, and the involvement by some members of the upper classes in political affairs. In the postwar 1956 present of the novel, Stevens, Lord Darlington's butler and the book's sole narrator, is trying to make sense of his life in the face of contemporary judgments that his employer was a Nazi sympathizer. Because Stevens believes he contributes "to the creation of a better world" not through direct action but through service to a gentleman who possesses great moral stature, the shift in society's judgment of Lord Darlington means that Stevens must rethink his identity and his beliefs.[1] Addressing difficult positions like Stevens's, Ishiguro explains to Graham Swift: "I'm interested in this business of values and ideals being tested, and people having to face up to the notion that their ideals weren't quite what they thought they were before the test came."[2]

Ishiguro's characters often face complex moral dilemmas and must work through the question "What happens if you give your energies and idealism to something which turns out to be rather foul?"[3] Through his depictions of Lord Darlington and Stevens, Ishiguro shows that people may desire to help humanity and to create a better, more just world but may not always be right about how to achieve these goals or be able to predict how their contributions to society might be used. Only retrospectively does Stevens acknowledge that Lord Darlington's actions were mistaken and dishonorable, and this new understanding puts Stevens in a difficult position in regard to his own complicity. Without Lord Darlington as his moral compass, Stevens must find a new way to give his life meaning, and his narrative is an attempt to convince himself and others that his behavior was, if not ethical, at least reasonable and dignified from a professional perspective. The reinterpretation of Lord Darlington's political involvement, Stevens's political and professional loyalty to Lord Darlington, and the British government's foreign policies form the shifting moral ground in *The Remains of the Day*.

In this chapter, I consider how questions of personal and social responsibility and morality are addressed in Ishiguro's book and in the 1993 Merchant-Ivory film adaptation. In particular, I address how the different representations of the characters, the shift in narrative perspective, and the changes in the time period affect readers' and audiences' understanding of the moral issues. The book and the film show characters' closely held beliefs being tested, and the depictions of the past and present settings show the instability of these belief systems over time. Collectively, the book and film offer a broader range of views about personal responsibility, social justice, and politics than either does on its own. My focus in this chapter is on moments in the book and in the film where ideological conflicts are foregrounded, and I address the characters' expressions of values and ideals and their actions in these complex historical moments. The scenes I discuss in detail are the following: (1) the three-day international Conference at Darlington Hall, including pre-Conference activities and the last dinner (1923 in the book; 1935 in the film); (2) the dismissal of the Jewish housemaids, including the added depictions in the film of Mr. Benn and his employer, Sir Geoffrey Wren (1932 in the book; 1936 or 1937 in the film); and (3) a small post-Conference meeting at Darlington Hall with high-ranking British and German officials (1936 in the book; 1938 in the film).[4] Despite its careful attention to moral issues, I argue that *The Remains of the Day* does not prescribe a particular worldview. Instead, by showing how different characters negotiate these complicated matters, *The Remains of the Day* offers a model for engaging with and living in the world that is socially responsible and that can adapt over time.

This adaptability is crucial to Ishiguro's ideas about the social and political function of literature. He maintains that although his stories have specific settings, he uses these locations to depict "universal metaphors."[5] This literary strategy encourages readers to see that the issues and problems he addresses "are happening over and over again" and that the stories he tells "can be applied to all sorts of human situations."[6] It also allows his work to accumulate meaning as the universal stories in *The Remains of the Day* about national identity, Britain's relationship with Europe, and its place in the global community remain relevant to twenty-first-century society and politics.[7]

The Conference at Darlington Hall to address the economic and social conditions in Germany following World War I is one of the pivotal political events in *The Remains of the Day* and sets up the ideological concerns about individual and social responsibility that permeate the book. Christine Berberich connects Lord Darlington's and his peers' interest in post–World War I politics to their class position. She argues: "Many members of the aristocracy longed for a strong leader to take Britain back to her former imperial glory, but there was also the sense that the Versailles Treaty went against England's perceived principles of fair play."[8] In *The Remains of the Day*, this dual set of interests gives rise to the Conference that Lord Darlington hosts. The specific goal of the Conference is to revise some of the harshest terms of the Versailles Treaty in order to help Germany recover politically and economically after the war. The larger goal is to establish greater stability in Europe. The twenty conference delegates, who are in a position to influence their countries' political policies, come from diverse backgrounds and have different reasons for aiding Germany, which include ensuring political and economic stability, facilitating social justice, and being morally responsible. Despite their varying motivations, the delegates are unified by a desire to create positive change and to preserve peace.

As the sole narrator, Stevens's memory of and reporting on the Conference significantly shapes the book's depiction of Lord Darlington's involvement in post–World War I foreign policy, and Stevens's presentation of the political issues has moral implications. Stevens prioritizes Lord Darlington's political views and highlights his noble intentions when he explains that Lord Darlington's interest in these great affairs comes from his "deep sense of moral duty" and "a desire to see justice in this world."[9] Because Lord Darlington's speech is the only one at the Conference that Stevens fully hears, understands, and presents to readers, Lord Darlington's moral position is foregrounded.

In his opening speech, Lord Darlington describes his postwar visits to Germany, where he witnessed the country's economic crisis and the effects of this economic instability on its citizens. Drawing on this firsthand know-ledge and wishing to alleviate the suffering he has seen, Lord Darlington makes a "strong moral case for a relaxing of various aspects of the Versailles treaty."[10] Lord Darlington's friendship with Karl-Heinz Bremann, which developed out of gentlemanly respect for one another even though they were on opposing sides during the war, also motivates him to advocate for political change. These details emphasize that Lord Darlington's personal and moral motivations are his primary reasons for supporting political change while specific foreign policies are only a secondary concern.

The other delegates to speak on the first morning of the Conference in favor of amending the Versailles Treaty include the Englishman David Cardinal, Lord Darlington's staunchest political ally, and representatives from Germany. Stevens observes that David Cardinal's "general gist seemed to be close to his lordship's, concluding with a call for a freezing of German reparation payments and the withdrawal of French troops from the Ruhr region."[11] Stevens's alignment of Cardinal's speech with Lord Darlington's perspective results in reinforcing Lord Darlington's ideas rather than adding depth to the political discussion. In addition, Stevens's absence for much of Cardinal's speech and his contention that what he does hear is too technical for him to fully comprehend mean that readers are only privy to an impression of Cardinal's ideas and miss potentially important details about the economic and social situation in Germany.

Stevens's professional duties prove even more detrimental to readers' understanding of German politics. The information might be crucial to the Conference proceedings, but Stevens is unable to represent this national perspective, because he must attend to other household matters. He leaves the room during the speech by one German gentleman and misses all of the German Countess's speech. When Stevens returns to the drawing room, there is an open discussion and debate about interest rates and commerce that is beyond his understanding and, therefore, remains unarticulated. Stevens's absences and inability to fully describe the content of these discussions effectively silences Germany's voice at the Conference. The result is that in these discussions about international relations any debate or disagreement regarding Germany's politics is kept to a minimum, and Lord Darlington's vaguer policy of goodwill continues to be foregrounded. These examples represent Stevens's rhetorical strategy more generally: he prioritizes Lord Darlington's views either by suppressing any that might conflict with Lord Darlington's or, as I will discuss, by presenting opposing views as wrong or unsound.

The political views of the French delegate, M. Dupont, are among the perspectives that are both silenced and maligned through Stevens's narrative. Early on, Stevens undermines M. Dupont's credibility when he articulates Lord Darlington's negative views about the French delegate. As Stevens recounts, Lord Darlington characterizes M. Dupont's French nationalist politics as "despicable," "increasingly barbarous," and the "most intransigent as regards releasing Germany from the cruelties of the Versailles treaty."[12] These depictions of France's punitive attitude toward Germany reveal Lord Darlington's and the other delegates' suspicion that M. Dupont will represent a dissenting view when it comes to revising France's foreign policy in regard to Germany. Even though France's support is vital to implementing the political goals of the Conference, Stevens does not represent M. Dupont's voice directly until the closing dinner when M. Dupont's views are better aligned with Lord Darlington's position.

At the closing dinner of the Conference, delegates from England, France, and America articulate their national commitments in light of the Conference discussions. Although France gets a voice here, Germany's position continues to be unrepresented in favor of the more powerful victor nations. The effect is threefold: (1) It makes Germany's political position less important than those of the countries trying to help it; (2) it makes readers more sympathetic to Lord Darlington's position, because Germany's nationalist, military, and expansionist policies are left unspoken (unlike in the film, where this rhetoric is included); (3) it keeps the discussion of foreign policy at the Conference focused on moral ideals rather than complicated political negotiations.

This latter point is evident in Lord Darlington's opening remarks at the dinner when he expresses his desire "to see good prevail" and proposes a toast to "peace and justice in Europe."[13] Lord Darlington's words emphasize his idealism; however, his lack of specificity about foreign policy suggests that he wields influence without fully understanding the intricacies and implications of his political agenda. Cynthia Wong points out that both Lord Darlington and Stevens are "[u]nable to foretell the probable harm that their allegiances might cause to a yet unknowable future. . . . They espouse their ideals with limited knowledge of a much larger picture. For Darlington, appeasement of German powers might stifle an impending war; for Stevens, good service to Darlington is of utmost importance to ensuring world peace. For both, service to a national cause is the order of the day."[14] Whether it is on a personal, national, or global scale, the difficulty of knowing the best course of action at a particular moment in time is one of the moral complexities addressed in *The Remains of the Day*.

M. Dupont, who speaks after Lord Darlington, addresses how one's cultural, national, and historical position affects the answer about what political approach is best. He contends that the other delegates' criticism of France's current foreign policy and attitude toward Germany shows a lack of understanding about the wartime atrocities that were committed in France. However, he acknowledges that the current situation in Europe is "very complex."[15] For this reason, he came to the Conference without a fixed agenda so that he could hear and consider other opinions. Although M. Dupont contends that there remain "differences of interpretation" about what is occurring in Europe at that moment, he maintains that he has listened carefully to what the other delegates have said, been impressed by certain ideas that were presented, and is convinced of the "justice and . . . practicality" of the main arguments made at the Conference.[16] M. Dupont may continue to hold some discordant political views, but he keeps these dissenting thoughts to himself in the interest of peace and progress. By the closing dinner, he is willing to support a more lenient position in regard to Germany and pledges to advocate for political change in France. Even if it is hard to determine the right policy toward Germany, M. Dupont offers a thoughtful model for how to approach the matter: one must listen to the ideas of others and be open to changing one's position.

M. Dupont's point about the importance of listening to other perspectives underlies his criticism of Mr. Lewis, who he believes comes to Darlington Hall with an inflexible political agenda. M. Dupont closes his speech by offering a personal and political condemnation of Mr. Lewis for taking advantage of Lord Darlington's hospitality and for "spend[ing] his energies solely in trying to sow discontent and suspicion."[17] He argues that people like Mr. Lewis "are not only socially repugnant, in the climate of our present day they are extremely dangerous."[18] The danger to which M. Dupont refers is the risk of renewed international conflict. He sees Mr. Lewis's divisive and deceitful behavior as a threat, because the destruction and loss of life caused by World War I are still too fresh and peace too tenuous. No one wants another war, and appeasement has not yet been shown to be a bad policy. Although M. Dupont is vehement about Mr. Lewis's poor behavior, he also tries to minimize Mr. Lewis's influence by discrediting him politically and personally. He claims that Mr. Lewis's opinions are less enlightened than those of other American officials that he knows, and he ends his speech with deliberate provocation when he implies that Mr. Lewis has been making disparaging remarks about the other delegates.

Rather than addressing M. Dupont's accusations, Mr. Lewis, who speaks next at the dinner, focuses on the current political issues. In particular, he argues that idealism, noble instincts, and good intentions do not always result in good foreign policy and that the actions of gentlemen amateurs can be irresponsible and have dangerous consequences. For these reasons, Mr. Lewis contends that international affairs should be left to politically experienced individuals, and he ends his speech with a toast to professionalism. Showing that he is alone in this perspective, no one except Mr. Lewis drinks to his approach to foreign policy. Mr. Lewis may sow discord at the Conference and in his dinner speech, but he tries to make people think critically, and airing disparate views is part of this process.

Lord Darlington closes the discussion by offering a rebuttal to Mr. Lewis's comments that indicates his continued commitment to what Ishiguro describes as an "English gentlemanly fair play ethic."[19] Lord Darlington redefines Mr. Lewis's assessment of gentlemanly political involvement as honorable rather than amateurish and goes on to argue that professionalism rather than amateurism is the problematic political approach. To Lord Darlington, professionalism means "cheating and manipulating" and "serving the dictates of greed and advantage rather than those of goodness."[20]

Mr. Lewis and Lord Darlington represent different national and class positions and present two distinct perspectives on how Europe and its allies should negotiate and work with Germany. Lord Darlington is a gentleman, committed to what Peter Childs describes as "the concept of *noblesse oblige*: the traditional belief that those in a socially privileged class have an obligation to be honourable and generous."[21] Mr. Lewis is a professional politician, who takes a more pragmatic approach to politics. Their disagreements about professionalism, Germany, and politics represent one of the primary ideological conflicts in the text, and as Lord Darlington's words about "goodness" and "justice" versus "cheating and manipulation" reveal, there exists a moral component to these political discussions. Further emphasizing this moral aspect, Stevens's depictions of the two men underscore that Lord Darlington's position is just, right, and honorable and that Mr. Lewis's views are dangerous and immoral.

Stevens first casts aspersions on Mr. Lewis's character when he recounts an informal pre-Conference meeting where Mr. Lewis is present. Among the topics of discussion are the differences between English and French views of Germany, and Mr. Lewis's questions and observations on the matter make Lord Darlington and his colleagues uncomfortable. Stevens marks this moment as the beginning of his feeling that Mr. Lewis was less honest than he appeared. Subsequently, Stevens makes repeated note of Mr. Lewis's covert, suspicious, and devious behavior and argues that Mr. Lewis's attention to M. Dupont is a ploy to turn the Frenchman against Lord Darlington and the other delegates. Stevens's proof is an overheard conversation between M. Dupont and Mr. Lewis. Although Stevens himself is acting covertly by eavesdropping, he makes a professional excuse for his behavior. He also claims that the secretive tone of Mr. Lewis's voice made him immediately suspicious and that the words he overhears confirm his opinion of Mr. Lewis's duplicitous character. Signaling that he only will be providing information that supports his position, Stevens begins his recitation with "[i]n effect" before summarizing the content of Mr. Lewis's remarks.[22] This summary eliminates any specific details that could be interpreted differently by someone else. Even though history would prove Mr. Lewis right about conceding too much to Germany, Stevens's account of Mr. Lewis's ungentlemanly manners in his private conversation with M. Dupont and his representation of M. Dupont's accusations about Mr. Lewis's abhorrent behavior at the final dinner work to situate Mr. Lewis personally, politically, and morally on the wrong side of the Conference discussions about negotiations with Germany.

The film complicates Stevens's depictions of Mr. Lewis and Lord Darlington and his presentation of the moral and political landscape through its larger narrative perspective (characters represent their views directly without Stevens serving as a narrative filter), its inclusion of more specific political details, and its temporal changes. The first two of these changes, the unfiltered portrayal of a wider range of political and ideological perspectives, add to the complexity of the political and national issues. In contrast, the depiction of a later time when the Nazis have more power makes the related moral concerns more clearly defined and accords with Robert Stam's contention that adaptations often "cleanse" a novel's "moral ambiguity."[23] In regard to the first Conference, the film shifts the setting from 1923, shortly after WWI, when another war seemed unthinkable, to 1935, when another war seems increasingly likely. Comparing the two settings allows audiences to consider how the same actions by Lord Darlington and Stevens in different time periods have dramatically different moral implications.

In particular, the film's later setting makes the extent and intent of Lord Darlington's involvement with the Nazis and Stevens's implicit support of Lord Darlington more problematic. In 1923, Lord Darlington's upper-class sense of fair play and effort to maintain peace can be understood as noble and well-intentioned. By 1935, his same ideas and actions seem not only naïve but also dubious and harmful. As Earl G. Ingersoll points out: "This decision to adjust 'history' . . . makes Lord Darlington even more clearly a dupe of the Germans than is the case in the novel where Darlington's view that the Versailles Treaty was a kind of slow capital punishment for Germany's 'crime' of being the enemy in the First World War would have been shared by many in England and elsewhere."[24] The film's representation of the political positions of the delegates at the Conference also shifts accordingly with the later setting.

A pre-Conference meeting that includes Lord Darlington and his allies reflects more dissenting views as it sets up the film's portrayal of the national tensions and political issues at the Conference. One focus of the group is to strategize about how to deal with some potentially disruptive delegates, including Mr. Jack Lewis, a young American congressman who is also a member of a foreign affairs committee, and the French delegate, M. Giscard Dupont D'Ivry. The pre-Conference meeting also addresses the current situation in Germany and reveals that Lord Darlington, who supports Hitler's leadership, and Reginald Cardinal, who questions Hitler's policies, hold opposing political views. In both the book and the film, Reginald Cardinal plays the same Conference role of secretary, but in the film he has more of a political voice. From the start, he is critical of Hitler's actions and of Lord Darlington's relationship with the Nazis. In the book, Cardinal does not question Lord Darlington's policy toward Germany or voice his dissent until the smaller post-Conference meeting at Darlington Hall; however, this change does not indicate a difference in the portrayal of Cardinal's character. Instead, it confirms the consistency of his political views, because the post-Conference meeting in the book and the first Conference in the film are both set in the mid-1930s, a time when Hitler's expansionist intentions and racial hygiene policies were becoming clearer.

At the pre-Conference meeting depicted in the film, Cardinal makes two significant objections to Lord Darlington's conciliatory policy toward Germany. Cardinal's first argument is about Germany's refusal to honor its agreements with other European countries. He contends: "I don't see how we can associate ourselves now with the Germans . . . with the Nazi Party. They have actually torn up and trampled on every single treaty and seem to be a worse threat than ever to the whole of Europe."[25] Cardinal's objection reflects the increasing power of the Nazi Party, Hitler's Chancellorship, and the threat posed by Germany's rearmament and open defiance of the Versailles Treaty. Lord Darlington dismisses these concerns with his narrow focus on the better economic conditions created by the Nazi Party. He notes that on a recent trip to Germany, he was pleased to finally see signs of rebirth in Germany and more prosperous German people. What Lord Darlington ignores is the cost of this "progress." This flaw in Lord Darlington's argument is Cardinal's second stated objection. "What about the Jews?" he asks.[26] The question resonates for the audience even more because it closes the scene and leaves time for thought during the transition to the next scene.

Revealing that Lord Darlington is not swayed by Cardinal's pre-Conference concerns, he opens the formal Conference with a speech about the benefits of a stronger Germany. Another delegate echoes Lord Darlington's views and argues that Europe needs to facilitate Germany's economic recovery by supporting "her fair demand for equality of armaments and universal military service for German youth." These speeches, which articulate more specific political details than in the book, indicate Lord Darlington's and the other delegates' political awareness and considered support for German nationalism. They are not merely proposing gestures of goodwill and fair play but are consciously advancing Hitler's political and social agendas. This active and knowing involvement is one of the ways the film demonstrates Lord Darlington's greater culpability.

The film also emphasizes the urgency and importance of Mr. Lewis's opposing political position. When M. Dupont leaves the room during the Conference speeches in order to get help from Stevens for his feet, Mr. Lewis follows on his heels in order to discuss a strategy to derail the proposed actions of the other delegates. The lengths to which Mr. Lewis is willing to go to solidify this political alliance is shown visually when Mr. Lewis begins to tend to M. Dupont's sore feet after Stevens is summoned to look after his ill father. Despite Mr. Lewis's efforts to create a diplomatic alliance between America and France so as to curb German expansionism and aggression, M. Dupont articulates a sympathetic position toward Germany. He explains to Mr. Lewis: "Germany wants peace as much as we do."[27] At the closing dinner, M. Dupont further contextualizes this position when he highlights Europe's shared experience of "the horrors of war" and the resulting desire never to experience them again.[28] Rather than calling out Mr. Lewis for his ungentlemanly behavior (as is the case in the book), the rest of M. Dupont's speech reflects his concern about maintaining peace. He emphasizes that he has been impressed by the goodwill he has witnessed at the Conference and has been convinced by the German delegates' speeches to amend the views he held before the Conference.

In another shift from the book, the film gives Germany a political voice through the Countess, the German representative to the Conference, and, later, through the German officials who visit Darlington Hall. The opinions of the Countess are given prominence at the final dinner when she gets to speak first. Physically and rhetorically, the Countess represents a soft, feminine, nonthreatening side of Germany. In her speech, she conveys this perspective through the descriptions of emotion that are intertwined with her political message. She observes that she has been heartened by the "spirit of goodwill that has prevailed. Goodwill for Germany."[29] Continuing to express her gratitude, she tells the delegates that it is *"with tears in my eyes*, I see that everyone here has recognized our right to be, once again, a strong nation. And *with my hand on my heart*, I declare that Germany needs peace and desires only peace."[30] The Countess's presentation of Germany's political agenda is filled with sentiment, but her mild tone masks the German aggression implied by her words about the country's right to be a strong nation. Her charming singing after dinner works in a similarly pacifying and sinister way. Ingersoll perceptively describes the Countess as the beguiling but dangerous Lorelei who "lure[s] the other representatives, with the exception of the American Lewis, into her trap."[31] In contrast to Lord Darlington and the other delegates who fall into this ideological trap, Mr. Lewis's ability to avoid it speaks to the film's portrayal of his ideas as sound, forward-thinking, and principled.

Mr. Lewis's final speech also reveals him to be prescient about the likelihood of further conflict with Germany and insightful about Hitler's agenda. The speech still includes a discussion of professionalism versus gentlemanly goodwill, but Mr. Lewis also offers a broader historical perspective on diplomatic relations with Germany. He argues that even if the goal of peace is noble, the personal and political consequences need to be carefully assessed. Expressing a view about this issue in line with Reginald Cardinal's earlier question about the human cost of Germany's economic recovery, Mr. Lewis contends: "the US doesn't want war," but "it doesn't care for peace at any price, because some prices are just too high to pay."[32] Mr. Lewis's words resonate with modern audiences who know from hindsight that his skepticism about Germany's political policies and about the efficacy of Lord Darlington's political involvement are well-founded.

This judgment is further reinforced in the film through Mr. Lewis's subsequent ownership of Darlington Hall. In the book, the new owner, a wealthy American named Mr. Farraday, is a character with no connection to the Conference or to any other part of the house's history. In the film, rather than the new owner only being emblematic of new American consumerism, economic power, and global influence, Mr. Lewis's acquisition of Darlington Hall also implies that the political views and values he articulates at the Conference are meant to take precedence over Lord Darlington's outdated ones.[33]

The film's opening similarly foregrounds the moral component of this victory and problematizes Lord Darlington's political involvement as Mrs. Benn's voiceover calls his reputation into question. She reveals that Lord Darlington has died and his heirs have put Darlington Hall up for sale. However, because there were no buyers, it is scheduled to be demolished. Although viewers soon find out that Mr. Lewis saves the house from destruction, the *Daily Mail*'s headline "Traitor's Nest to Be Pulled Down" accurately describes Lord Darlington's tarnished postwar image.[34] The paper and the public see him as having been complicit with the Nazis and his political negotiations with them as harmful, even treasonous, rather than well-intentioned.

Even Stevens must acknowledge that from the perspective of the 1950s present (1956 in the book; 1958 in the film) Lord Darlington's ideas are difficult to fathom and seem "rather odd—even, at times, unattractive."[35] Despite his understanding of the public's negative sentiments about Lord Darlington, Stevens still tries to reconcile Lord Darlington's fascist sympathies with his moral goodness. James Lang describes Stevens's conflict when he notes: "Stevens attempts to construct a narrative of Lord Darlington's life which can encompass both poles of the man's persona—the publicly reviled Nazi sympathizer and the privately kind and generous employer."[36] Although he expends considerable effort, Stevens cannot always reconcile these disparate images of Lord Darlington. His doubts about Lord Darlington's judgments and actions are evident in his internal dialogue and in his public defensiveness about Lord Darlington's character.

The dismissal of the Jewish housemaids is one of the moments that undermines Stevens's narrative about Lord Darlington's moral nature. Stevens may deny the significance and meaning of the event, but readers can see that his logic does not work. Stevens employs several strategies to defend Lord Darlington against charges that he dismissed two Jewish housemaids because he was anti-Semitic and supported fascism. First, Stevens tries to distance Lord Darlington from fascist organizations and ideas. He disputes accusations that Lord Darlington had a close association with Sir Oswald Mosley and the British Union of Fascists, claiming that Mrs. Carolyn Barnet was Lord Darlington's main connection with Mosley and this group. Stevens also makes the point that "Lord Darlington came to abhor anti-Semitism."[37] However, Stevens's wording belies his denial. That Lord Darlington "*came to abhor anti-Semitism*" implies that Lord Darlington was not always opposed to it, and his dismissal of the housemaids illustrates this point.

As his second strategy, Stevens tries to excuse Lord Darlington's anti-Semitic behavior and involvement with the Nazis by explaining the contemporary historical context. In regard to Lord Darlington's relationship with the German diplomat and Minister of Foreign Affairs, Joachim von Ribbentrop, Stevens argues that he was a popular figure in the 1930s and that many people were taken in by his charm. Stevens offers the same type of defense—other people were fraternizing with the Nazis—for Lord Darlington's trips to Germany where he accepted their hospitality. Stevens further argues that the change in public opinion is a retrospective historical revision. He notes that "[a]nyone who implies that Lord Darlington was liaising covertly with a known enemy is just conveniently forgetting the true climate of those times."[38] Rather than mitigating Lord Darlington's responsibility, Stevens's arguments reveal that Lord Darlington's involvement with the Nazis may not have been extraordinary, but it existed.[39]

Finally, Stevens tries to defend Lord Darlington's questionable views by minimizing them. Although Stevens maintains that the "allegations that his lordship never allowed Jewish people to enter the house or any Jewish staff to be employed" are "utterly unfounded," he concedes a precedent: "except, perhaps, in respect to one *very minor* episode in the thirties which has been blown up out of all proportion."[40] The "minor" employment episode to which Stevens refers is Lord Darlington's decision that there cannot be any Jewish people on staff at Darlington Hall. Like Stevens's observation about Lord Darlington's association with the Nazis, Stevens's exception shows that these allegations have an established basis and are not negligible.

Kathleen Wall argues that the structural disruption to the travel narrative section also signals the significance to Stevens of Lord Darlington's decision about the household staff. She observes: "The segment entitled DAY

History, Morality, and Social Responsibility 23

THREE—EVENING; *Moscombe, near Tavistock, Devon* begins not, as the other chapters do, with some mention of the present, but with Stevens's attempt at once again addressing Lord Darlington's attitude toward 'Jewish persons.' Stevens's total lack of pretense of keeping up his travel narrative calls startling attention to what follows."[41] What follows is Stevens's continued justification of Lord Darlington's behavior in regard to the dismissal of the housemaids. Stevens may intend to defend Lord Darlington's reputation, but his disclosures end up having the opposite effect: they reveal Lord Darlington's unethical behavior and Stevens's willful blindness.

Although Lord Darlington claims that having to let the housemaids go is "regrettable," he does so anyway. Then he tries to justify this decision by telling Stevens: "we have no choice."[42] Lord Darlington's rhetoric implicates everyone. His use of "we" rather than "I" signifies his belief that not only does he have no choice but also that Stevens, the rest of the household, and his gentlemen peers have no choice. Similarly, Lord Darlington's insistence that "[i]t's in all our best interests" is an attempt to make his decision more excusable, because it implies that his staffing directive is a political necessity and a social imperative rather than a personal choice.[43] Stevens's only response to Lord Darlington's order to terminate the housemaids' employment is "I beg your pardon, sir?"[44] Even if Stevens's question implies more than that he needs confirmation he has heard correctly, Stevens does not further challenge Lord Darlington. Similarly, Stevens may retrospectively claim that he was upset by the dismissal, but he does not voice his opinion at the time, and he dutifully carries out Lord Darlington's orders. In fact, Stevens seems more upset about informing the housekeeper, Miss Kenton, about the change in her staff than about the fate of the housemaids.

Stevens's acquiescence raises the question of whether Stevens is in a position to disagree with his employer. His refusal to carry out these orders could jeopardize his job, and because his job is an integral part of his identity, it also could threaten his sense of self. In addition, he trusts his employer to make morally correct decisions. According to Stevens, a butler of any worth must believe that his employer represents everything good and honorable. Because Stevens believes that Lord Darlington fits this ideal, he is willing to serve him with devotion, and his unquestioning professional loyalty is one of the ways that Stevens rationalizes his personal decisions.

Stevens also excuses his deference by maintaining that gentlemen inherently know more about the world than their staff. His rationale, which implies a class-based social hierarchy, illustrates Ishiguro's contention that "[t]he butler is a good metaphor for the relationship of very ordinary, small people to power."[45] Ishiguro's sympathetic depiction of Stevens reveals two conflicting ideas. Ishiguro shows the difficulty of acting in an extraordinary way and questioning authority while making the point that an individual's lack of power does not mitigate his or her social responsibilities. Comparing Stevens's reaction to Lord Darlington's decision to dismiss the housemaids to Miss Kenton's response emphasizes the complexity of the situation.

In contrast to Stevens's acquiescence, Miss Kenton openly objects to the dismissal of Ruth and Sarah and makes a personal and a professional appeal to save their jobs.[46] She also argues that Lord Darlington's decision is morally wrong. "Does it not occur to you," she asks Stevens, "that to dismiss Ruth and Sarah on these grounds would be simply—*wrong*? . . . a sin as any sin ever was one."[47] Rather than acknowledging Miss Kenton's point or letting her know that he shares her concerns, Stevens staunchly defends Lord Darlington's position by citing their employer's greater knowledge of the world and in particular of "the nature of Jewry."[48] Stevens may be content to defer to Lord Darlington's better judgment, but Miss Kenton is not and threatens to quit her job in protest. Although Miss Kenton ultimately does not leave Darlington Hall, which shows the difficulty of acting in an extraordinary way, her verbal objection and plan to act on her convictions represent another course of action that a staff member could take and highlight her different sense of social responsibility. Unlike Stevens, Miss Kenton realizes that her inaction has consequences. As Lydia R. Cooper argues, Miss Kenton "may have limited autonomy, but she understands her complicity and is able to identify immorality and reject its corrosive attitudes."[49] Miss Kenton's different response further suggests that Stevens's contention that he has no real choice in the matter is simply an excuse for his failure to act in a situation that calls for him to question convention and authority.

Moreover, Stevens does in fact make a choice when he carries out Lord Darlington's wishes and dismisses the housemaids. Peter Childs uses the Nuremberg trials to elucidate the moral implications of Stevens's willingness to comply with Lord Darlington's directive. He argues: "*The Remains of the Day* asks: to what extent did those who appeased or followed the Nazis believe they were doing good and to what extent could any individual abrogate moral responsibility by following the orders of their 'superiors'—which was the argument given by several German officers indicted for war crimes at the 1945-46 trials at Nuremberg, the setting of Nazi rallies in the 1930s and in particular of anti-Semitic decrees in 1935."[50] Childs's comparison of Stevens's actions to those of a Nazi enforcer suggests that Stevens bears some responsibility for what he does. Christine Berberich makes a similar point about Stevens's culpability when she argues: "The more pernicious collusion with the fascists in *The Remains of the Day* does not take place via the active support of Darlington, but through Stevens's unquestioning dedication to his master."[51] Both Berberich and Childs point to the dangerous potential of

Stevens's fixed ideas about duty, service, and loyalty. In the case of the housemaids, sending them away takes only a few minutes, but the consequences are enormous and irrevocable. When more than a year later, Lord Darlington decides that he wants to trace them and make amends, Stevens promises to try but he is not optimistic of success. The amount of time it took for Lord Darlington to realize "[i]t was wrong what happened" further demonstrates that his anti-Semitic views were not just a passing phase as Stevens has claimed.[52] In addition, Lord Darlington's use of ambiguous and neutral language in his admission, "what happened" was wrong and "one" would like to do something, extends his failure to take responsibility for his role in their fate.

When Stevens conveys Lord Darlington's new sentiments to Miss Kenton, he also puts this life-altering decision in benign terms when he characterizes it as a "terrible misunderstanding."[53] Stevens then recasts his reaction to the dismissal by claiming that he was as upset by what happened as Miss Kenton. Miss Kenton's memory differs significantly, and she challenges Stevens's self-representation: "As I recall you thought it was only right and proper that Ruth and Sarah be sent packing."[54] When Stevens protests and she asks why he did not express his concerns to her at the time, Stevens has no ready reply. He admits: "For a moment [I] was rather at a loss for an answer. Before I could formulate one, Miss Kenton put down her sewing."[55] That Stevens cannot "formulate" an answer quickly suggests his disingenuousness. Furthermore, when he does come up with an answer, it remains vague and evasive like Lord Darlington's. "Naturally," he says, "one disapproved of the dismissals."[56] Kathleen Wall suggests that Stevens's narrative shift from "I" to "one" indicates a kind of self-consciousness "when distance from a feeling or a judging self is operating, or when Stevens feels a need to erase some part of himself."[57] In this instance, Stevens's use of neutral language indicates both his continued refusal to take responsibility for his opinions and his desire to rewrite the past by erasing his personal feelings. Because Stevens's opinions shift as he attempts to portray Lord Darlington and himself in a better light, his truthfulness is hard to gauge. Questions remain: Did Stevens believe the dismissal was wrong at the time or does his change of heart simply reflect Lord Darlington's current perspective?

The film raises similar questions about Stevens's sincerity, but the narrative sequence involving the dismissal of the Jewish housemaids makes the moral judgment on Lord Darlington more explicit. The set of scenes I want to consider begins with the arrival of the two new housemaids, Elsa and Erma (Ruth and Sarah in the book), and ends with Stevens telling Miss Kenton about Lord Darlington's remorse for dismissing the young women. In the book, the housemaid sequence is compact: Lord Darlington decides to dismiss Ruth and Sarah, Stevens tells Miss Kenton about the dismissal,

Miss Kenton objects to the decision and threatens to leave, Stevens teases Miss Kenton about giving her notice, Lord Darlington expresses regret, and Stevens tells Miss Kenton about Lord Darlington's change of heart. In the film, a greater number of scenes make up the housemaid sequence. Among the additional scenes are the Moscombe scenes with Harry Smith, the Taylors, and Dr. Carlisle and a scene in which Stevens is being quizzed about politics by one of the guests at Darlington Hall. In the book, these scenes exist but are not connected through their proximity. Their different placement in the film offers an additional commentary on the dismissal of the housemaids. The scenes in the film's full housemaid sequence represent the people, political climate, and ideologies that influence Lord Darlington; provide a scathing commentary on Lord Darlington's treatment of the housemaids; reveal Stevens's complicity in Lord Darlington's actions; depict the larger implications of Lord Darlington's and other characters' support of Hitler; and demonstrate the far-reaching effects of an undemocratic society.

The sequence in the film begins with Lord Darlington using his German to welcome Elsa and Erma to Darlington Hall. Although their refugee status is made explicit later in the film, it is implied here through their gratitude for Lord Darlington's asylum.[58] At this point, Lord Darlington shows no reservations about having the young women work for him. However, in spite of this positive start, the housemaids' status in the house is destabilized in the next scene when Sir Geoffrey Wren arrives at Darlington Hall.

Sir Geoffrey is a character added to the film who articulates strong support for Hitler and for fascism. At a luncheon with Lord Darlington and several other politically powerful men, Sir Geoffrey describes the Race Laws of the fascists as progressive and sanitary measures. He also argues that every country needs a penal system and that the difference between prisons and concentration camps is merely a matter of semantics: "Over here we call them prisons. Over there they call them concentration camps. What's the difference?"[59] Sir Geoffrey may not see the difference, but the audience does, and this attempt at easy elision quickly alerts them not only to the danger that Sir Geoffrey represents but also to the danger of uncritically accepting the tenants of fascism. The inclusion of Sir Geoffrey's racist and anti-Semitic remarks makes clear that the gentlemanly way of dealing with the Nazis that Lord Darlington and many of his contemporaries supported is not innocuous. Sir Geoffrey's stated political opinions may be more extreme articulations of fascism than Lord Darlington's, but by showing Lord Darlington's support for Hitler, the film shows his good intentions and political naivete to be as harmful as Sir Geoffrey's zealotry. Including this scene between the arrival of the housemaids and their dismissal also implies Lord Darlington's tacit approval of Sir Geoffrey's ideas and his willingness to act on them.

One of the few characters who questions Lord Darlington's and Sir Geoffrey's fascist views is Sir Geoffrey's butler, Mr. Benn. Mr. Benn is a character in the novel, but he a shadowy figure who serves primarily as a love interest for Miss Kenton rather than as a political conscience. The film develops Mr. Benn's character in both of these regards. Although the fuller characterization of Mr. Benn is an important part of the film's romantic plot, my focus in this chapter is on the implications of Mr. Benn's expanded political role. Just as Sir Geoffrey offers a counterpoint to Lord Darlington that allows viewers to better assess Lord Darlington's opinions and actions, Mr. Benn serves as a counterpoint to Stevens and his views about service. In particular, Mr. Benn represents a challenge to Stevens's assertion that being a butler in a great house is incompatible with holding an opinion different from one's employer. In contrast to Stevens, Mr. Benn is outspoken about politics and about his employer's political views.

The film includes two scenes that highlight the ideological tensions between Mr. Benn and Stevens. One scene takes place in Stevens's parlor and is part of the sequence about the Jewish housemaids. The other takes place later in a pub with Miss Kenton. In both, Mr. Benn articulates his disagreement with Sir Geoffrey's politics. In the first scene, Mr. Benn has accompanied Sir Geoffrey to Darlington Hall. While the gentlemen upstairs discuss politics, Mr. Benn and Stevens enjoy some time to themselves. Admiring Stevens's comfortable situation at Darlington Hall, Mr. Benn observes that Stevens must be very content.[60] Stevens's reply, which focuses on his service rather than on his individual contentment, demonstrates his inability to separate his personal identity from his professional duties. For him, contentment means serving to the best of his abilities an employer who is "a superior person not only in rank or wealth but in moral stature."[61] Stevens may believe that Lord Darlington possesses all of these markers of superiority, but Mr. Benn challenges Stevens's judgment by alluding to Lord Darlington's and Sir Geoffrey's fascist views. He asks: "In your opinion, what's going on up there has moral stature, does it? I wish I could be so sure, but I'm not. I've heard some very fishy things."[62] Although Mr. Benn implies that the negotiations taking place at Darlington Hall are not morally sound, Stevens refuses to engage with Mr. Benn about these political issues and makes a professional argument for his discretion. "I hear nothing," he tells Mr. Benn. "To listen to gentlemen's conversations would distract me from my work."[63] Mr. Benn may not pursue the matter, but he appears disconcerted by Stevens's reticence.

Mr. Benn not only voices his political convictions but also claims to act on them. Even though it is not part of the housemaid sequence, I want to briefly discuss the second scene that highlights the professional and ideological differences between Mr. Benn and Stevens, because it further contextualizes the expected relationship between servants and their employers. While they have drinks in a pub, Mr. Benn tells Miss Kenton that he has left his job with Sir Geoffrey and implies that he left because he does not support Sir Geoffrey's politics. "There was something about Sir Geoffrey and his blackshirts that gave me the creeps," he explains.[64] Mr. Benn's political and moral motivation may become more questionable when he admits that he does not want to return to service and would prefer to work for himself; however, like Miss Kenton, he articulates a different way that someone in service can act. As Mr. Benn and Miss Kenton debate the relationship between politics and professionalism, Miss Kenton voices Stevens's opinion that politics and service are incompatible. Then both she and Mr. Benn argue against this philosophy. Mr. Benn puts it candidly: "If I don't like something I want to be in a position to say stuff it."[65] Even if Mr. Benn allows that he is "not a real professional like Mr. Stevens," his contention that servants should be able to have their own political opinions and act on them serves as a counterexample to Stevens's reserve and belief that a good butler is discrete, loyal, and trusting.[66]

This philosophical difference becomes even more important in the scenes that follow the parlor discussion between Stevens and Mr. Benn. In the first of these scenes, audiences see the further development of Lord Darlington's anti-Semitism when he enters the library as the housemaids are cleaning the fireplace and begins reading from Houston Stewart Chamberlain's *Foundations of the Nineteenth Century* (1899), a book that expresses prejudicial views about Jews that would influence Hitler. As Roderick Stackelberg and Sally A. Vinkle note, "In Hitler's Germany he [Chamberlain] would be officially celebrated as the 'seer of the Third Reich.'"[67] A voiceover provides some of the content of what Lord Darlington is reading in which Chamberlain argues that because Jewish people have "fundamentally different natures," there exists a "deep cleft that separates us Europeans from the Jew . . . a real gulf."[68] In the 1930s, the Nazis would use this naturalization of difference to justify oppression and genocide. As Lord Darlington considers Chamberlain's views, his gaze falls on the housemaids who are cleaning the fireplace. The next scene in which Lord Darlington orders Stevens to dismiss the Jewish housemaids shows him applying this philosophy to the people around him and directly connects Lord Darlington's actions to Chamberlain's and Hitler's dangerous ideas.

As in the book, Lord Darlington's choice of words to explain his decision, "It is regrettable" and "We have no choice," conveys his attempt to evade personal responsibility.[69] Stevens eventually carries out Lord Darlington's orders, but his initial response differs from that in the book. Rather than letting the matter rest, he offers a defense of the girls: "My Lord, may I say, they work extremely well, they're intelligent, polite, and very clean."[70] Although

Stevens's attempt to make sense of the matter from a professional point of view does not challenge Lord Darlington's misguided politics, his reply represents an implicit challenge to Lord Darlington's authority. Emphasizing the significance of the interaction, Anthony Hopkins, who plays Stevens in the film, argues that this conversation represents the first time Stevens recognizes "something is wrong."[71] Lord Darlington's response is patient but decisive. He tells Stevens that he has thought carefully about the matter but that "[t]here are larger issues at stake."[72] Although the audience only sees Stevens's back as he faces Lord Darlington, Stevens presumably questions this point through his expression, because Lord Darlington must bluntly acknowledge his prejudices: "They're Jews."[73]

Stevens's words about the housemaids and questioning look represent a brief moment where he obliquely resists the established order, which is an extraordinary act for Stevens. However, because these subtle protests also reveal that he can see another side to his employer's decision, Stevens's objections make his subsequent acquiescence more of a choice and, therefore, more troubling. Moreover, as in the book, when Stevens tells Miss Kenton about Lord Darlington's instructions to dismiss the housemaids, he not only stifles his dissenting opinion but also defends Lord Darlington's position. Using the same language as Lord Darlington, Stevens tells Miss Kenton, "We have no choice."[74] This expression of Stevens's lack of choice serves the same function as Lord Darlington's: it is a way to evade responsibility. Stevens not only uses this language to absolve himself but also tries to make the decision to follow Lord Darlington's orders greater than an individual choice by invoking "we" in his paralysis of the will.

Miss Kenton's objection to Elsa and Erma's dismissal "because they are Jews" and much of the dialogue, including Miss Kenton's threat to resign, closely matches that of the book. What differs are the added details about the girls' fate if they are dismissed.[75] Miss Kenton tells Stevens that if they do not have jobs, "they could be sent back to Germany."[76] That a return to Germany implies a death sentence goes without saying. Stevens ignores the meaning of Miss Kenton's words when he hides behind his professional duty and firmly states: "It is out of our hands."[77] Stevens's acceptance of Lord Darlington's position relies on his continued belief that his employer has superior knowledge about politics and about the world. Miss Kenton, however, is neither satisfied by Stevens's reasoning nor does she accept that because of his class and social position Lord Darlington's actions are inherently right and moral. She challenges both men when she presents an ethical argument for keeping the girls. John J. Su makes a good point when he argues that because Miss Kenton only voices her objection to Stevens rather than confronting Lord Darlington, "[her] protests operate within the social hierarchy without ever threatening it."[78] Nevertheless, Miss Kenton's conversation with Stevens remains important in its articulation of an alternative course of action.[79]

The climax of Lord Darlington's decision, the actual dismissal of the Jewish housemaids, is done off screen.[80] This hidden moment highlights the precariousness of the girls' position. They can be let go at any moment, without professional cause, and quietly enough to make the event nearly invisible. The audience only knows for sure that the housemaids are gone when, in the next scene, Miss Kenton and Stevens interview a new girl for the housemaid position. As they are debating the merits of the new hire, Stevens asks Miss Kenton about her earlier threat to leave if the Jewish housemaids were dismissed. Miss Kenton must admit that despite her intentions, she is not leaving. She tells him: "All I see out in the world is loneliness, and it frightens me. That's all my high principles are worth."[81] Miss Kenton may not follow through with her protest because she has no place to go and is afraid to leave, but her remorse indicates a sense of responsibility that Stevens must suppress in order to carry out Lord Darlington's orders.

Three present-day scenes in Moscombe further problematize Stevens's submission to authority. These scenes portray the political issues of the 1930s in starker terms than in the book and present a challenge to Stevens's contention that professional duties outweigh personal responsibilities. When Stevens gets into a discussion with some of the local residents about politics and democracy, Harry Smith and Mr. Taylor articulate the idea that all individuals have a right to their opinions and a responsibility to vote their consciences. Both also make the connection between the loss of democracy and the rise of fascism. As Mr. Taylor says to Stevens when he shows him his room for the night: "Democracy is what we fought Hitler for."[82] Making the moment more poignant, Stevens stays in the room of Mr. Taylor's son, who was killed at Dunkirk.[83] This scene and a later mention of Reginald Cardinal's wartime death highlight the personal costs of the war. They also demonstrate that Lord Darlington's appeasement politics, fascist sympathies, and undemocratic views have damaging consequences beyond Darlington Hall.

A similar point about democracy is made when one of Lord Darlington's guests, Mr. Spencer, quizzes Stevens about politics in order to prove that the common man does not know enough to participate in national governance and to argue against universal suffrage. In the book where the scene comes later, Lord Darlington contends: "Democracy is something for a bygone era. The world's far too complicated a place now for universal suffrage."[84] The book also shows how these ideas about suffrage and democracy can lead to fascism. This point can be seen in Lord Darlington's praise of Germany's and Italy's effective political and social policies that have made these countries orderly and efficient. He contrasts the benefits of "strong leadership" and a lack of "universal suffrage nonsense" with the English government's tendency to make decisions slowly because its representatives debate matters.[85] By juxtaposing this flashback scene with the present-day postwar discussion of democracy in Moscombe and by making it part of the Jewish housemaid sequence, the film emphasizes the larger implications of Lord Darlington's and Mr. Spencer's positions: the suppression of democracy, represented as a minor class issue—gentlemen disregarding the opinions of ordinary men—can lead to fascism, war, and suffering.

A final present-day scene in Moscombe in which Dr. Carlisle questions Stevens about his role at Darlington Hall also calls into question Lord Darlington's politics. In the book, Dr. Carlisle talks with Stevens about village politics and asks about his definition of dignity but does not say anything about Lord Darlington or Darlington Hall. In the film, Dr. Carlisle voices strong opinions about Lord Darlington and connects him with Hitler, appeasement, war, and treason. Dr. Carlisle's rhetoric implies that Lord Darlington's actions were not just personal mistakes but crimes against the nation, and his depiction of Lord Darlington as a traitor mirrors the newspaper headlines shown at the beginning of the film. In order to defend Lord Darlington's reputation, Stevens must admit to Dr. Carlisle that he knew and worked for Lord Darlington. However, when Dr. Carlisle asks if Stevens shared Lord Darlington's opinions, Stevens is reluctant to continue discussing the subject. He replies with his standard professional argument that avoids the moral issue: "I was there to serve him. Not to agree or disagree."[86] Dissatisfied with this response, Dr. Carlisle reframes his question and asks if Stevens trusted Lord Darlington. Stevens concedes that he did, but also acknowledges that, in retrospect, his trust may have been misplaced. Stevens then redirects the discussion away from himself and back to a defense of Lord Darlington's character. He contends that, in the end, Lord Darlington came to rethink his actions. He "admitted that he'd been mistaken. . . . That he'd allowed himself to have been taken in."[87] Like the language used to describe Lord Darlington's change of heart about the housemaids, Stevens's description of Lord Darlington's passive role—he had "been taken in"—is one more attempt to mitigate Lord Darlington's responsibility and, by extension, his own. The film's sequencing then connects Stevens's statement to Dr. Carlisle about Lord Darlington being mistaken about his association with the Nazis to his specific mistake about dismissing the Jewish housemaids.

Lord Darlington's moment of recognition about the dismissal being a mistake is prefaced with a shot of Stevens ironing a newspaper, one of many scenes in the film that show the machine-like domestic duties of the staff and depict the servants as part of the household mechanics rather than as individuals. Even Stevens, who is more identifiable than most of the servants in the film, is depicted as relatively invisible. Scenes like the Charlgrove hunting meet where Stevens holds out a drink to a mounted rider who simply ignores him or the dinner service where he tries to "achieve that balance between attentiveness and the illusion of absence" visually emphasize the expectation that Stevens and the other servants should quietly and imperceptibly carry out their duties.[88] These scenes contextualize Stevens's persistent rationale that he is there "to serve . . . not to agree or disagree" and imply that Stevens's reticence in regard to the dismissal of the Jewish housemaids may be disappointing but is in keeping with how he understands his professional duties.

Stevens is similarly professional and accommodating to his employer when Lord Darlington changes his position on the dismissal of the housemaids and attempts to make amends. Engaging Stevens's help, Lord Darlington explains: "One would like to do something for them. It was wrong what occurred. I'm sorry about it."[89] Lord Darlington may feel regret, but the language he uses continues to distance him from the error in judgment. By describing the matter neutrally and passively—"one" would like to do "something," and "it was wrong" rather than "I was wrong"—he persists in denying his responsibility. As in the book, Stevens offers to try and trace the young women, but his subsequent comment marks an important difference from the book. He recounts to Lord Darlington that at the time, he attempted to help the housemaids by getting them another position at a house in Surrey. Unfortunately, he explains, "there was room only for one, and the girls didn't want to be separated."[90] Although this effort is not enough to save the young women and Stevens feels constrained from doing more, his act goes beyond Lord Darlington's orders to dismiss them and shows an internal conflict between his personal feelings and his professional duties. Because Stevens values his professional identity above all else, he ultimately suppresses this inner conflict at the time and continues to do so.

In the scene that closes the housemaid sequence, Stevens does not reveal to Miss Kenton that he attempted to help the housemaids. He simply tells her that Lord Darlington conceded it was a mistake to dismiss them. As in the book, Stevens voices his misgivings about the dismissal. "I was upset," he tells her. "I don't like to see that sort of thing happening in this house."[91] Like Lord Darlington's expression of remorse, Stevens's claim that he was distressed at the time is vague. "[T]hat sort of thing" could mean anything from letting competent housemaids go to Lord Darlington's anti-Semitic behavior. His regret also does not change the fact that he still followed Lord Darlington's orders and dismissed the housemaids. Stevens may truly believe that he could act in no other way, but his inability to question Lord Darlington's decisions does not fully absolve him from personal responsibility. As Andrew Teverson suggests, Stevens's "true failing . . . is that he denies his freedom to choose, and denies the responsibility involved in the act of choosing."[92] Moreover, Miss Kenton's and Mr. Benn's protests against their employers' actions and politics and Dr. Carlisle's pointed questions about Stevens's opinions show that there are other ways that Stevens could have acted.

Lord Darlington's culpability and Stevens's implicit support of his employer's political agenda become even clearer at a meeting to negotiate secret talks between the British Prime Minister and Hitler that takes place at Darlington Hall approximately thirteen years after the Conference in the book and three years after in the film. At the time of this meeting between British and German officials, Reginald Cardinal is a newspaper columnist who reports on international affairs. As such, Cardinal is aware of Lord Darlington's continued political involvement with the Nazis. Cardinal does not believe that Lord Darlington's intentions are bad but rather that he is a bad judge of the situation and that his noble instincts are being exploited. His assessment of how Lord Darlington has been manipulated by the Nazis echoes Ishiguro's observation about how Hitler manipulated the "old English gentlemanly fair play ethic" and skillfully used "these old English gents as pawns."[93] Both Cardinal and Ishiguro emphasize that at this point in history, Lord Darlington's naivete has harmful consequences. Cardinal cares deeply about Lord Darlington, but his loyalty is not unquestioning, and whatever the cost to their relationship, he feels a moral obligation to help Lord Darlington see the truth about Hitler.

Cardinal's desire to persuade Lord Darlington to break his ties with Hitler represents an important change from his perspective at the 1923 Conference (the book's setting for the Conference) when a renegotiation of Britain's relationship with Germany at least seemed reasonable to consider. Cardinal's official role at the first Conference is small but his participation shows that even as a young man, he is engaged and well-prepared. He may comically misinterpret Stevens's awkward prelude to a discussion about sex, "Sir David wishes you to know, sir, that ladies and gentlemen differ in several key respects," as Stevens trying to ensure he is prepared for the Conference delegates, but his answer shows a thoughtful and methodical approach to politics.[94] Cardinal assures Stevens he has "done extensive reading and background work on this whole area" and that he is "very well briefed indeed."[95] "This attaché case," he observes, "is chock-full of notes on every possible angle one can imagine.... I really think I've thought through every permutation the human mind is capable of."[96] This detailed explanation shows that Cardinal is capable of entertaining many different political positions and their consequences. His careful preparation exemplifies the "ideological process" Ishiguro wants his readers to experience: "to become more aware, more sympathetic, to marginalised ways of seeing and alternative ways of thinking."[97]

Crucially, Cardinal's point of view on Germany changes because he remains politically aware and socially conscious.

By the time of the smaller meeting at Darlington Hall, Cardinal has reconsidered the viability of helping Germany and has ethical concerns about Lord Darlington's negotiations with British officials on behalf of Hitler. Demonstrating a continuation of his earlier engagement, Cardinal's opinions about Lord Darlington's actions are based on a close examination of the circumstances. He insists: "No one with good judgement could persist in believing anything Herr Hitler says after the Rhineland."[98] As Cardinal suggests, particularly after German expansionism has become more evident and Hitler has openly defied the terms of the Versailles Treaty, Lord Darlington's inability or refusal to rethink his views in light of this new evidence is irresponsible and dangerous. Cardinal speculates that if he were still alive, even his father, Lord Darlington's friend and great ally during the earlier Conference, would try to dissuade Lord Darlington from his current course of action. In place of his father, Reginald Cardinal tries to do just that.

When Cardinal fails to change Lord Darlington's mind, he attempts to enlist Stevens's help, but Stevens politely refuses on professional grounds. He also denies that he knows any details about the current meeting despite the minute knowledge of the household his position requires. Stevens's denial and stated position "It is not my place to be curious about such matters" reflect his trust in Lord Darlington's judgment and the loyalty that prevents him from questioning his employer's actions or decisions.[99] Even when Stevens admits the possibility that he *may* be curious, he represses this impulse because it conflicts with his understanding of duty.

Unlike Stevens, Cardinal understands that curiosity is not just about information but, more importantly, about caring and being engaged with the world, which he sees as part of being politically, morally, and socially responsible. Although Cardinal fails to get Stevens to act, he makes some critical points. Cardinal emphasizes that Stevens's lack of curiosity is more than a professional decision; it is a tacit endorsement of Lord Darlington's views. He also points out that when Stevens lets things happen without questioning them, he becomes partially responsible for the events that take place in the household and in the world. Berberich offers a similar indictment of Stevens's behavior when she argues that Ishiguro offers "a subtle analysis of how appeasement flourished not just because of the active involvement of key players in large country houses, such as Lord Darlington, but also because of the passive acquiescence of the general populace, such as Stevens."[100]

Reginald Cardinal's death during the war further highlights the idea that "passive acquiescence" can cause irreparable harm. Cardinal is killed in Belgium, and the setting for his death is fitting in terms of his argument in favor of taking a stand against what seems to be wrong rather than doing nothing. In an effort to avoid conflict, Belgium declared neutrality in the 1930s and then again at the beginning of the war in 1939. However, King Leopold III's decision did not prevent Germany from invading Belgium in 1940 and occupying it until December 1944. His inaction also led to accusations that he was collaborating with the Nazis. This history suggests that in these circumstances trying to be neutral either as a country or as an individual is not a viable political position.

Cardinal may not have a solution to the current political crisis, but he proposes the means to one: curiosity, concern, and a willingness to act on one's beliefs. "Quite frankly," he admits to Stevens, "I don't know what's to be done. But you might at least be curious."[101] Rather than advocating for a specific political position, it is this model of engagement for dealing with difficult moral and political issues that is central to Ishiguro's message about social justice. Stevens, however, cannot make this ideological leap. Admitting that Lord Darlington may not have been a superior person in knowledge and in moral stature means that his own actions may have been misguided as well. As a result, Stevens continues to go to great lengths to justify Lord Darlington's efforts.

The film with its later 1938 setting for the meeting further complicates Stevens's defense of Lord Darlington, who is portrayed as willfully ignorant and, therefore, more culpable. The film also represents the German Ambassador and the German Embassy officials who accompany him to Darlington Hall as arrogant and sinister, particularly when they proprietarily admire Lord Darlington's art and when they talk about foreign policy. The audience is presented with an omniscient perspective on this closed-door meeting during which British and German officials discuss the fate of Czechoslovakia. Articulating the British government's appeasement policy of the 1930s, the Prime Minister assures the German Ambassador that Britain does not intend to go to war over German expansion into Czechoslovakia. Supporting the Prime Minister's position, Lord Halifax characterizes the occupation of the Sudetenland as Germans taking back what is rightfully theirs, and the foreign office official, Mr. Fraser, argues that the fate of this region is not worth losing British lives over. By minimizing Germany's actions and defining them as beyond the scope of Britain's concerns, these government officials rationalize their willingness to appease Germany in order to avoid war.

Responding to these statements and sentiments, the German Ambassador observes that "[t]he Fuhrer is a man of peace."[102] However, he clarifies that Hitler "will not allow a small second-rate country to thumb its nose at the one-thousand-year German Reich."[103] The Ambassador's words make explicit Germany's feelings of righteous superiority and emphasize that international stability and peace are contingent on people and nations meeting Hitler's terms. With its depictions of the Germans as arrogant, self-righteous, and prepared for war, the film telegraphs historical events and foreshadows the mistake the world would make by not acting sooner and more decisively to curb Hitler's aggressive German nationalism. These political details provide the further context in the film for Reginald Cardinal's concerns about Lord Darlington's negotiations with Germany and are the impetus for his discussion with Stevens. In an attempt to convince Stevens of the need to act, he explains that Lord Darlington is "trying to persuade" British officials to enter into a "pact" with "criminals."[104] Cardinal's characterization of the German officials as "criminals" highlights that their actions, and by extension Lord Darlington's, are morally wrong. In addition, his description of Lord Darlington "trying to *persuade*" British officials positions him in an active political role whereas in the book Lord Darlington simply "bring[s] together" British and German officials "for secret talks."[105]

Despite Cardinal's strong arguments, Stevens continues to deny that it is his place to question Lord Darlington's decisions.[106] Instead, Stevens defends Lord Darlington by maintaining that his motives are noble and, echoing Neville Chamberlain's Munich Agreement rhetoric, that Lord Darlington is "working to ensure peace in our time."[107] Cardinal may agree with Stevens's assessment of Lord Darlington's motivation, but he insists that Lord Darlington's association with the Nazis remains abhorrent. Moreover, Cardinal suggests that good intentions are not enough to make a political action correct and contends that the problem with the peace Lord Darlington is working toward is that it will be "on their beastly terms."[108] Confirming the error of Lord Darlington's efforts, the film visually and rhetorically links his political actions to his physical and emotional decline. In addition, as I argue earlier, Mr. Lewis's present-day ownership of Darlington Hall represents a physical and ideological replacement of Lord Darlington and signifies that Lord Darlington's actions were morally flawed and that Mr. Lewis's Conference views were the correct ones.

In spite of these implied moral judgments, the film ends with an interesting note of ambiguity about pre–World War II politics, which suggests the difficulty of knowing at the time which course of action in regard to Germany would have been right. While playing with a Ping-Pong ball on the game table that has replaced the banquet table, Mr. Lewis reminisces to Stevens about the Conference dinner speeches that took place in this room. He observes: "We all stood up and delivered ourselves of our principles. God knows what I said." Then he asks Stevens: "What did I say anyway?"[109] Mr. Lewis's claim not to remember what he said is both curious and significant. There are several potentially contradictory reasons for his stated lack of memory about such an important moment. First, if he is being disingenuous and does remember, his words may be an attempt to erase the differences Mr. Lewis had with Stevens's previous employer, Lord Darlington, and to put Stevens at ease with the new household structure. Second, just as Stevens has been recasting his relationship to Lord Darlington, Mr. Lewis may be trying to recast his role in the past to be more diplomatic. Third, Mr. Lewis may be suggesting that the past should be left in the past. On the other hand, if Mr. Lewis truly does not remember, this lapse suggests the difficulty of foreseeing the best action in a politically complex situation. Although each delegate was passionate about his views, anyone could have been right about how events would play out.[110] This point is visually suggested by the Ping-Pong ball Mr. Lewis is playing with as he talks and by the back-and-forth game it represents in which a single move can win the match but, while the ball is in play, the victory can go to either side. What remains important to the subject of personal and social responsibility is that at the Conference dinner Mr. Lewis and others were true to their principles and expressed their views.

Stevens's memory of the event is as questionable as Mr. Lewis's. He tells his current employer that he does not remember what Mr. Lewis said because he was "too busy serving to listen to the speeches."[111] However, Stevens's hesitation suggests that he is not being entirely truthful. There are a couple shots at the original dinner that show Stevens listening while Mr. Lewis is speaking. The audience also knows that Stevens has a subsequent conversation with Reginald Cardinal where he seems to remember the content of Mr. Lewis's speech. Therefore, Stevens's noncommittal response allows Mr. Lewis a clean slate in their current relationship and implies that although it is important to be aware of one's mistakes so that one can act thoughtfully and not make the same mistakes again, the past should not destroy the present.

This point resonates in the book when Stevens comes to a new awareness of himself and his position. His first revelations about the past have tragic implications as he realizes that he blindly followed Lord Darlington rather than thinking for himself. However, Stevens finds a way to shift his outlook to something more positive when he considers the advice the person on the pier gives him, "that I should cease to look back so much, that I should adopt a more positive outlook and try to make the best of what remains of my day."[112] From here, Stevens arrives at his most forward-thinking idea. "Surely," he argues, "it is enough that the likes of you and I at least *try* to make our small contribution count for something true and worthy."[113] It is not clear in the book or in the film that Stevens will achieve this contentment, but he ultimately does recognize the importance of being true to one's principles, making one's own decisions and mistakes, and thoughtfully trying to make a positive contribution to the world.[114] This engagement with the world, however, cannot remain static.[115]

The different presentations of moral complexities in the book and in the film are the means to help readers and audiences think critically about their beliefs, actions, and responsibilities.[116] Although as Cynthia Wong argues, "Ishiguro seems sympathetic to the limitations of what humans can know," *The Remains of the Day* also shows that people must be willing to rethink their beliefs in order to remain empathetic, socially engaged, and responsive to a changing society.[117] Ishiguro's point about *The Floating World* applies to *The Remains of the Day* as well: "The floating world comes to refer, in the larger metaphorical sense, to the fact that the values of society are always in flux."[118] Rather than providing set moral imperatives, in *The Remains of the Day*, Ishiguro provides the model for becoming a socially responsible individual, which means caring about others, engaging with people and ideas (described by Reginald Cardinal as curiosity), consciously choosing one's path, being willing to carefully think about one's actions, and remaining open to rethinking one's views.

NOTES

1. Kazuo Ishiguro, *The Remains of the Day* (New York: Vintage Books, 1993), 116. In a more recent interview, Ishiguro also addresses individuals' fundamental desire to make the world better. This impulse, he tells Mary Laura Philpott, is "what I love about human beings. . . . We're not content just to feed ourselves and reproduce and then die. We've got to keep asking ourselves, 'Have I made a contribution? Have I been good . . . ?' Even if I'm a criminal, I'd ask myself 'Have I been a good criminal? Have I been loyal to my gang members?' It's just hard-wired into human beings. We want to say that we did it well, not just in terms of career, but in terms of being a parent or being a sibling or being a friend or being a spouse" (Ishiguro, "Some Awful Things Have Happened").

2. Kazuo Ishiguro, interview by Graham Swift, *BOMB* 29 (Fall 1989): 22.

3. Kazuo Ishiguro, quoted in Eleanor Wachtel, "Kazuo Ishiguro," in *More Writers & Company: New Conversations with CBC Radio's Eleanor Wachtel* (Toronto: Knopf Canada, 1996), 18.

4. For each scene, I begin with a discussion of the book and then discuss the film.

5. Kazuo Ishiguro, "'I'm Sorry I Can't Say More': An Interview with Kazuo Ishiguro," interview by Sean Matthews, in *Kazuo Ishiguro*, ed. Sean Matthews and Sebastian Groes (New York: Continuum Books, 2009), 119.

6. Ibid.

7. Contextualizing the novel in terms of the 2016 referendum in which the UK voted to leave the EU, Kristian Shaw contends that *The Remains of the Day* serves as a good example of "how contemporary manifestations of post-imperial melancholia

were evident in British literature long before the referendum" (Kristian Shaw, *Brexlit*, 29). Shaw also reads Ishiguro's more recent novel *The Buried Giant* (2015) in relation to Brexit, arguing that "[t]hrough the guise of fantasy literature, Ishiguro has unintentionally produced perhaps the most prescient and hauntological Brexlit novel, dramatizing how the interdependent ties of community can be threatened or undone by the myopic violence of nation states and the yearning temptation to recover the past. In reading *The Buried Giant* against recent cultural and cosmopolitical developments, the narrative engages with contemporary manifestations of post-conflict resolution and suggests ways by which England—a country disrupted by the hauntology of its past within the British constellation—can come to terms with its historical legacy. Ishiguro gestures to the folly in assuming a backward-looking national perspective, or sustaining an illusion of grandeur to protect us from our diminished position, and insinuates the need to tear down a fabricated national mythology in seeking reconciliation and restitution for the transgressions of the past" (96).

8. Christine Berberich, "Kazuo Ishiguro's *The Remains of the Day*: Working Through England's Traumatic Past as a Critique of Thatcherism," in *Kazuo Ishiguro: New Critical Visions of the Novels*, ed. Sebastian Groes and Barry Lewis (New York: Palgrave Macmillan, 2011), 122.

9. Ishiguro, *Remains*, 61, 73.

10. Ibid., 92.

11. Ibid.

12. Ibid., 87, 76.

13. Ibid., 98, 99.

14. Cynthia F. Wong, "Kazuo Ishiguro's *The Remains of the Day*," in *A Companion to the British and Irish Novel 1945–2000*, ed. Brian W. Shaffer (Malden, MA: Blackwell Publishing, 2005), 498.

15. Ishiguro, *Remains*, 99.

16. Ibid., 100.

17. Ibid.

18. Ibid., 100–101.

19. Kazuo Ishiguro, quoted in "Blind Loyalty, Hollow Honor: England's Fatal Flaw," in *The Remains of the Day*, directed by James Ivory (1993; Culver City, CA: Columbia Tristar Home Entertainment, 2001), DVD.

20. Ishiguro, *Remains*, 103.

21. Peter Childs, "Kazuo Ishiguro: Remain in Dreams," in *Contemporary Novelists: British Fiction since 1970* (New York: Palgrave Macmillan, 2005), 135.

22. Ishiguro, *Remains*, 95.

23. Robert Stam, "Introduction: The Theory and Practice of Adaptation," in *Literature and Film: A Guide to the Theory and Practice of Film Adaptation*, ed. Robert Stam and Alessandra Raengo (Malden, MA: Blackwell Publishing, 2005), 43.

24. Earl G. Ingersoll, "Desire, the Gaze and Suture in the Novel and the Film: *The Remains of the Day*," *Studies in the Humanities* 28, no. 1–2 (June–December 2001).

25. *The Remains of the Day*, directed by James Ivory (1993; Culver City, CA: Columbia Tristar Home Entertainment, 2001), DVD.

26. Ibid.

27. Ibid.
28. Ibid.
29. Ibid.
30. Ibid. (emphasis added).
31. Ingersoll, "Desire."
32. *Remains*, directed by Ivory.
33. Adam Parkes also addresses the implications of making Mr. Lewis "a composite of two different Americans in the novel." He argues that "[t]he effect of this merger is a sharp irony at the expense of Lord Darlington that also makes Lewis look grimly prophetic. . . . The price of sharpness, however, is complexity: by keeping Lewis and Farraday separate, Ishiguro subtly indicates a larger sense of historical movement, as English culture finds itself displaced even on home soil by the ascendant American culture of the postwar era" (Parkes, *Kazuo Ishiguro's* The Remains of the Day, 79–80). For more on the implications of this change and on the decision to cast Christopher Reeve in the role of Mr. Lewis, see Jeffers and Ingersoll.
34. *Remains*, directed by Ivory.
35. Ishiguro, *Remains*, 199.
36. James M. Lang, "Public Memory, Private History: Kazuo Ishiguro's *The Remains of the Day*," *Clio* 29, no. 2 (2000): 156.
37. Ishiguro, *Remains*, 137.
38. Ibid.
39. Robert Emmet Long and Christine Berberich also offer good cultural contexts for Lord Darlington's beliefs. Long describes the class-based views of the "'Cliveden set' of English Tories who wanted to accommodate Hitler as far as possible" and those of "Sir Oswald Mosley, whose views and those of other members of the British aristocracy, were eerily close to Hitler's" (Long, "England," 227). Berberich evaluates the status and influence of Lord Darlington's guests, which include "Lady Astor, of Cliveden Set notoriety (*RD* 134); Lord Halifax, the infamous Foreign Secretary at the time of the Munich Agreement and one of the architects of British Appeasement (*RD* 135); Herr von Ribbentrop, Hitler's ambassador to London, successful at charming his way into the British upper classes (*RD* 135); and Oswald Mosley himself (*RD* 137, 145)" (Berberich, "Kazuo Ishiguro's *The Remains of the Day*," 123).
40. Ishiguro, *Remains*, 137 (emphasis added).
41. Kathleen Wall, "*The Remains of the Day* and Its Challenges to Theories of Unreliable Narration," *The Journal of Narrative Technique* 24, no. 1 (1994): 33.
42. Ishiguro, *Remains*, 147.
43. Ibid.
44. Ibid.
45. Ishiguro, interview by Swift, 22.
46. Describing Rob Atkinson's use of legal theory to assess Stevens's and Miss Kenton's "different moral stances" in relation to Lord Darlington's directive about the housemaids, Matthew Beedham notes that "Atkinson evaluates the reactions of Stevens and Kenton by applying two contemporary theories of lawyer professionalism: Stevens's 'neutral partisanship' and Kenton's 'moral activism'" (Beedham, "*The Remains of the Day* 3," 98).

47. Ishiguro, *Remains*, 149 (original emphasis).

48. Ibid.

49. Lydia R. Cooper, "Novelistic Practice and Ethical Philosophy in Kazuo Ishiguro's *The Remains of the Day* and *Never Let Me Go*," in *Kazuo Ishiguro: New Critical Visions of the Novels*, ed. Sebastian Groes and Barry Lewis (New York: Palgrave Macmillan, 2011), 112.

50. Childs, "Kazuo Ishiguro," 136. Adam Parkes emphasizes this connection to the Nuremberg defense as well when he argues that "Stevens passively accepts Lord Darlington's word on political matters, even when young Cardinal tells him point-blank that his employer is the dupe of the Nazis; the only defense Stevens offers to explain the dismissal of the two Jewish maids is that he was (in a chilling echo of the Nuremberg trials) simply obeying orders" (Parkes, *Kazuo Ishiguro's* The Remains of the Day, 51).

51. Berberich, "Kazuo Ishiguro's *The Remains of the Day*," 123. Emily Horton similarly contends that Stevens's "wilful quietism in the name of obedience" represents Stevens's moral failure. She argues: "Stevens works as a Nazi complicit, silently approving his master's racism through his refusal of condemnation. . . . [W]hile he promises loyalty, he delivers collusion" (Horton, "A Genuine Old-Fashioned English Butler," 20). Richard Rankin Russell extends the critique of Stevens to argue that he is not only culpable but also "monstrous" in his support of fascism and anti-Semitism. In order to address the full ethical implications of Stevens's actions, Russell analyzes the novel through the lens of fantasy fiction. In this context, Russell asserts that "Stevens's motorized quest across the rolling, beautiful countryside of southern and southwestern England to find Miss Kenton and bring her back to Darlington Hall allows him to go on a second quest with deep ethical import: an assessment of whether he served a distinguished household, a concern that must be viewed through his duplicity on the intertwined issues of anti-Semitism, fascism, and Nazism" (Russell, "Monsters of Anti-Semitism," 441).

52. Ishiguro, *Remains*, 151.

53. Ibid., 153.

54. Ibid.

55. Ibid.

56. Ibid., 154.

57. Wall, "*Remains* and Its Challenges," 23. Rebecca L. Walkowitz argues that the shift from "I" to "one" serves as an aesthetic and an emotional strategy in *The Remains of the Day*: "Ishiguro has the wit to notice that the choice of 'one' over 'I' unites an 'impersonal' grammar with the rhetoric of English impersonality. Stevens's language seems at once natural—what a butler sounds like—and yet tactical. 'One' negates the claim to personal feeling Stevens's statement would otherwise offer, and it is stilted, an attempt to sound like the gentleman that Stevens, in his indifference, fails to be" (Walkowitz, "Ishiguro's Floating World," 1068). Lydia R. Cooper also sees Stevens's lack of feeling as ethically significant. She argues that his "complicity [in unethical systems] derives from a fundamental empathetic failure. . . . In believing himself to be entirely powerless, Stevens abdicates moral responsibility and so

becomes ethically guilty of all that he does *not* do" (Cooper, "Novelistic Practice," 111–12, 113 [original emphasis]).

58. Refugees from Germany started arriving in Great Britain in 1933. According to the Association of Jewish Refugees, "by September 1939 about 70,000 Jews had been granted refuge in [Great Britain]. Among those who obtained entry visas were many women who came as domestic servants" (Association of Jewish Refugees). For more on the situation of Jewish refugees in Britain, see London.

59. *Remains*, directed by Ivory.

60. In the book, the context for this discussion is different. Miss Kenton voices the opinion that Stevens must be content in order to give him the opportunity to declare her importance to him. Stevens, however, fails to make a declaration of love, and, as in the film, links his contentment to his employer's achievements.

61. *Remains*, directed by Ivory.

62. Ibid.

63. Ibid.

64. Ibid.

65. Ibid.

66. Ibid.

67. Roderick Stackelberg and Sally A. Vinkle, eds., *The Nazi Germany Sourcebook: An Anthology of Texts* (New York: Routledge, 2002), 11.

68. Stewart Chamberlain, *The Foundations of the Nineteenth Century*, Volume 1 (London: Ballantyne and Company, 1911), 338.

69. *Remains*, directed by Ivory.

70. Ibid.

71. Anthony Hopkins, quoted in "Love and Loyalty: The Making of *The Remains of the Day*," in *The Remains of the Day*, directed by James Ivory (1993; Culver City, CA: Columbia Tristar Home Entertainment, 2001), DVD.

72. *Remains*, directed by Ivory.

73. Ibid.

74. Ibid.

75. Ibid.

76. Ibid.

77. Ibid.

78. John J. Su, "Refiguring National Character: The Remains of the British Estate Novel," *Modern Fiction Studies* 48, no. 3 (2002): 569. Su's idea could be applied to Mr. Benn as well. Mr. Benn voices his discontent about his employer's political opinions to Stevens and to Miss Kenton, but there is no scene in which he directly confronts Sir Geoffrey.

79. The conversation between Stevens and Miss Kenton is followed by a brief shot of Lord Darlington in the rain, perhaps suggesting a guilty conscience or a wrong decision; however, if that is the case, his regret, like the scene, is fleeting.

80. Jennifer Jeffers claims that screenwriter Ruth Prawer Jhabvala "makes Stevens morally weak by removing him from the responsibility of telling the girls that they must leave" (Jeffers, "Heritage and Nostalgia," 62).

81. *Remains*, directed by Ivory.

82. Ibid.

83. The book is less dramatic in this regard. The room where Stevens stays is that of the Taylors' son, but he is still alive. Although the son may not have been killed in the war, which gives an individual face to Hitler's victims, the book emphasizes the community cost of the war when Mrs. Taylor observes that their village gave more than their share of young men.

84. Ishiguro, *Remains*, 198.

85. Ibid., 198, 199.

86. *Remains*, directed by Ivory.

87. Ibid.

88. Ibid. This point resonates with the advice Anthony Hopkins was given about his character by Cyril Dickman, steward of the Queen's household. Dickman told him: "When the butler is in the room, the room must feel even more empty" (Hopkins, quoted in "Love and Loyalty").

89. *Remains*, directed by Ivory.

90. Ibid.

91. Ibid.

92. Andrew Teverson, "Acts of Reading in Kazuo Ishiguro's *The Remains of the Day*," *Q/W/E/R/T/Y: Arts, Littératures & Civilizations du Monde Anglophone* 9 (1999): 256.

93. Ishiguro, quoted in "Blind Loyalty."

94. Ishiguro, *Remains*, 84.

95. Ibid.

96. Ibid.

97. Teverson, "Acts of Reading," 258.

98. Ishiguro, *Remains*, 225.

99. Ibid., 222.

100. Berberich, "Kazuo Ishiguro's *The Remains of the Day*," 118.

101. Ishiguro, *Remains*, 222.

102. *Remains*, directed by Ivory.

103. Ibid.

104. Ibid.

105. Ishiguro, *Remains*, 222.

106. In "A Phenomenological Analysis of Existential Conscience in James Ivory's (1993) *The Remains of the Day*," George Berguno discusses the importance of this moment in terms of ethics. Berguno argues: "In the context of the present discussion on conscience, Mr. Stevens' conversation with Mr. Cardinal represents a very important moment. Suddenly, we are struck by the realisation that, though Mr. Stevens is a humble servant, he has, potentially, a very important role to play in the political events that are unfolding across Europe. As Lord Darlington's butler, he holds the possibility of entering into ethical dialogue with his employer. In other words, this scene, more than any other, illustrates the potential for *existential conscience*. Mr. Stevens, as a unique human being, encounters a unique historical situation that demands from him a unique, compassionate response. Mr. Stevens, however, tells Mr. Cardinal that it is

not his place to intervene or question his employer's political judgement" (Berguno, "A Phenomenological Analysis," 98).

107. *Remains*, directed by Ivory.

108. Ibid.

109. Ibid.

110. Addressing the politics of the novel's 1956 present moment, John Sutherland makes a similar observation when he suggests that Lord Darlington's politics would have been well-suited to the mid-1950s: "Ishiguro delicately points to an irony. Eden was driven in his mad Suez adventure by the demons of Munich—the sense that there must be no 'appeasement'. His favourite rallying call was that Nasser was Hitler all over again. But, unlike 1938, this was an occasion in which diplomacy, international co-operation—'appeasement', if you like—was exactly the right policy to have adopted. Lord Darlington's policies of discussion and *détente*, so tragically wrong in the 1920s and 1930s, would have been precisely right in autumn 1956" (Sutherland, "Why Hasn't Mr. Stevens Heard," 188–89).

111. *Remains*, directed by Ivory.

112. Ishiguro, *Remains*, 244.

113. Ibid. (original emphasis).

114. Ishiguro emphasizes the complexity of Stevens's situation in an interview by Brian W. Shaffer. He notes: "Stevens, at his novel's close, is perhaps deluding himself in thinking that he still has time to lead his life in a different way or become a new person. We sense that he's going to be hopeless at bantering or joking or whatever. He's never going to be one of the lads; we can see that he's far too set in his ways. But I wanted to suggest somehow that even the fact that he finally comes to see himself clearly is an achievement and a sort of dignity in itself. There is something noble—even heroic—in his ability to face up to those very painful things about himself. There is something positive about Stevens's triumph over that impasse, even though there is still something sad about him" (Ishiguro, interview by Shaffer, 11–12).

115. Emily Horton's analysis of the novel in relation to twenty-first-century national politics and global conservatism shows that the book's meaning is not static either. In this contemporary context, she argues that the novel serves as an affirmation of the values of cosmopolitanism. Addressing the idea implied by Dr. Carlisle that "England itself has adopted a stalwart political quietism, preferring stasis to uncertainty and global engagement," Horton contends that "if there is one positive message to be gained from *Remains*, it is that the novel itself registers this error, refusing to be duped by popular modern 'new world' banter, as Thatcher presents it. In this critical persistence, *Remains* demonstrates its continuing importance as response to conservative politics: in place of both nationalism and consumer libertarianism, it affirms cosmopolitanism's centrality as the basis for present democracy" (Horton, "A Genuine Old-Fashioned English Butler," 24).

116. For more on the social function of active reading and how Ishiguro's writing engages the reader in the production of meaning, see Teverson.

117. Wong, "Kazuo Ishiguro's *The Remains of the Day*," 498.

118. Kazuo Ishiguro, interview by Gregory Mason, *Contemporary Literature* 30, no. 3 (1989): 344.

Chapter Two

Destabilizing Institutional and Social Power in Patrick McGrath's *Asylum*

In his novel *Asylum* (1996), Patrick McGrath chronicles the relationship and aftermath of an illicit love affair between Stella, the wife of a forensic psychiatrist and deputy superintendent at a hospital for the criminally insane, and Edgar, a patient who has been convicted of murdering, decapitating, and enucleating his wife. This relationship and McGrath's fictional depiction of Broadmoor Lunatic Asylum provide the lens for his commentary on the politics of mental illness, marriage, and motherhood in post–World War II Britain. *Asylum* also offers a critical examination of how deviant behavior, ranging from unconventional to criminal, is defined and judged based on traditional ideas about gender and power. Through explicit comparisons between mental health patients and women, mental health professionals and husbands, and mental health institutions and the institution of marriage, McGrath highlights the problems with women's lives, marriage, and motherhood within a social system that mirrors the hierarchies of the asylum. These parallels expose the social and gender inequalities of both institutions that often are masked and naturalized by a philosophy of benevolent paternalism.

McGrath's use of an intelligent, engaging, and professional narrator who is also unreliable and pathological is an integral part of this project and crucial to his argument about power and gender. People tend to base their moral position about transgression on conventional gender role expectations and to make judgments based on a person's social and professional standing. McGrath challenges these ideological "truths" by allying the reader with the narrator and his personal, professional, and narrative power and then destablilizing the narrative position. Readers' realization about the narrator's unreliability unsettles their firmly held moral beliefs and encourages them to consider how they came to hold these beliefs. In this chapter, I explore the relationship between morality, naturalized social hierarchies, and narrative unreliability in order to argue that while the time period and hospital setting are key elements in setting up the novel's moral framework, the unreliable narrator, particularly one in which readers have put their trust, is critical to dismantling this framework and upsetting readers' moral judgments about transgression.

In *The Rhetoric of Fiction*, Wayne C. Booth defines two types of narrators: "*reliable* when he repeats for or acts in accordance with the norms of the work (which is to say, the implied author's norms), and *unreliable* when he does not."[1] In relation to *Asylum*, what is particularly important in this definition and described in more detail throughout Booth's book is the connection he makes between the unreliable narrator and moral and ethical issues. Vera Nünning observes of this link: "The significance of unreliable narration is . . . located at the point where narratological and ethical categories intersect: a decision as to whether a narrator is to be considered unreliable or not always entails a judgment as to what is considered 'normal,' that is, what the reader's world view and his or her ethical convictions are based on."[2] James Phelan and Mary Patricia Martin further emphasize the reader's role in evaluating the ethics of a text and argue that "while a text invites particular ethical responses through the signals it sends to its authorial audience, our individual responses will depend on the interaction of those invitations with our own particular values and beliefs."[3] McGrath's point in *Asylum* is for the reader to become cognizant of the ways in which "our own individual ethical standards influence our view" and how these views are historically and culturally constructed.[4] Like Heinz Antor who offers a perceptive reading of the unreliable narrator in McGrath's *The Grotesque*, I am interested in "the cultural functions of the use of such a device as that of the unreliable narrator," particularly in relation to morality and ethics.[5]

McGrath's unreliable narrators who seem trustworthy are an important part of his work. What differentiates the narrator in *Asylum* from those in McGrath's earlier fiction is the length of time it takes readers to recognize the narrator's unreliability and the extent and breadth of his power.[6] *Asylum*'s psychiatrist narrator, Dr. Peter Cleave, initially appears to be a moral individual who has personal, institutional, and social power because he is a man and a doctor but who seemingly uses this power carefully and for the good of those around him. McGrath notes that "[w]e perceive him as somebody who is wise, sympathetic, a doctor, a mature, professional man. So, as he tells us his story, we're lulled at first into complete confidence that he is giving us the facts."[7] In spite of readers' confidence in Peter, there are early indications that he is unreliable. For example, Peter's comment that "Stella Raphael's story is one of the saddest I know" echoes the opening words used by Ford Madox Ford's famously unreliable narrator in *The Good Soldier*.[8] However, while readers of *The Good Soldier* quickly suspect the accuracy of John Dowell's tale and his motivation for telling it, readers of *Asylum* trust Peter and his narrative until late in the text, because his narrative is plausible, he wields cultural power, and his desire for absolute control is hidden, in part even from himself. Readers' willingness to accept Peter's version of events makes him all the more dangerous. Peter has full social and narrative authority, and he abuses both.

Peter is representative of the paternalistic, hegemonic order that McGrath criticizes, and Peter's language and presentation of the story are part and parcel of the worldview that McGrath calls into question. Everything readers learn is filtered through Peter. He is the one describing, characterizing, and judging the events and characters of the narrative. Even when Peter ostensibly gives Stella's or Edgar's perspectives by reporting what they (supposedly) said or felt, he controls their voices, at least the voices readers hear. Peter's reputation, authority, and sense of self are all at stake in his narrative representation. Only gradually do readers realize that his narrative is not as accurate or as impartial as it initially appears to be. It also is important to note that Peter's moral framework is firmly rooted in the mainstream views of 1950s and 1960s psychiatric practices and marriages. Therefore, his unreliability is a result of his limited vision as well as his deliberate manipulations.

Peter contextualizes his account of Edgar and Stella's affair by explaining: "It was the summer of 1959 and the Mental Health Act had just been passed into law."[9] The time period is important to understanding contemporary gender expectations and social responses to transgressive behavior, and the reference to a specific piece of legislation elucidates how mental illness was conceived of and treated. The Mental Health Act of 1959 sought to liberalize policies regarding the incarceration of mental patients and to professionalize the commitment process by giving control of detention to psychiatrists rather than to magistrates. This legislation was an attempt to protect patients' rights, improve hospital conditions, and give psychiatrists more autonomy to treat their patients.[10] Although this Act helped to humanize the mentally ill and to make the hospital a place of treatment rather than a place of confinement, it also gave psychiatrists much more power. Both the compassionate philosophy about mental illness and the institutional hierarchies and power inequalities embedded in the legislation are reflected in McGrath's portrayal of the hospital in *Asylum*.

McGrath's commentary on naturalized power inequalities is also a reflection of the changes occurring in psychiatry and society more contemporary to the novel's publication. Whereas the 1959 Mental Health Act gave psychiatrists more power, a 1983 Mental Health Act sought to balance this new power with patients' rights. As Joanna Moncrieff notes: "The Mental Health

Act of 1983 reflected a renewed concern with protecting patients' interests, reflecting the influence of the civil rights movements on the 1960s and 1970s. It narrowed the definitions of certain categories of mental disorder and placed restrictions on the administration of psychiatric treatments in the absence of consent. It also reintroduced an inspectorate, the Mental Health Commission."[11] In part, the Act was a response to a series of hospital scandals that revealed the poor treatment of patients. The Act was also a response to "the lack of clarity about the legal position of doctors to treat detained patients without consent and the lack of any safeguards on the assumption of such powers."[12] McGrath delineates the problems of doctors' unchecked power in *Asylum*. Further affecting the efficacy of mental health treatment and patient care, there were substantial financial cuts to health care that took place in the 1980s and 1990s. McGrath argues that "the mental hospital system as a whole has been greatly harmed by Thatcher policies, cutbacks, and a move towards privatization. [British Prime Minister] Major is continuing the dismantlement of the national health system."[13] In McGrath's depiction of *Asylum*'s hospital, he reflects on the history of Victorian asylums, changes to the mental health system taking place in 1959, current concerns about patients' rights, the impact of economic cuts, and "balancing social control with care and treatment."[14]

The hospital in *Asylum* is modeled on Broadmoor Lunatic Asylum, which in 1959 was "one of three special hospitals . . . available for patients subject to detention under the Mental Health Act, who in the opinion of the Minister required treatment under conditions of special security because of their dangerous, violent or criminal propensities."[15] McGrath's familiarity with Broadmoor and his views about mental illness derive from his childhood experience of living in a house on the hospital grounds where his father was medical superintendent from 1957–1981. He also returned to Broadmoor briefly in 1973 to work in the psychology department.

Broadmoor was opened in 1863 in response to the Criminal Lunatics Act of 1860 in order to house and treat the criminally insane.[16] Its objective was treatment rather than punishment. Broadmoor's philosophy about mental illness was "one of sympathy and compassion and the desire of the psychiatrist to know and to understand but always to sympathize and never to make moral judgements."[17] When Dr. McGrath became Broadmoor's tenth medical superintendent, the hospital had come to resemble an overcrowded prison where containment was the primary goal. Trying to honor the original intent of Broadmoor, Dr. McGrath "converted a grim, forbidding institution into a caring, efficient psychiatric hospital."[18] Because of his father's work, McGrath learned early on not to judge the insane in moral terms. McGrath explains that "all question of responsibility becomes very difficult once you have somebody who's mentally ill. . . . [C]ertain crimes are committed when the person responsible is *not* responsible for his or her actions because of a state of insanity."[19]

The openness of Broadmoor's landscape reflected this philosophy that criminally insane patients were sick rather than bad. The architecture also had a therapeutic value. It was a "moral architecture" based on the premise that "spatial arrangements were . . . quite central to any serious effort to remoralize the dangerous and defective."[20] Andrew Scull describes how this moral architecture works:

> Beyond the utility of physical barriers to enforce moral divisions in the patient population, the building's design was important for the reformers in countless other ways. Their ideal institution was to be a home, where the patients were known and treated as individuals, where the mind was constantly stimulated and encouraged to return to its 'natural' state. . . . The building itself should emphasize as little as possible the idea of imprisonment or confinement. It should be sited where the patients could enjoy the benefits of fresh, bracing country air, and where there was an extensive and pleasing view of the surrounding countryside to divert the mind from its morbid fantasies.[21]

Despite the openness of Broadmoor's setting and the relative freedom some of the patients experienced, the grounds and architecture also included structural borders—gates, locked doors, and a perimeter wall—that signified limitations to patients' interactions with the outside world and implied a power structure.

In *Asylum*, Peter Cleave's description of the hospital conveys this contradiction: "It embodies regularity, discipline, and organization. All doors open outward to make them impossible to barricade. All windows are barred. Only the terraces, descending by flights of stone steps to the perimeter wall at the foot of the hill, and planted with trees, grassy banks, and flower gardens, soften and civilize the grim carceral architecture standing over them."[22] Although it confines without appearing to do so, this landscape encourages conformity and contains madness. Peter acknowledges this mechanism of control but still approves of the policies and practices of the asylum.

The seeming openness and compassionate patient philosophy of Broadmoor and its *Asylum* counterpart are predicated on keeping unruly people confined to the hospital grounds, thereby distancing the larger community from criminal or deviant behavior. In other words, the existing power structure at the hospital—and, as I will discuss later, in the marital home—is only invisible until boundaries are breached. Then the structure becomes visible, moral judgments are made, and bad behavior must be punished. This system functions ideologically to separate the deviant from the sane. Scull argues that the institution reinforced this division: "confinement provided its own rationale" for separating asylum inmates from the rest of the community. "Why else were lunatics locked up in the first place, unless it was unsafe for them to be at large. Since the public was convinced . . . that 'these establishments are the necessary places of detention of troops of violent madness, too dangerous to be allowed outside the walls,' asylums were now seen as an essential guarantor of the social order, as well as an important symbolic reminder of the awful consequences of nonconformity."[23] As part of this mechanism of control, when an inmate tries to escape, alarms quickly sound to prevent the patient from leaving the hospital. If the patient succeeds in leaving the grounds, his or her actions and reason for incarceration, which are sympathetically understood inside the hospital, are reassessed as something bad and dangerous, because the patient is no longer separate from the community.

In *Asylum*, Peter's response to Edgar's crime effectively illustrates this point about how and why social perspectives about crime change. As Edgar's psychiatrist, Peter knows the graphic details about the murder Edgar commits: "he bludgeon[s]" his wife "with a hammer," takes out her eyes, and tries to sculpt her head like it was made out of clay.[24] This brutal act remains the same whether Edgar is inside or outside of the hospital, but when he is isolated from the community, Peter can portray Edgar as sick rather than bad and treat the illness rather than punish Edgar for his crime. Once Edgar escapes and his madness is no longer contained, Peter and other hospital officials—individuals who hold institutional power—emphasize the criminal element of Edgar's behavior and his extreme threat to the community.

McGrath's depiction of the shifting judgments about Edgar's crime shows how people's moral beliefs are formed, how these beliefs become socially accepted, and how they are integrated into society and reinforced by law. It reveals that crime and responsibility become moral issues when people want to distance themselves from criminal or deviant behavior. One way to differentiate themselves from the "bad" elements is to define the world in binary terms, us/them, inside/outside, good/bad, and to make sure that the borders between these ideological and physical spaces are policed. In *Asylum*, these borders are physical (community and hospital) and moral (right and wrong). By exposing that these judgments are both made by and reinforce the power of those like Peter who hold social and institutional authority, McGrath prompts readers to see how ideologies of authority and morality are naturalized and to recognize that these ideologies are neither neutral nor inherent.

Power is also naturalized by hiding the structural hierarchy. One moment in *Asylum* when patients, staff, and doctors are on seemingly equal footing is at the annual dance, which encourages the idea that the inhabitants of the asylum are one big happy family: "Parole patients from both the male and female wings of the hospital may attend, and for this one evening they and the staff become an extended family without distinction of rank or status."[25] The sense of community fostered by the dance, staff living on the hospital grounds, and patient work details allows for informal interactions between patients and nonpatients and veils power relations. McGrath fondly recalls that as a boy he spent time with the patients who had work privileges: "These were the friends of my early boyhood, men who twenty years earlier would still have been called 'criminal lunatics'. The first I met was Frank, who built me a swing that hung from an iron bar that he made in the hospital workshop and set high between a pair of tall pines. I treated Frank as an uncle, following him around when he went about his work, chattering away."[26] This childhood experience is the model for Charlie's relationship with Edgar in *Asylum* and illustrates how relationships between patients and nonpatients seemingly erase the boundaries between the sane and the insane. In reality, however, they do not. This flattening of status is only an illusion. Broadmoor, as McGrath observes, "was a closed world, a hierarchy where everything had its place."[27] Everyone also had his or her proper place: "The superintendent was this benign despot, the feudal overlord of this large estate. He had the psychiatric staff, the attendant staff and the nursing staff, and finally there was the great population of patients at the base of this pyramid."[28] Should an incident occur to challenge the hierarchy, the power structure with doctors on top, staff in the middle, and patients on the bottom would be shown to be firmly in place.

In *Asylum*, McGrath highlights this issue of power through Peter's description of the hospital system as "Victorian paternalism on the grand scale."[29] Although McGrath's point of view here corresponds with Peter's observations about the structure of the hospital, Peter remains a representative of the kind of paternalism McGrath wants to critique. That critique can be seen in the difference between how Peter and McGrath perceive the Victorian paternalism embedded in the hospital's structure. Peter revels in the naturalized authority and power that his paternalistic role gives him. In contrast, McGrath shows that even if the superintendent's and psychiatrists' power is masked by the benevolent idea that structure and hierarchy benefit patients and make institutional life function efficiently and effectively, their authority always exists and is absolute. In addition, McGrath reveals that the institutional family structure, with the superintendent in the position of patriarch, does not erase but rather depends on power inequalities; childlike patients are entirely dependent on father figure doctors and motherly nurses for their privileges and everyday needs. Like the hospital landscaping that "soften[s] and civilizes the grim carceral architecture," this benevolent paternalism, a softer more civilized form of patriarchy, remains a mechanism of control.[30]

The moral architecture is not just a physical space but also reflects a particular philosophy and social structure. Foucault makes this point in "The Birth of the Asylum" when he argues that the asylum came to "represent the continuity of social morality. The values of family and work, all the acknowledged virtues, now reign in the asylum."[31] In this work, Foucault describes the ways in which Samuel Tuke's York Retreat helped to normalize institutional power dynamics by tying asylum life to a simulation of the family.[32] Integral to this configuration is the physician. Beginning in the eighteenth century, Foucault notes, the physician in the asylum system "becomes the essential figure of the asylum."[33] He comes to embody judicial and moral wisdom, and the family structure thus takes on a moral component. Foucault emphasizes how the physician's power is then naturalized in the nineteenth and twentieth centuries: "The authority he [the doctor] has borrowed from order, morality, and the family now seems to derive from himself; it is because he is a doctor that he is believed to possess these powers."[34] These power dynamics and the position of psychiatrists as moral judges is part of the Broadmoor model as well. It is precisely this idea that "because he is a doctor" he "possess[es] these powers" and the implied "because he is a doctor, he *should* possess this authority" that McGrath wants to dismantle in *Asylum*. McGrath achieves this goal by revealing how this professional power and the corresponding moral values are created rather than natural.

Stella comes to understand the full extent of this patriarchal authority at a dinner party hosted by medical superintendent Jack Straffen[35] and his wife, Bridie. In this scene, McGrath reveals the discrepancy between the ideal for Broadmoor—a therapeutic environment—and the custodial reality where power hierarchies prevail. As Stella listens to the discussion between Jack, Peter, and Max (Stella's husband and deputy medical superintendent) about Edgar's parole status and chance for discharge, she realizes that doctors have full power to decide patients' fates and to suppress their voices. She also recognizes that this professional and masculine authority has been institutionalized and naturalized:

> It was the raw bare face of institutional power she was seeing on the back lawn that night, she was hearing the voice of the master. It hurt her cruelly . . . and what was worse was that that voice would not be contradicted, because Edgar *had* no voice; he was silent, just as she was now silent on his behalf, unable, although here in the inner council of hospital authority, to speak for him because to do so would not help him. So in her silence she grieved for their lost voices.[36]

Stella mourns not only Edgar's powerlessness because he is a patient but also her own. She has no voice in this discussion because she lacks professional authority. Even more so, Stella is excluded from institutional power because she is a woman.

Through his depiction of marriage, McGrath illustrates this gender-based dynamic in the larger society as well. The marriages of Jack Straffen and Max Raphael conform to the patriarchal social and institutional model, which denies women power. Bridie goes so far as to describe her marriage to Jack specifically in terms of a doctor-patient relationship. As she explains to her dinner guests, she insisted to Jack when they married: "Think of me as a patient . . . and we'll survive. And we have."[37] Bridie's testimony suggests that Jack's paternal role at the hospital and at home serves him well. It makes their roles clear, and it puts Bridie in the position of being cared for. This type of relationship may work well for Bridie and Jack, but not for Stella who is troubled by Max's greater power in their marriage and in the world simply because he is a man. She rebels against the situation in which marital and gender relations, like institutional society, are defined and controlled by patriarchal authority.

Max's patriarchal authority is evident in his desire to control and civilize the landscape, his patients, and his family. According to Peter, Stella explains: "His ambition was to tame and cultivate both the hospital and the estate, make them over as his twin gardens."[38] The parallel between the hospital and the marital home emphasizes Max's authority in both spaces. Extending the parallel, Stella, like Max's patients, is trapped: her view from the garden is "defined by the wall," and her life is circumscribed by marriage.[39] It also is circumscribed by the social expectations of the time period, which McGrath describes as "a highly structured and predictable society. It is very easy to see . . . the hierarchies, the compartments, the rules, the conventions, the uniforms, the distinguishing marks of rank, status, class." This setting provides him with an "orderly, grid-like" structure that highlights Stella's "conflict with reality."[40]

Stella may be socially and economically safe, but she is not free. As Julie Wheelright observes, Stella's "is every woman's story from the postwar era. . . . Stark's imprisonment is juxtaposed with Stella's entrapment in her loveless marriage."[41] Reflecting the time period and her social position, Stella is expected to privilege her role as a wife and mother over work outside of the household, to be self-sacrificing, to put her family's needs before her own, and to be content with this life. "Implicit in this socially sanctioned ideal" about the family structure in this cultural context "is a moral judgment about good and bad wives and mothers: good women are patient, love their families, and are grateful for the lives their husbands have given them."[42] In this ethical paradigm, failing to prioritize the family's needs and failing to be happy with this arrangement make women bad or mad.[43]

Although for many women of Stella's generation marriage was the best means of attaining financial security and social respectability, many discovered that they were not satisfied with their domestic lives.[44] Not only were women miserable, but some were also beginning to resist these prescriptive gender roles. As Sheila Rowbotham observes: "The 1950s appeared to be the epitome of the conventional decade, yet paradoxically it generated resourceful rebels."[45] Stella's rebellion takes the form of an affair. In Peter's words, she "jeopardize[s] it all for a sexual relationship with a patient."[46] Her adulterous act represents more than an attraction to another man. It is a way for her to escape the confines of her marriage and the related social expectations. Stella's might be "a normal marriage. . . . A husband, a home, a child, reasonable contentment," but being a "good" wife and mother is not enough to make her happy.[47] She finds her life to be stifling and unsatisfying, and she eventually becomes depressed and desperate. As Sue Zlosnik contends: "Stella's story throws into relief the way in which social attitudes constrained women in the mid twentieth century. The boundaries of the asylum are paralleled by the ideological boundaries that contain her as a middle-class married woman and which she breaches, just as surely as Edgar breaches the physical boundaries of the asylum."[48]

There also is a parallel between how Stella's and Edgar's transgressive behavior is judged. Like the shift in perspective about Edgar's crime when he escapes from the hospital, Stella's behavior is judged more harshly when she openly attempts to escape her marriage and her role as a mother. In marital and hospital environments, women and patients are acceptable if they are quiet and invisible. However, once they become visible—and unruly women and escaped patients are indeed visible—they challenge traditional authority, and their subversive behavior has the potential to disrupt the social order. As a result, their transgressions become moral issues. That the community judges Stella's nondomestic behavior in this way is evident in their perception of her as "a tramp and a slut and an unfit mother."[49] For them, Stella's relationship with Edgar challenges conventional gender roles and the assumed safety of marital and familial domestic space. Having internalized proper behavioral roles—the ones against which she is now judged—even Stella is shocked by her actions. She feels "horror at the appalling transgression she'd committed—having sex with a *patient*, not fifty yards from the house."[50] This description suggests that the sexual relationship with Edgar is even more scandalous, because of its proximity to the household, which is a crucial part of the family's moral architecture. This domestic space represents family values and social stability. As a result, when Stella consummates the relationship near the marital home and then brings Edgar into the marital bed, she violates these ideological structures.

Stella's shock at her own actions makes her vow to end the relationship with Edgar, but she cannot and the relationship intensifies. After Edgar's escape to London, their trysts move away from the marital home. This distance from the family's moral center would seem to lessen the threat to the family, but the offense worsens because the act of volition it takes for Stella to travel to London makes the affair a continued conscious decision rather than just a relationship of convenience. As Peter sees it: "The transit [to London] . . . put her on the other side, that's what shifted her beyond the law, not just the criminal law but the law of her marriage, her family, and her society, which of course was the hospital."[51] Peter's description, which traces the range of Stella's transgressions, confirms that Stella's affair is not simply a personal indiscretion but also a legal matter and an affront to society. From Peter's perspective, Stella's story is that "of selfishness, of self-indulgence, of the willful destruction of a family." She is "a woman who pursues her own appetites and thereby destroys the fabric of the community in which she had a place. In that sense she is in the tradition of Anna Karenina or Madame Bovary."[52] This tradition is one in which transgressive women are punished by death for their threat to the social structure. That this narrative fate occurs in so many different settings and time periods emphasizes the pervasiveness and gender-specific nature of this problem. Stella's sexual transgression and later her "unnatural" behavior toward her child represent direct challenges to society and its morality.

Ironically, Stella's adultery requires her to more faithfully perform her domestic and conjugal duties and, at least superficially, to conform to traditional marital and maternal roles in the interest of Max "find[ing] her invisible again."[53] From Max's perspective, good wives and mothers are nice, proper, and do not "make an exhibition" of themselves.[54] Their role is to quietly support the family rather than to be in charge of it. This formulation naturalizes marital inequalities based on gender roles. McGrath does not simply describe the plight of the powerless. Instead, he reveals the mechanisms behind these power inequalities: how the marital and medical institutions he depicts in *Asylum* maintain these "patriarchal arrangements."[55]

The paradox of women's invisibility is that they are always being watched. Max, Jack, and Peter all watch Stella with their "terrible psychiatric gazes," which makes her "feel like a specimen!"[56] Even Charlie, Stella and Max's son, watches Stella and scrutinizes her behavior. Stella notes that as she cooks dinner after a trip to see Edgar, "Charlie was sitting at the table, swinging his legs and watching her. His gaze was clinical."[57] Charlie's gaze, even though he is only a child, represents male power. That Charlie already exercises this male privilege accords with McGrath's idea that "so much of our personalities is conditioned by the gender typing we've been subject to right from day one."[58] In *Asylum*, McGrath exposes how gender roles are learned and perpetuated. Charlie not only watches Stella but also reports to his father, the highest authority in the household, that she has come back from London drunk. Stella's anger about Charlie's assumed power is evident when on another trip to London, she becomes apathetic about her late return. Stella initially panics that she will not be home in time to pick up Charlie from school, which indicates an ingrained feeling of maternal responsibility. However, her next thought reveals her bitterness toward Charlie: "She discovered she didn't care. She didn't care if she missed her train. She didn't care if she was late. Charlie could go home on the bus and she would tell him some story, and it wouldn't matter. She was alert enough to recognize the hostility in the thought, and to understand that she hadn't forgiven him for betraying her to Max."[59] Beyond resenting Charlie's actions in this one situation, Stella's anger stems from feeling powerless in the male-centered household.

In contrast to this stifling situation, Stella's relationship with Edgar allows her to cast off her "old, stale identity" and explore a role besides mother and wife.[60] Stella believes that shedding these roles will give her more freedom and power. However, she is mistaken. She cannot escape male authority or a maternal role. When Edgar's illness returns, she must mother him—"She had to treat Edgar as a child now, a touchy, clinging child, and she wondered why she was looking after this child and not her own"—and as Edgar's mistress, Stella continues to be defined by a man and her actions circumscribed.[61] Moreover, when they leave the hospital environment, a place where Stella has marginally more authority than a patient, she loses her advantage over Edgar. Outside of the hospital, Edgar wields considerably more power: "He was stronger now. No longer constrained, he spoke and acted with an authority she had never known in him on the estate."[62] Through Stella's relationships with Max and Edgar and her interactions with Jack and Peter, McGrath documents the ubiquitousness of male authority. Mitchell R. Lewis emphasizes this point when he argues that Stella is a victim of patriarchy: "The reader comes away with the sense that Stella is a victim in relationship to all three men in her life, Edgar, Peter, and Max, among whom she is passed back and forth like a commodity, without whom she has no money, home, means of support, friends or family."[63] The circumstances of Stella's life may change, but the gender roles available to Stella do not.

Further confirming her lack of social and personal authority, Stella is often invisible in her relationship with Edgar just as she was with Max. She, or at least her head, may be at the center of his artistic project, but her role as a model is one of passive object. She also recognizes that "Nick's reaction [to Edgar's work] mattered as hers did not."[64] These instances of invisibility highlight Stella's powerlessness in her relationship with Edgar, but there are also times, as with Max, when Stella uses invisibility to her advantage. When Edgar's behavior becomes more erratic and she becomes the locus for Edgar's jealous delusions, Stella tries not to be noticed. When she leaves him out of fear, her status as a poor woman makes her unworthy of attention and allows her to successfully avoid detection in the working-class London neighborhood where she has been living. Despite her desire to stay hidden, Stella's concern for Edgar's well-being prompts her to risk visibility, and she returns to his flat to check on him. He is gone, but the police are there, and they take her into custody and bring her back to her family.

In her role as an adulterer—a sexually deviant woman—Stella's behavior becomes highly visible, and she is scrutinized and judged by the community. Stella "flout[s] not only the rules of her marriage but also the most serious ethical imperatives of the institution and ultimately the law."[65] In an attempt to distance themselves from Stella's bad acts, the members of the community initially shun Stella for leaving her family. "[S]he was an affront to their sense of decency," and she is condemned for this behavior.[66] However, Stella's return from Edgar and from London seemingly indicates a return to the bounds of her marriage. In this socially acceptable position, she is less of a threat and can be viewed more sympathetically. In contrast, Edgar, who remains outside the bounds of the hospital, continues to be a social threat and is therefore held fully responsible for Stella's socially inappropriate acts. Stella's behavior has not changed, but Peter's description of it has. In the new narrative based on Stella's and Edgar's changed positions, Peter portrays Stella as "the victim, seduced and abandoned, a pitiful woman led astray by a cunning man who had manipulated and entrapped her and then cast her aside."[67] This version denies her agency but mitigates her responsibility in the affair.

Stella's "passiv[ity] and plian[cy]" after her arrest further serve to diminish her responsibility: "She became . . . like a child or a sick person. . . . All she wanted now was to be looked after."[68] Once Stella gives up control and tacitly agrees to be voiceless and powerless, the community can be more compassionate, because her disruptive behavior can be understood as a sign of illness rather than as a direct challenge to the social order. In moral terms, a nervous breakdown is better than Stella's willful disregard for marriage and motherhood. In accordance with this point of view, Peter advises Max to foreground his "psychiatric perspective" and to see Stella's actions as a result of "hysterical illness."[69] This condition means: "Therefore she was not entirely culpable. Therefore, she needed not punishment but care. Therefore, she would get better."[70] Peter's rationale that Stella is mad rather than bad relieves her of responsibility, but more importantly in terms of gender roles, means that Stella can be "cured" and successfully return to her marital and domestic duties.

As a psychiatrist, Max may be able to understand Stella's behavior; however, as a husband he remains hurt by her actions and wants her to feel guilty for her conduct. That Max continues to feel wronged can be seen in his dismissal of Stella's intense misery when she tries to resume her former life: "When the tears came . . . nobody came down to see if she was all right, it was just the slut in the kitchen who'd ruined their lives, getting drunk on neat gin and howling for her lost lunatic lover."[71] Stella may have returned home, but she has not been cured in the sense that she happily returns to her domestic role. Instead, she withdraws from her family and moves from active transgression (physically leaving the household) to passive resistance (emotionally leaving the household).

Max wants Stella to be a good wife, but even more so he wants her to be a good mother, and this is the primary reason he tries to reconcile with Stella. As he explains: "I stay here, with you, for one reason only, and that's because I think that child needs a mother. But if you never show him any warmth there isn't much point."[72] Max's words reflect contemporary psychological theories about the importance of the mother-child relationship in which "the mother, long relegated to the wings of psychoanalytic thought, moved to center stage."[73] Donald Winnicott's 1940s radio broadcasts helped to make these ideas accessible and fashionable to the public. Another popular psychologist at the time was John Bowlby. In *Child Care and the Growth of Love* (1953), Bowlby argues: "What is believed to be essential for mental health is that the infant and young child should experience a warm, intimate, and continuous relationship with his mother . . . in which both find satisfaction and enjoyment."[74] This discourse about the importance of the mother to her children's development created a climate in which mothers were an essential part of their children's success. However, if they failed to be good mothers, this same rhetoric positioned them as the cause of children's problems: "The mother was thus immensely responsible and immensely to blame if she reared misfits, oddballs or trouble-makers."[75] As they became part of the culture, these theories about the mother's relationship with her baby or young child were being applied to mothers' relationships with their older children as well. Although Charlie is older than the children that Bowlby describes in his book, Stella's failure to connect with her child and her incapacity for consistent maternal warmth can still be deemed "maternal deprivation" and have harmful effects.[76] In accordance with Bowlby's theory, Max implies that Charlie's anxiety, sadness, and social withdrawal can all be attributed to maternal deprivation. Stella may be reproached for being a bad wife, which is an embarrassment to her husband and family, but in line with with these theories about the mother-child relationship, she is condemned for being a bad mother, which is a social evil. That Stella has inculcated these views is evident in the guilt that she feels in relation to Charlie.

Stella does love Charlie, but her domestic and marital discontent interferes with the maternal expectations prescribed by a postwar society[77] and popularized by psychoanalytic theories about the mother-child bond. Stella, in contrast to these ideals, is distanced and distracted, which translates into a lack of vigilance about Charlie's safety. For example, after warning Charlie once about getting too close to the edge of a pond, she lapses into inattention and does not pursue the matter when Charlie remains precariously perched. Another moment of carelessness on Stella's part occurs after Edgar escapes from the hospital and a search ensues. Until Stella's mother-in-law, Brenda, asks about Charlie, Stella does not even notice that he is missing, because she is too preoccupied with Edgar's safety. Then, Peter observes, she "promptly simulated extreme anxiety."[78] This simulation shows that Stella is aware of how she should act but only does so when she realizes someone is watching.

Stella's depression and resulting disregard for upholding social conventions is even more evident when Charlie drowns on a school trip on which Stella is one of the chaperones. This event echoes the scene of Charlie near the pond, but now Stella is too numb to feign concern or to act. On the field trip, Stella is physically present but mentally withdrawn. She goes with Charlie when he wants to explore the water. However, when he "los[es] his balance" and falls in, she blankly watches instead of trying to save Charlie "who was in deeper water now, trying to scramble upright and flailing around and shouting."[79] Stella's depression manifests itself as indifference to Charlie and to the world around her and is horrifyingly emphasized by her calm demeanor as she observes Charlie drowning. Instead of acting, Stella just sits, "smoking her cigarette, turning her head away, then back, then away again, as an indistinct figure struggled in the water."[80] Stella's vague awareness and continued apathy convey the depth of her despair about her married life and her life without Edgar.

After Charlie's death, the community initially feels sympathy for Stella, because she is a mother who has lost her son and because they interpret her lethargy as shock at the loss. However, when Hugh Griffin, another chaperone on the trip, reveals that Stella watched Charlie drown and did nothing to save him, the community's sympathy is replaced by disbelief and anger that a mother would willfully fail to protect her child. As a result, they find her morally culpable: "What horrified them was that she had made no noise and hadn't moved. When they properly understood this it all changed, because then she was a mother who'd watched her child drown and done nothing to save him. It was unnatural, they said. It was evil. They couldn't understand it; she has no feelings, they said, she isn't human, she's a monster. Or perhaps she's mad."[81] When Max tries to make sense of her behavior and asks: "But why didn't you shout?" Stella defends her conduct as culturally being in line with how women are expected to act.[82] Good women, she knows from experience, should be quiet and invisible: "Usually they want you to keep your mouth shut, but sometimes they want you to shout, and they expect you to know the difference. This was what amused her."[83] Although Stella's excuse points to the problem with expecting women, wives in particular, to be passive and submissive, she fails to account for social expectations about mothers. A good mother is expected to be watchful, protective, and self-sacrificing, and it is for this failure that she is judged. Because Stella's behavior diverges so much from how a good mother should act, the community can only make sense of Stella's inaction by seeing her as monstrous or mentally ill.

Peter emphasizes the latter, arguing that Stella suffers from clinical depression. His diagnosis resonates with why many women were incarcerated at Broadmoor: they were convicted of murdering their children while suffering from postnatal psychosis and acquitted by reason of insanity. From Peter's psychiatric perspective, which he claims frees him from moral judgments, Stella should be pitied and helped rather than denounced. Despite his contention that he does not judge people in moral terms, Peter's narrative *always* foregrounds morality, and he constantly assesses individual responsibility. Moreover, whether readers deem Stella mad—not subject to moral judgment under the Broadmoor model—or bad directly relates to how Peter portrays Stella and how readers perceive her level of responsibility. When Peter wants readers to judge Stella less harshly, he ascribes her actions to something beyond her control, using narratives like romance or illness that situate her in a passive role and thereby lessen her responsibility. In contrast, when Peter wants readers to be more critical of Stella's actions and to see her as morally culpable, he describes her active control of a situation and her conscious choices.

These shifting narratives can be seen in Peter's description of the affair. Initially, he portrays Stella as the active party. Edgar may suggest a sexual encounter—"he had bluntly suggested she come into the conservatory with him"—but Stella takes the physical initiative.[84] She "pull[s] him into the conservatory," "[takes] his head in her hands," and "kisse[s] him fiercely on the lips."[85] She also finds a meeting place and "plan[s] to bring a man . . . [there] for sex."[86] In this version of events, Stella is to blame for advancing the affair.

In contrast, when Peter invokes a romance narrative to describe these same events, Stella becomes a victim of circumstance: "She saw him as her charming rogue. She couldn't argue with him. She couldn't oppose him at all, it wasn't possible, for she had begun to surrender herself and no longer felt distinct and separate from him, rather that she was incomplete without him. She understood what was happening, she was falling in love, and she didn't want to stop it. She said she couldn't stop it. . . . No control."[87] Peter's explanation that Stella's actions are beyond her control makes her less culpable. Stella also becomes less culpable when Peter describes Edgar as the active party in the relationship. He maintains that Edgar consciously influences Stella's feelings: "Much more pertinent from my point of view was that he [Edgar] was behaving manipulatively and, at the outset at least, attempting to use his considerable sexual attraction as a means of control."[88] In this formulation, which implies that Stella is weak, suggestible, and easily manipulated, Edgar is the responsible party.

Peter then advances another hypothesis that again shifts the blame. He argues that the affair might have been beyond both of their control: "They seemed powerless to control this hunger they had for each other."[89] This language makes passion rather than either individual responsible. Significantly, each of Peter's theories and narratives prompts the reader to judge the affair and its repercussions differently, and these judgments shift throughout the text. Through these examples, McGrath's unreliable narrator works "to reveal . . . the gap between appearance and reality, and to show how human beings distort or conceal the latter."[90] Here the distortion comes through Peter's storytelling. What eventually becomes clear is not whether Edgar or Stella is responsible for the affair or whether either or both are mad or bad, but rather how an individual's moral judgments are derived from conventional narratives, gendered expectations about behavior, and unequal power relations.

Like the calculating behavior he ascribes to Edgar, Peter's manipulative narrative is "a means of control," and it is effective. Because Peter is a figure of authority, even when he admits that he is not privy to firsthand knowledge about the relationship between Edgar and Stella and that he must speculate about what happens and what people are feeling, his acknowledgment of conjecture does not immediately discredit his account. Instead, as in novels like McGrath's *The Grotesque* (1989) and *Trauma* (2008), books in which the narrator's credibility becomes increasingly questionable yet cannot entirely be discounted, Peter's credibility is built up by providing verifiable details. For example, Peter fills in the emotional particulars when he describes the first sexual encounter between Stella and Edgar: "I *imagine* it was urgent and primitive, a thing of hunger and instinct."[91] The phrase "I imagine" is one example of how Peter's unreliability is revealed "in the discourse of narrative, in the verbal habits of the narrator."[92] Yet McGrath deemphasizes the linguistic markers here by focusing on the reliable parts of Peter's narrative. Peter may have to "imagine" parts of the sexual encounter, but he knows the minutiae of the bathroom where Stella washes up afterwards: "I know that bathroom. The original fittings are all intact. The big tub with its tarnished brass taps on clawed feet on a floor of discolored tiles. A fern that flourishes in the steamy atmosphere of that large damp room overflows its terra-cotta pot by the door, and beside it there's a large wicker laundry basket."[93] These precise details give credence to the invented part of his story. The plausibility of Peter's account also helps him maintain his narrative credibility. He uses familiar narratives and characters—the love story, an unhappy marriage, forbidden relationships, a fallen woman, a mad artist—in order to make the events understandable and convincing to the reader.

Peter's professional authority and in-depth psychiatric knowledge further makes his narrative trustworthy and, ultimately, much more sinister. His position as a respected forensic psychiatrist and later the hospital's medical superintendent inspires the reader's confidence. Moreover, his willingness to share his professional knowledge with the reader creates a bond; if Peter can trust the reader with sensitive, confidential information—the details about his medical cases—the reader can trust him.

Although Peter ultimately represents what Booth describes as a "most vicious character," McGrath initially "builds sympathy" for him by providing an "inside view" of Peter.[94] Magali Falco elaborates on the effect of this personal interaction between narrator and reader when she notes:

> McGrath's narrators usually express themselves casually and frequently address the reader in order to create an intimate space so that they delude the reader into believing in their wild imaginings. McGrath's deceptive narrative techniques are mainly based on the pseudo-confession style . . . as the narrator is telling himself stories, trying to convince himself and the reader, the latter is plunged into the narrator's imagination and fantasies. He then becomes his witness, his accomplice, even.[95]

This close ideological connection between Peter and the reader is precisely what occurs in *Asylum* as readers put their trust in Peter's version of the truth.

Peter further draws in the reader and demonstrates his authority with his psychological explanation of the stages of a "catastrophic love affair characterized by sexual obsession": "Recognition. Identification. Assignation. Structure. Complication."[96] As Stella moves from one stage to the next, Peter educates the reader by identifying each shift, explaining in detail Stella's actions, and offering psychiatric reasons for her behavior: "She became involved. Identification, hazy at first, hedged around with friendly detachment, quickened. . . . Now, predictably, as they moved toward assignation and structure, Stella began to create a sort of arabesque in her mind, a pattern of thought and feeling whose function it was to lead her back to him. . . . Assignation, this was the next stage. Establishing the times and places, giving the thing a structure."[97] Being privy to this information aligns the reader with

Peter and his clinical perspective. Additionally, it puts the reader in a position of authority to assess and judge Stella's behavior, and as a result, Stella must endure the reader's gaze as well as Peter's. It is this position of power that McGrath wants to question and destabilize by showing the mechanics behind it.

Despite readers' early connection with Peter's point of view, Peter's narrative becomes more suspect later in the text, and readers "grow suspicious of the objectivity of his account."[98] McGrath then explains the effect he wants this suspicion to have on the reader: "What I hope happens is that the reader's sense of disorientation and disillusion, is quite strongly disturbed, because the initial confidence had been so firmly established; and we'll then see that this man is none of the things that we first thought him to be: he is not wise, he is not detached, he is not sympathetic."[99] Peter may begin as the representative of normalcy, social standards, mental stability, and professional authority, but by the end of the novel he is shown to be dangerous and corrupt. The revelation that such a seemingly upstanding member of the community is pathological disrupts readers' habitual conflation of social power and moral authority. Moreover, once readers realize that Peter is an unreliable narrator who is blind to his own obsessions, they must question their own moral position and the foundations of their ethical positions and belief systems.[100]

Peter's ability to easily impose his view of the world and to suppress all other voices emphasizes the lack of power women and patients have and highlights the problems with granting moral and social authority solely on the basis of one's social, gender, and professional position. These cultural markers traditionally grant power, but as McGrath shows, they are not a guarantee of moral rectitude. By the end of *Asylum*, the reader learns the extent of Peter's delusions and must question his professional authority, his decisions about patients' treatment, and his level of responsibility in the tragedies that occur.

Among Peter's questionable choices is to arrange for Stella to become a patient at the hospital where Max was deputy superintendent (until her relationship with Edgar forced him to resign) and where Peter is currently superintendent. This "unorthodox" decision marks the moment when Peter's seemingly neutral narrative position begins to unravel for the reader.[101] His professional interest in Stella is suspiciously personal, and his choice to treat her is a manifestation of his need for power. Peter's love of power becomes clear in his reaction to Stella's return to the hospital as a patient: "Now that I had her here in the female wing I relished the prospect of stripping away her defenses and opening her up, seeing what that psyche of hers really looked like. I understood of course that she would resist me, but we had time."[102] As this description suggests, Peter's desire for control is the motivating force in his personal and professional life. Exercising control is also part of his sexual fantasies. He wants to subdue Stella, to mentally undress her, and so long as she eventually yields to his "treatment," her resistance is part of a game of seduction for him, part of her appeal.

The doctor-patient relationship that he fosters at the hospital mirrors the unequal power dynamics that Stella experiences in her marriage. Both are spaces where men have power and women do not, and both are spaces where women's behavior is scrutinized and judged. As a patient and as a woman, Stella understands that she must not "risk nonconformity," and her survival in the hospital, like in her marriage, depends on adhering to conventional gender roles and behavioral expectations.[103] These parallels allow Stella to recognize that many women share her domestic discontent and that "mad" women are often ordinary women who simply deviate from or defy social conventions: "She no longer saw the other women as so very mad or strange or different from herself."[104] Stella's new perspective suggests that women's madness can be a response to the strictures of marriage, motherhood, or gendered social expectations. Stella's recognition accords with the literature of the time in which madness and institutional punishment are connected to women deviating from socially prescribed gender roles.

The antipsychiatry movement also gave feminism a language and social context for women's deviance. Elaine Showalter argues that "Labeling theory provided a way of looking at female insanity as the violation of sex-role expectations. Laingian theory interpreted female schizophrenia as the product of women's repression and oppression within the family. Madness itself became intelligible as a strategy, a form of communication in response to the contradictory messages and demands about femininity women faced in patriarchal society."[105] Although not schizophrenic, Stella's oppression, resistance, and sentence to a mental hospital resonate with these ideas about gender roles, and the population of women that Max works with in Wales—the "block he was responsible for housed a high proportion of female schizophrenics, women in middle age or older who had been institutionalized so long there was no real hope of change"—suggests that Stella's transgressive behavior is not unique.[106]

Stella's double powerlessness because she is a woman and a patient becomes even more apparent when Peter imagines Stella as his wife. He explains: "She was my patient, but she was also a woman of taste, a woman of my own class, and I was not blind to her qualities. In recent days I had more than once imagined her in my house, as she once so frequently had been, among my furniture, my books, my art. Oh, she had a place there, among my fine *objets*."[107] Emphasizing women's expected passivity in marriage, Stella becomes little more than an object in Peter's fantasy. Her lack of power is further highlighted when Peter talks not to Stella but to Max about his plans and asks Max to grant Stella a divorce so that he can marry her. At this moment, Peter truly crosses moral boundaries and his blindness, arrogance, and unethical professional behavior become even clearer and more shocking.

Peter's conversation with Max also highlights the problems for women in this patriarchal environment. When Peter proposes, Stella recognizes that the proposal is a bargain struck between men and that she is the object of exchange: "She felt like a consignment of damaged but retrievable womanhood, in the process of being transferred from old owner to new, after being stored for a while in a warehouse."[108] Peter's proposal—his offer of "[s]afety. Asylum"—is even more disturbing, because he presents it under the guise of kindness and concern and because he proposes while Stella is still his patient.[109] That Peter couches his offer of marriage in terms of "asylum" continues to emphasize the parallels between marriage and institutionalization and the power inequalities between doctors and patients and between husbands and wives. Peter believes his feelings for Stella are dispassionate and his proposal logical. However, Stella can see Peter's offer for what it is: "A romantic proposition from the medical superintendent, with her husband's complicity."[110] Although Stella clearly recognizes the patriarchal implications of the proposal, she also realizes that within this institutional and social structure, she is powerless to refuse the offer. Technically, of course, she could; however, she knows that refusing puts her in a precarious position. Peter is still in charge of certifying that she is sane and applying to the Home Office for her discharge, which affects when or whether she is released. Because of her lack of power, Stella understands that it is in her best interest to comply with his wishes. Her experiences reveal the hospital and the institution of marriage to be places of misused power and authority disguised as benevolent paternalism.

If the patients in *Asylum* are presented sympathetically, the doctors are not. All of them hold power over the lives of others, and all to some extent misuse it. Max is cold, aloof, and patronizing (although the reader must also remember that he is being described by Peter who has romantic feelings for Stella); Jack is kind but more concerned about maintaining appearances than solving problems; and Peter is radically deficient in medical and moral judgment. Moreover, Peter's irresponsible and unethical behavior has lethal consequences. Only after it is too late to prevent Stella's suicide does Peter realize he has misinterpreted Stella's actions at the hospital dance: "Oh, I had been blind! It was not for us, that dress, it was not a gesture of pride, or defiance, thrown in the face of the hospital community, it was for *him* [Edgar], she'd worn it for *him*, it was her wedding dress, she'd worn it the night she became wedded to him. . . . I'd deluded myself: I had allowed my judgment to be clouded by private concerns, and in the process lost my objectivity. Classic countertransference."[111] Significantly, even in the midst of his concern about Stella's well-being, Peter attempts to mitigate his responsibility by using medical language to describe his moment of failure.

In a further attempt to evade his moral culpability, Peter places responsibility for his blindness on Stella. Rather than continuing to portray Stella as the grateful and graceful recipient of his paternal care, he manipulates and rewrites the narrative to suggest that her rational and quiescent behavior at the hospital was a conscious act: "A calm, good-tempered demeanor, amiable but not hysterical, composed but not depressed, this she knew was what we wanted to see."[112] Stella's performance of sound mental health is effective and, Peter implies, is an active attempt to fool him:

> She'd have known then that she must pretend not to care [about Edgar]. Everything that followed—asking for a job in the laundry, sitting alone on her bench—*even the dreams of a screaming child*—all a performance, a distraction, invented to keep me from the truth. And the truth was that her suffering these last weeks was not remorse for the death of her child, the truth was that she was still obsessed with Edgar Stark, to the virtual exclusion of everything else.[113]

Although Peter earlier protects Stella from the community's indictment that she is a bad mother, he invokes this bad mother narrative—she lacks remorse for her child's death and puts her desires above those of others—and its moral imperative when he feels he has lost control of Stella.

Peter also claims that Stella's acceptance of his proposal was part of the masquerade, "the desperate duplicity of a woman still passionately in love with another man and frantic to conceal it."[114] Through his description of Stella's "desperate duplicity" and the refrain "she led me to believe," Peter positions himself as the victim of Stella's manipulations.[115] He does not question his own actions nor does he take any responsibility. Instead, he hides behind his professional, social, and narrative authority. By the end, however, readers can see through Peter's façade and can see the system of power that sustains his authority.

Troublingly, only through her death does Stella escape from Peter and the social and institutional oppression he represents. Symbolizing this freedom, she is buried "outside the Wall."[116] However, Stella's escape is only partial, and her suicide is hardly a victory. Peter still controls her story and her image, and his need for control is apparent both in his villainization of Stella when she resists him and in his valorization of her death. Like Bram Stoker's disturbing description of the vampire Lucy's purification through violence, Peter describes Stella's sexual and social purification through death in similar terms: "As she relaxed, as she let go all effort of deception and repression, her face changed, her beauty became even more remarkable, and once again she was as pale and lovely as when we'd first known her."[117] Peter's words are meant to shift the reader's perception of Stella one final time; in death, and therefore no longer disruptive, she is once again a pure figure deserving of sympathy.

McGrath's novel explores the complex relationship between pathological states, oppressive social norms, and the construction of narrative. The shift in the reader's perception about Peter from a wise and kind father figure to a deluded and dangerous individual emphasizes McGrath's indictment of Peter and his misused power as well as his indictment of the society which unquestionably grants authority to people in Peter's social and professional position, issues that continue to be relevant to contemporary society. More importantly, McGrath's unreliable and pathological narrator is meant to unsettle readers' entrenched social beliefs and make them rethink their moral judgments about paternalism, mental illness, criminal insanity, and deviant women.

NOTES

1. Wayne Booth, *The Rhetoric of Fiction* (Chicago: The University of Chicago Press, 1961), 158–59. Using Booth's definition as a starting point, subsequent narratological work has expanded and complicated this definition of the unreliable narrator. Rhetorical and cognitive approaches have been two main ways of understanding unreliable narration. More recently, critics such as Vera Nünning and Bruno Zerweck have expressed a "cultural-narratological theory of unreliable narration" (Zerweck, "Historicizing Unreliable Narration," 151). They emphasize that "because the ascription of (un)reliability involves interpretive choices and strategies, it is culturally and historically variable" (Angsar Nünning, "Reconceptualizing Unreliable Narration," 99). In addition, there have been efforts by Ansgar Nünning in his 2005 study (his early work articulates a strictly cognitive approach), J. Alexander Bareis, and Per Krough Hansen to synthesize some of these approaches. Bareis, for example, "consider[s] unreliable narration to be an interpretive effect that takes place in the interplay between the text, the author, and the reader" (Bareis, "Ethics, The Diachronization of Narratology," 47).

2. Vera Nünning, "Unreliable Narration and the Historical Variability of Values and Norms: *The Vicar of Wakefield* as a Test Case of a Cultural-Historical Narratology," *Style* 28, no. 2 (2004): 236–37.

3. James Phelan and Mary Patricia Martin, "The Lessons of 'Weymouth': Homodiegesis, Unreliability, Ethics, and *The Remains of the Day*," in *Narratologies: New Perspectives and Narrative Analysis*, ed. David Herman (Columbus: Ohio State University Press, 1999), 88–89.

4. Ibid., 103.

5. Heinz Antor, "Unreliable Narration and (Dis-)Orientation in the Postmodern Neo-Gothic Novel: Reflections on Patrick McGrath's *The Grotesque* (1989)," *Miscelánea: A Journal of English and American Studies* 24 (2001): 13.

6. For more about narrative unreliability in McGrath's work see his interviews by Crittenden and by Menegaldo. Also see Antor; Falco; and Zlosnik.

7. Patrick McGrath, interview by Gilles Menegaldo, *Creative Voices* (1998): 123.

8. Patrick McGrath, *Asylum* (New York: Vintage Books, 1998), 3.

9. Ibid., 4.

10. Joanna Moncrieff, "The Politics of a New Mental Health Act," *The British Journal of Psychiatry* 183 (2003): 9.

11. Ibid.

12. Jeffrey Cohen, "Tracing the Developments of the Mental Health Act Commission and Its Predecessors," in *Understanding Treatment without Consent: An Analysis of the Work of the Mental Health Act Commission*, written by Ian Shaw, Hugh Middleton, and Jeffrey Cohen (London: Ashgate, 2008), 28.

13. Patrick McGrath, interview by Lindsey Crittenden, *Turnstile* 3, no. 2 (1992): 36.

14. Ian Shaw, "A Short History of Mental Health," in *Understanding Treatment without Consent: An Analysis of the Work of the Mental Health Act Commission*, written by Ian Shaw, Hugh Middleton, and Jeffrey Cohen (London: Ashgate, 2008), 9.

15. Susanne Dell and Graham Robertson, *Sentenced to Hospital: Offenders in Broadmoor* (New York: Oxford University Press, 1998), 1.

16. For in-depth histories of Broadmoor, see Partridge; Black; and Dell and Robertson.

17. Patrick McGrath, quoted in Magali Falco, "Patrick McGrath's Case Histories or the Ruin(s) of Psychoanalysis," *Anglophonia: French Journal of English Studies* 15 (2004): 95–96.

18. Nicholas Freeman, "Patrick McGrath," in *Dictionary of Literary Biography: British Novelists since 1960 Fourth Series*, ed. Merritt Moseley (Detroit: Gale Group, 2001), 146.

19. McGrath, interview by Crittenden, 45.

20. Andrew Scull, *Social Order/Mental Disorder: Anglo-American Psychiatry in Historical Perspective* (Oakland: University of California Press, 1989), 214.

21. Ibid., 226, 228.

22. McGrath, *Asylum*, 4. Hélène Machinal makes the important point that the hospital in *Asylum* is structured like Jeremy Bentham's Panopticon (Machinal, "'The Turn of the Screw' in McGrath's *Asylum*," 66). Her chapter "'The Turn of the Screw' in McGrath's *Asylum*" offers an insightful discussion of this idea and spatiality more generally.

23. Scull, *Social Order/Mental Disorder*, 231. Similarly, Christine Ferguson argues: "In constructing and quarantining images of disease with the confining barriers of art, the mainstream forges its identity through the processes of contradistinction. We know ourselves by what we are not; the more monstrous and raving the 'Other', then, by reverse definition, the more healthy and rational the society which is able to identify it as such" (Ferguson, "Dr. McGrath's Disease," 240).

24. McGrath, *Asylum*, 10.

25. Ibid., 6. For more details about the parole dances, see Partridge, 257–61, and Black, 163–66.

26. Patrick McGrath, "A Childhood in Broadmoor Hospital," *Granta* 29 (1989): 158.

27. Patrick McGrath, "In Pursuit of Sublime Terror," interview by Suzie MacKenzie, *The Guardian*, September 2, 2005.

28. McGrath, interview by Menegaldo, 121.

29. McGrath, *Asylum*, 46.

30. Ibid., 4.

31. Michel Foucault, "The Birth of the Asylum," in *Madness and Civilization: A History of Insanity in the Age of Reason* (New York: Vintage Books, 1973), 257.

32. Ibid., 254–55.

33. Ibid., 270.

34. Ibid., 275.

35. Jack Straffen's name echoes child-killer John Straffen, the "longest-serving prisoner" in England whose escape from Broadmoor was unprecedented (Lowe, *Escape from Broadmoor*, 182). McGrath's invocation of John Straffen suggests not that the medical superintendent is actually a murderer but rather that his decisions about the hospital may not be as morally sound as readers automatically believe them to be. The name casts doubt on his character and encourages readers to question their assumption that Jack is good simply because he is in a position of authority. Character names are important to McGrath who argues that "a name in a piece of fiction has quite a bit of work to do. . . . It's got to be not only that which identifies a character but also that which suggests the meaning and the metaphorical implications of that character" (McGrath, interview by Crittenden, 37). In another interview, McGrath explains the implications of Peter Cleave's name: "His name in fact is Cleave, which is one of those words that has two meanings, diametrically opposed to each other: 'cleave' meaning to cut in half, to sever, to chop out, to divide; but 'to cleave' also means to cling to, to hold to" (McGrath, interview by Menegaldo, 123). These contradictions are part of McGrath's strategy to complicate moral and ethical issues.

36. McGrath, *Asylum*, 50 (original emphasis).

37. Ibid., 47.

38. Ibid., 28.

39. Ibid., 52.

40. McGrath, interview by Menegaldo, 121.

41. Julie Wheelright, "No Hiding Place," review of *Asylum*, by Patrick McGrath, *New Statesman*, September 13, 1996.

42. Mara Reisman, "Complicating a Feminist Reading of Fay Weldon's Fiction," in *Fay Weldon, Feminism, and British Culture: Challenging Cultural and Literary Conventions* (New York: Lexington Books, 2018), 55.

43. Ibid.

44. Reflecting this postwar domestic discontent, the "mad housewife" novel flourished in the 1960s and early 1970s (Greene, "Mad Housewives and Closed Circles," 58).

45. Sheila Rowbotham, *A Century of Women: The History of Women in Britain and the United States* (New York: Viking Press, 1997), 281.
46. McGrath, *Asylum*, 214.
47. Ibid.
48. Sue Zlosnik, *Patrick McGrath* (Cardiff: University of Wales Press, 2011), 80.
49. McGrath, *Asylum*, 187.
50. Ibid., 27–28 (original emphasis).
51. Ibid., 81.
52. McGrath, interview by Menegaldo, 122.
53. McGrath, *Asylum*, 86.
54. Ibid., 137.
55. Patrick McGrath, "Problem of Drawing from Psychiatry for a Fiction Writer," *Psychiatric Bulletin* 26 (2002): 143.
56. McGrath, *Asylum*, 49, 213.
57. Ibid., 90.
58. McGrath, interview by Crittenden, 45.
59. McGrath, *Asylum*, 95.
60. Ibid., 107.
61. Ibid., 125.
62. Ibid., 109.
63. Mitchell R. Lewis, "The Gothic Gaze: The Politics of Gender in Patrick McGrath's *Asylum*," *Anglistik & Englischunterricht* 69 (2007): 164.
64. McGrath, *Asylum*, 130.
65. McGrath, "Problem," 142–43.
66. McGrath, *Asylum*, 148.
67. Ibid., 145.
68. Ibid., 146.
69. Ibid., 184, 189.
70. Ibid., 189.
71. Ibid., 184.
72. Ibid., 180.
73. Janice Doane and Devon Hodges, *From Klein to Kristeva: Psychoanalytic Feminism and the Search for the 'Good Enough' Mother* (Ann Arbor: The University of Michigan Press, 1995), 7.
74. John Bowlby, "Some Causes of Mental Ill-health," in *Child Care and the Growth of Love* (Melbourne: Penguin Press, 1953), 11.
75. Rowbotham, *Century of Women*, 292–93.
76. Bowlby, "Mental Ill-health," 12.
77. World War II added to the imperative that women be good mothers: "The war, with the evacuation of children and the separation of families, and the destruction of young lives in the bomber raids, seems to have put a new premium on the importance of children and the need to provide them with loving care" (Marwick, *The Penguin Social History of Britain*, 68).
78. McGrath, *Asylum*, 61.
79. Ibid., 200.

80. Ibid., 200–201.
81. Ibid., 202.
82. Ibid., 201.
83. Ibid.
84. Ibid., 24.
85. Ibid., 25.
86. Ibid., 33.
87. Ibid., 36.
88. Ibid., 23.
89. Ibid., 109.
90. David Lodge, "The Unreliable Narrator (*Kazuo Ishiguro*)," in *The Art of Fiction: Illustrated from Classic and Modern Texts* (New York: Penguin Press, 1994), 155.
91. McGrath, *Asylum*, 25 (emphasis added).
92. Kathleen Wall, "*The Remains of the Day* and Its Challenges to Theories of Unreliable Narration," *The Journal of Narrative Technique* 24, no. 1 (1994): 20.
93. McGrath, *Asylum*, 25.
94. Booth, *Rhetoric of Fiction*, 378.
95. Falco, "Case Histories," 98.
96. McGrath, *Asylum*, 3.
97. Ibid., 17, 28, 31.
98. McGrath, interview by Menegaldo, 123.
99. Ibid.
100. Heinz Antor makes a similar point about *The Grotesque* when he notes that "unreliable narration, the use of the grotesque and the exploitation of gothic elements all come together in this novel in so far as they are means of transgression the function of which it is to create epistemological and epistemic defamiliarization with the aim of making the reader stop and look and think again" (Antor, "Unreliable Narration," 30). Antor further argues that McGrath uses transgression (of which one component is the unreliable narrator) in order to make a point about ethics in the postmodern world: the purpose of transgression "is to achieve an effect of defamiliarization as a catalytic tool designed to get the reader started towards the negotiation of a new ethics for the postmodern period" (Antor, "Unreliable Narration," 32).
101. McGrath, *Asylum*, 204.
102. Ibid., 212.
103. Ibid., 244. The patient Sarah Bentley serves as a counterpoint to Stella and shows the problems with challenging the system. Sarah continues to act out, which prolongs her incarceration. In contrast, Stella knows the importance of masquerade. She also knows that even if she agrees with Sarah about the unfairness of the institution, of marriage, and of the world, it is in her best interest to distance herself from Sarah, because this association would lessen her chances of release.
104. Ibid., 210.
105. Elaine Showalter, *The Female Malady: Women, Madness, and English Culture, 1830–1980* (New York: Penguin Press, 1987), 222.
106. McGrath, *Asylum*, 186.

107. Ibid., 222.
108. Ibid., 232–33.
109. Ibid., 232.
110. Ibid.
111. Ibid., 250–51 (original emphasis).
112. Ibid., 220.
113. Ibid., 251 (original emphasis).
114. Ibid., 252.
115. Ibid., 237.
116. Ibid., 252.
117. Ibid. Lucy's crimes are those of female deviance. She openly expresses her sexuality before she becomes one of the Undead and afterwards represents extreme wantonness. As a vampire, she is also unmaternal, sucking blood from young children. Her punishment consists of having a stake driven through her heart, her head cut off, and her mouth filled with garlic. These acts "save" her from damnation and redeem her goodness, which is reflected in her changed physical appearance: "There, in the coffin lay no longer the foul Thing that we had so dreaded and grown to hate . . . but Lucy as we had seen her in her life, with her face of unequalled sweetness and purity" (Stoker, *Dracula*, 255).

Chapter Three

The Language of Transgression and Empathy in Graham Swift's *The Light of Day*

Graham Swift may reject the label of moralist, but he believes that writing has an important moral function. "[G]ood writing," he contends, "is in a sense a kind of escape: a liberation from the narrowness of what you know, and your own experience and your limited perspective on the world. Writing should open things up."[1] Through the imaginative act of understanding new perspectives, readers can develop empathy, and it is this process that Swift defines as a moral act. Like the other authors in this study, Swift makes a distinction between authors imposing moral judgments on their readers and authors creating an environment in which readers can consider new ideas and better understand their world and others. In order to upset a prescriptive way of thinking about the world and to effect social change, Swift encourages readers of his 2003 novel, *The Light of Day*, to think about how language affects their moral judgments about transgressive acts.

The Light of Day depicts multiple moral dilemmas related to a range of traditionally designated transgressive behaviors including adultery, murder, and professional misconduct. Each story of transgression carries with it a set of moral assumptions about good and bad behavior and good and bad people. Correlated to these moral judgments, much of the language in the book is morally-inflected language: right/wrong, fair/unfair, justice/injustice, corrupt/honorable. This oppositional language, which "[p]rivileg[es] one binary over the other becomes easy shorthand for determining right from wrong" and "naturalize[s] moral judgments" about behavior.[2] It also naturalizes social hierarchies that divide people. Through his careful attention to language, both specific words and larger narratives, and his depiction of multiple perspectives on transgressive acts, Swift disrupts this narrow and divisive view of the world and challenges readers to think critically about their closely held beliefs.

In this chapter, I examine Swift's narrative and linguistic strategies in relation to the conventional stories and stereotypes about adultery, murder, and professional misconduct. In particular, I look at the adultery narratives about George's father and Carol, George's clients and their spouses, and Kristina and Bob; the murder narrative about the Nash Case; and the corruption narrative about George's professional misconduct. I conclude by arguing that through detective narrator George Webb's meticulous deliberations about words, which reveal and foster connections between people, Swift offers his readers a social and narrative model that does not rely on binaries.[3]

Among his linguistic strategies, Swift uses the language of chance and change to encourage readers to better identify with those who have committed a transgressive act. Even if readers have not committed adultery, murder, or professional misconduct, most have had experiences that unexpectedly and dramatically change their lives. Recognizing the links between themselves and others on this basic level gives readers the opportunity to consider people who have behaved transgressively in a more empathetic way. Swift's other techniques that unsettle the stereotypes about transgressive acts and the related moral judgments about them include (1) emphasizing the multiple and fluid meaning of words; (2) showing how culpability shifts depending on language; (3) depicting transgressive acts as either neutral or chance moments; (4) offering several, even contradictory, perspectives on an event in order to make the transgressive act morally ambiguous; and (5) highlighting parallels between people and events through the use of repeated words, phrases, and images. In regard to this repetition, phrases like "Something's come over you," "Something happens," "You cross a line" recur at regular intervals in the novel, refer to and connect disparate transformative moments and people, accumulate meaning as they are repeated, and disrupt a singular and static interpretation of a situation. The adultery narratives, which I discuss first, include all of these techniques for subverting traditional judgments about transgression.

George's views about adultery and marital relationships are shaped by his boyhood discovery of an affair between his father, Frank, and a woman named Carol. George's recollection of the affair reveals both his conventional moral judgments about adultery as well as the moments that prompt a change in his perspective. It is chance that George overhears one of his father's golf partners ask his father: "Are you still seeing Carol Freeman?"[4] Yet with this simple question, George crosses a line of understanding that changes everything for him: his outlook on life, his relationship with his parents, his future profession, and his adult relationships with other women, including Sarah. As he describes, after that moment, "everything was as it was, but not."[5] This phrase represents the duality of George's new reality, but it also relates more broadly to people's lives and their relationships with others. There often is a discrepancy between appearances and what lies below the surface, and it is important to understand both positions in order to make sense of one's own life and to be more compassionate toward others. In *The Light of Day*, this idea becomes especially important in regard to transgressive acts.

When the young George learns about his father's affair, he carefully considers whether he should divulge the truth or keep quiet. This question of knowledge and the responsibility of telling represents a moral dilemma not only for George but also, Swift argues, for people in general: "There is a kind of moral duty to the truth, whatever the truth is. But sometimes the truth is very painful, very harmful."[6] Even as a boy, George understands that telling his mother about Carol would cause her pain so he decides that it would be better if he keeps his father's affair secret. For many years, he adopts a strategy of silence and secrecy: he "[k]eep[s] mum."[7] This phrase has the dual meaning of staying quiet and protecting his mother and is one of many places in the book where readers' attention is drawn to the multiple meanings of a word or phrase so that they can consider carefully and critically all of the implications.[8]

George's first thoughts about the affair reveal that he judges it in the binary terms of right and wrong and cannot see beyond this strict moral framework. He deems infidelity to be "wrong" and realizes that "words, that were just bits of air, could turn scary and black and hard."[9] With a specific act to attach to it, "wrong" becomes a tangible and powerful word for George that evokes a visceral emotional response. It is a "hard" word with a distinctly moral meaning that does not allow George to feel much sympathy toward the parties he deems in the wrong. In that way, "wrong" is a divisive word, because it situates the person judging on the other side of the moral divide, "right" rather than "wrong." When George later finds himself in the wrong with his professional conduct, readers can see even more clearly the detrimental effects of this binary moral view of the world. In regard to his father's relationship with Carol, George never loses this right/wrong frame of thinking, because he only can see the affair from the conventional perspective in which his mother, Jane, is a victim of her husband's infidelity.

When his father falls gravely ill, George is comforted by the thought that his father's death will ensure that his mother will never find out about the affair. He explains: "I couldn't help thinking: well at least she'd be safe now. . . . Her memories wouldn't have any scars."[10] This peaceful dream of safety and wholeness is destroyed when, hours before he dies, George's father utters "Carol." Just as the single question by his father's golf partner changes everything for George as a boy, this single name changes everything for the adult George and for his mother. George's secret about the affair is no longer safe, and he must confront the idea that his mother now knows about the affair and is devastated by it. George describes her hurt in terms of physical pain, of being "stabbed . . . by a name."[11] He also believes that this knowledge will irrevocably change his mother's memories of the marriage and of her life. With one word, she is cheated out of the happy marriage she has worked hard to create and maintain. His father's dying declaration also means that George must confront the idea that his mother's memories of the past and of her marriage will have scars and that the relationship will be "as it was, but not."

Although everything changes for Jane in this moment, what remains the same is George's commitment to protecting his mother. He must again "keep mum," but in a different way. "I'll have to pretend, for her sake, to be shocked, bewildered," he thinks.[12] He also tries to comfort her by offering the excuse that his father did not know what he was saying, but George sees the skepticism in her face. This look and the fact that his mother does not ask who Carol is also reveals a disruption to the narrative George has constructed over the years in which his mother is an unknowing victim of her husband's affair and, most importantly, that he has protected her from heartbreak during this time. George must now consider the possibility that his mother already knew about the affair and that, like George, she has been pretending for all of these years. Significantly, readers are not given a definitive answer, and this ambiguity allows for a range of possible truths to exist beyond the one that George himself believes or wants to believe.

Faced with knowing at the very least that his mother now knows about the affair (if she has not known all along), George continues to interpret the adultery and his mother's response in conventional terms. He imagines that her knowledge about the affair means that her sorrow at her husband's death must be an act and that she just pretends "[t]o be the brave grieving widow."[13] However, George's next question, "But was it such a pretence?" unsettles this prescriptive role, George's initial perspective on his mother's feelings, and his narrative about his parents' relationship.[14] It shows that even if George continues to prioritize his boyhood interpretation of how the affair affects his mother, he is able to consider alternative views as well. Simply by asking the question, George allows his mother's brave front to represent a different role from that of the conventional scorned and vengeful woman or the woman deserted and pitied.

The question "Was it such a pretence?" also challenges the standard adultery narrative wherein a spouse's cheating completely nullifies the marital relationship and any good memories about it. It upsets the presumptions that because someone cheats, the marriage is bad, the spouse is devastated, and the affair is more important than the marriage. In the divergent narrative that George's question invokes, his mother's grief for her husband may be real, they may have had a good marriage, and the affair may not have diminished their relationship.

The requests Jane makes of George after Frank's death also prompt George to rethink his views about his parents' relationship. For Jane, the public image of the marriage—what family, friends, and the community know about the couple—is just as important to her as the private relationship she had with Frank, because it, too, shapes how she understands the relationship and her role in it. In order to control this public narrative, Jane asks George to get an inscribed bench to honor Frank's memory. She also requests that after she dies, George will put her name on the bench as well "[s]o it says 'Frank and Jane.'"[15] The bench serves as a memorial to Jane's husband and to what Peter Widdowson describes as "a public fiction of the fidelity of their relationship."[16] Jane wants others to know that she and Frank were committed to one another, that the marriage was a good one, and that she was loved by and important to Frank, just as he was loved by and important to her.

The bench also symbolizes another important revision to the adultery narrative. Rather than the conventional narrative in which an adulterous relationship singlehandedly dismantles and nullifies an entire marriage, Jane symbolically refuses to grant such importance to her husband's affair. She has applied this way of thinking to Frank's other flirtations as well. "Never mind all of them," she tells George, "he knew how to make me smile."[17] Rather than focusing on her husband's potential infidelities, Jane prioritizes Frank's ability to make her happy and his desire to marry her. By putting her name on the bench alongside Frank's, Jane excludes and erases Carol and any nameless others from their marital history. Only George's knowledge of the affair with Carol disrupts the completeness of his mother's gesture, but his continued commitment to keeping mum ensures that, at least publicly, her choice of narratives will remain the official one.

By thinking carefully about his mother's response to her husband's affair, George learns that there are multiple ways of understanding the world beyond his own views. Whatever he personally may believe, George starts to acknowledge and accept other perspectives as well, including that he and his mother may not have shared the same beliefs about her marriage or about the affair. George's internal monologue and thoughts about language function in a similar way for readers; they give readers access to a wider range of perspectives and allow them to form their own conclusions about the specific story George is relating and about the act of adultery more generally. Through Swift's narrative construction, George's and the reader's interpretations of people or events become simply one of many, and this diversity represents an important strategy in Swift's work. Speaking of novels, but applying more broadly to life, Swift observes: "Novels are not about this *or* that but about this *and* that and about varieties of possibilities and contradictions and paradoxes, all these things which, as everybody knows, our real experience of life is. . . . I am a novelist. Which means I accept complication."[18] By making George and readers attentive to the nuances of language, Swift shows the process through which George learns to accept complication and, by example, shows readers how to do the same.

George's work as a private detective specializing in marital infidelities also gives him a different perspective on adultery from the binary right and wrong lens he has applied to his father's affair, and he is able to articulate alternative narratives about his cases that challenge the rigid moral view that adultery is inherently bad and that there are only guilty parties and victims. This new view is represented in George's neutral portrayal of the photographic evidence he collects for his clients. He describes the photographs as depicting "[a] man and a woman doing things with each other."[19] By presenting an outsider's interpretation of the images, George defamiliarizes the transgression. His vague description of what takes place in the photographs also neutralizes the act. Pascale Tollance contends that "[t]o a certain extent, the multiplication of words like 'things' or 'something' has a blurring and dulling effect. The extraordinary also feels ordinary, banal."[20] The commonplace language that George uses to describe the act of adultery similarly minimizes the moral element by representing the transgression as something "ordinary, banal" rather than as something scandalous.

George continues the process of detaching the act from its moral context when he suggests that rather than the photographs inherently representing evidence of betrayal, they also can be seen as something inoffensive and innocent, even something good. He observes: "They're not photos of horrors, atrocities. Just of two people being—nice to each other."[21] Although George understands that his clients may see the pictures of their spouses in a different way than he presents here and may be upset by them (just as he would be upset by seeing pictures of his father and Carol), he also can articulate another way of thinking about the act—two people being nice to one another—that is outside of the traditional moral framework.

George's neutralizing descriptions about and multiple ways of interpreting pictures of adultery also apply to the photographs of Kristina and Bob that Sarah brings him for identification purposes. Looking at their pictures side-by-side, George subversively observes that Kristina and Bob were "like a couple" and wonders "Was that how it was meant to be?"[22] The implication that this adulterous relationship might be natural and right, how things were "meant to be," and that Kristina might be Bob's natural partner rather than a "marriage buster" disrupts the usual way of looking at an affair and its participants.[23] As with George's other clients, Sarah's closer relationship to the people in the photographs may change her assessment of the relationship, but her judgment is only one of many possible views that George's musings about words and transgressions open up. On a larger scale, George's presentation of these alternative interpretations challenges the natural immorality of traditionally defined transgressive acts. If how a person interprets whether an act is bad or good depends on the context, the observer, the people involved, and the language used to describe the event or act, then meaning is unstable and the corresponding moral judgments about a situation are neither inherent nor fixed.

George's perspective on his clients' agency rather than on their victimization is another challenge to the conventional adultery narrative. In particular, he upsets the set roles people play in which the cheated-on spouse is always a victim and the cheater is always a villain. George notes that the moment his clients come to him, the binary moral framework that their spouse is bad and that they are good breaks down, because when they hire him, they turn into participants and coconspirators in the investigation. Albeit for different reasons, his clients begin to enjoy the same clandestine pleasure as their adulterous spouses: the "tingle of conspiracy" and the "thrill of the chase."[24] George's descriptions emphasize how the moral responsibility shifts depending on the language used to describe one's involvement in the infidelity and in the investigation, passive and injured or active and guilty. However, rather than switching roles—becoming the transgressor as their spouses become the wronged parties—George's clients simultaneously play two different roles, and these positions are neither mutually exclusive nor static. In moral terms, George's point that people's actions are not usually clearly defined applies more broadly in the text as well. Tollance argues that "transgression expands in various directions, adopting various forms but at the same time involving little by little almost every character."[25] The pervasiveness and fluidity of the transgressions Tollance describes is another way that Swift effectively upsets conventional moral evaluations about people's actions and natures.

Sarah, Kristina, and Bob are among the characters involved in transgressions where moral responsibility is difficult to assess because it fluctuates. Like George's other clients, Sarah begins her interview with a traditional script about adultery, which includes morally-inflected language and stereotypical roles for husbands, wives, and mistresses, but she soon abandons it in favor of a different narrative that challenges the familiar story and standard set of roles. Sarah explains that her marriage was not an unhappy or troubled one and that Bob did not have a history of having affairs. Furthermore, their life was emotionally and economically stable enough that they were willing to share their good fortune with someone in need like Kristina, a refugee from Croatia who cannot return home because of the war there. In the context of

Kristina and Bob's subsequent affair, whether Sarah and Bob's decision to take Kristina into their home was a good or a bad one becomes less certain. This ambiguity is reflected in a narrative chorus of contradictory judgments about Sarah and Bob's actions: Sarah was asking for marital trouble by inviting a young woman into her home, Sarah and Bob giving Kristina a place to live was a nice piece of charity and what people should do, and Sarah and Bob taking in Kristina was really an act of exploitation because they got free help around the house. This strategic multiplicity undermines a set judgment about the decision, which then complicates the moral issues surrounding the affair.

George's account of the affair in which he articulates multiple perspectives similarly disrupts an easy understanding about who is the victim and who is the villain. Trying to make sense of Kristina and Bob's affair (as well as his own feelings for Sarah), George begins by thinking about why people fall in love: "How does it happen? How do we choose?"[26] The questions show his need for a logical explanation about attraction, but their juxtaposition also speaks to a difference in how responsibility and culpability are judged in regard to relationships that fall outside of conventional social boundaries. Within a moral framework about adultery, "choose" is active and suggests considered decisions that make an individual more morally responsible while "happen" is passive and suggests a situation beyond one's control that diminishes an individual's moral responsibility. By considering Kristina and Bob's affair in both active and passive terms and by emphasizing the role language plays in the construction of meaning, George complicates readers' moral judgments about the affair and about the people involved.

George starts traditionally by positioning Sarah as the main victim of the affair, because, like his mother, she is the passive party. The affair "happens" to her; she does not "choose" to be part of that situation. However, when Bob confesses his feelings about Kristina to Sarah, he presents himself as a casualty of circumstance and makes it sound like "he was the helpless victim now."[27] Implicit in the description of Bob's helplessness is that Kristina holds the power in the relationship. In this version of the narrative, Kristina chooses and seduces Bob. George's speculation that the difficult personal and political circumstances Kristina faced made her ruthless—"you were robbed, now you take"—fits into this same narrative about Kristina's active role in instigating the affair.[28]

Using the same political context in regard to Kristina's life but representing Kristina as a victim of this instability and violence offers a different perspective on the person responsible for initiating the relationship. In this version of the narrative, Bob takes advantage of Kristina's refugee status, her isolation, and her lack of power in the household and in the country. Passively positioned, "poor and helpless" Kristina is to be pitied.[29] George also presents two other narratives about Kristina and Bob's relationship: Kristina and Bob may have had an equal role in choosing to pursue the affair or both may have been victims of passion whose feelings for one another were beyond their control. Each of these narrative possibilities changes the portrayal of the characters and how readers judge the affair. By encouraging readers to empathize with each character in turn, Swift complicates simple moral judgments about this affair and about adultery in general.

The language of concessions and sacrifices also affects readers' assessments of the characters and their actions. In each iteration, the person described as making a concession or a sacrifice is positioned as the most helpless and vulnerable of the trio and the one to be pitied; however, like the representation of who is the active or passive party in the affair, this position shifts. Sarah may be the person who chooses to invite Kristina to stay with her and Bob, but she loses some of her power in the household after the affair begins. Kristina's asylum status also complicates Sarah's possible responses to the affair. "Once the affair begins between the husband and the girl," Swift explains, "it is not possible to do what is often done in such a situation: when the wife discovers it, the husband goes, the girl goes, both go. But because there is the obligation to protect, the charitable obligation, it is not as simple as that."[30] Even if Sarah's options are limited due to the commitment she and Bob made to Kristina, letting Kristina stay in the house is not one of them. In order to negotiate this unusual set of circumstances, one of the concessions Sarah must make is to allow Bob to find and pay for a different place for Kristina to live. Another of her concessions is to let Bob and Kristina spend regular time together. Sarah recognizes that this permission represents an extraordinary sacrifice on her part and wonders: "When does a concession become a surrender?"[31] Sarah's question is an example of how using different words can change the meaning of an act. Concession suggests that she actively chooses to give up something or someone for a particular reason, whether that is reconciliation, fairness, or obligation. Surrender positions Sarah more passively: she gives up, gives in, accepts that she has lost the battle to keep her marriage.

In her attempt to better understand her own actions and emotions, Sarah makes the imaginative effort to try to understand Kristina's and Bob's positions and what they might be feeling after the political situation changes and Kristina is finally able to return home. In practical terms, her return would bring the affair to an end.[32] Sarah suggests that Kristina leaving and sacrificing her relationship with Bob may be her concession to Sarah and to Bob for their asylum. As Sarah explains to George, Kristina's decision to go allows her "to look as if she's doing it for us."[33] Alternatively, Sarah posits that letting Kristina leave could be Bob's concession, his sacrifice to Sarah and to their marriage. Sarah also recognizes that rather than a concession, Kristina leaving could be an active strategy for Kristina and Bob to escape together and continue the relationship. There remains the additional possibility that Kristina and Bob have not yet made a decision about what to do.

Sarah's inability to know if Kristina and Bob are conceding or escaping when Bob takes Kristina to the airport is the primary reason why Sarah hires George. Unlike his other clients who hire him to provide confirmation and photographic evidence that their spouse is cheating on them, Sarah wants confirmation that the affair is really over. She engages George to follow the couple to the airport so that she knows for sure that Kristina gets on a plane and that she leaves alone. Sarah also asks George to report on how Bob and Kristina part so that she knows the affair is over emotionally as well. After watching the couple, George can truthfully tell Sarah that Kristina gets on the plane alone, but he keeps mum about Bob's emotional state, because he wants to protect Sarah from pain. George recognizes that even with Bob's return home, the marriage will not be the same. A line has been crossed, and echoing the effect of other life-changing moments in the text, "everything was as it was, but not." An even more irrevocable line is crossed when Sarah kills Bob after he comes home.

By linking the affair and the murder through their temporal proximity, Swift raises questions about what justice means in this case and who, primarily, is responsible. Even with Sarah's confession, George's focus on the intricacies of language and his articulation of disparate views about the Nash Case complicate a straightforward assessment of the act and of Sarah's guilt. That Bob is dead may not change, but how the murder and the participants are judged can and does change based on George's choice of words and on the narratives he presents. George first destabilizes the familiar murder narrative through his description of the unusual circumstances surrounding the case. He then upsets the crime's seriousness and the related moral implications of the act through his linguistic playfulness. Finally, he challenges an easy moral judgment about the case and those involved by raising questions about the nature of the crime.

George begins his account of the Nash Case with generalizations about class and murder that he has derived from his professional experiences. He observes that murders tend to be "bleak, grim, depressing affairs" that happen in neighborhoods "where we don't have to go."[34] The upscale suburban location of the Nash home and Sarah and Bob's upper-middle-class status upset the class stereotypes implied in George's observation that violence is more prevalent in impoverished locations and among the lower classes. The Nash murder takes place in a beautiful home in a fashionable neighborhood, and the people involved are respectable, professional, and educated. Bob is a gynecologist, and Sarah, the person who commits the murder, is a "college lecturer and translator: words were her thing."[35] Except for her class privilege, Sarah seems ordinary, someone who would be unlikely to kill and especially unlikely to kill in such a physical manner.

The warm, fragrant kitchen where the murder takes place also challenges George's preconceptions about the "grim, depressing" spaces where murders ordinarily occur. When he arrives, the Nashes' kitchen is a "scene of perfect welcome" where Sarah has lovingly made Bob's favorite meal, coq au vin, and has dressed up to greet him.[36] George's description of the murder weapon, "a kitchen knife, a good one and recently sharpened," also highlights its criminal unconventionality, because his main focus is on the "green smears and flecks of parsley" that remain on the knife.[37] These mundane details draw attention to the knife's normal kitchen utility, chopping herbs, rather than to the harm it does to Bob's body. The murder may be bloody and gruesome, but George's attention to the unusual elements—the inviting kitchen, the delicious food prepared with high-end culinary equipment, the beautiful black velvet dress that Sarah wears—rather than to the murder itself makes the crime seem less terrible and more puzzling. It becomes a mystery to be solved rather than a murder to be judged.

The playful language used to describe the murder, Sarah, and the crime scene also works to undercut the initial horror of the act and disrupts a simple judgment about the murder and the murderer. In the following examples, the clichéd words used to describe the murder are given prominence over the violence that they describe:

> [S]he'd got all dressed up to welcome him. She was dressed—don't say it—to kill.[38]

> Mrs. Nash, the papers would note . . . was a striking woman. If that's not an unfortunate word.[39]

In these passages and numerous others about the crime, words have a literal and figurative meaning that are both apt. The refrain "if that's not an unfortunate word" draws attention to the literal meaning of the phrases, but the practical effect is to divert the reader's attention away from the crime and onto the words themselves. As a result, these descriptions undermine the severity of the crime and redirect the horror into humor. Readers, therefore, can view the murder as (groaningly) fun rather than just morally wrong.

Even the investigating officers have a hard time taking the crime seriously. George speculates that one might have been tempted to taste the delicious-smelling abandoned food. Another cop makes "a tasteless joke" about Sarah's decision to take off her apron, remarking that "she should have kept it on."[40] Although the words convey lightheartedness, they remain a serious matter, because they not only describe a situation but also create its meaning. As Regina Barreca notes, it is important to recognize, as Swift does, that "[l]anguage has a formative, not merely an evaluative function."[41] In *The Light of Day*, the word play changes the investigators' response to the crime, because it masks the damage.

On the other end of the spectrum, certain words can be as damaging as murder. For example, Sarah is devastated when Bob says of Kristina, "I can't live without her."[42] Like George's description of his mother being "stabbed" by the name Carol, these words cause severe emotional harm. Tollance remarks of Sarah's pain and subsequent actions that "if words can hurt as much as a knife, the knife turns out to be the last resort when words are of no avail."[43] Sarah may be a teacher, but her professional relationship with words cannot fix her private life. When she kills her husband, Bob's words, like the word play about the crime scene, take on a literal meaning. Bob's claim that he cannot live without Kristina ends up defining his life. In this example, the meaning of the phrase shifts in its repetition and context from an expression of emotion (Bob's love for Kristina) to a physical description (Bob's death), which adds complexity to the cliché and demands closer attention by readers. In Barreca's words, Swift "makes literal what has come to be disregarded as simply conventional, reconnecting the signifier and signified in order to explode meaning."[44]

Just as Sarah teaches George about the seriousness of words, George's narrative shows readers the importance of looking critically at language in order to better understand that the world it describes is a complicated one. Stef Craps argues that George's deliberations on the power of words "forces the reader to reflect on the meaning of the most innocuous of words by introducing an element of ambiguity."[45] George's introduction of ambiguity into the larger narratives he invokes has the same effect. His accounts of Sarah's motive, the nature of the crime, and the person responsible for Bob's death include multiple theories—one way of creating narrative ambiguity—that prompt readers to rethink (as George, too, must do) their preconceived notions and judgments about transgressive acts like murder.

The unclear motive is among the details that disrupts a simple moral judgment about the crime. The primary theory by DI Marsh and the community is that Sarah killed Bob as an act of revenge for the affair; however, the elements of the case differentiate it from other crimes of passion and revenge. The conventional love-and-violence narratives tend to involve either a spontaneous act of violence upon the discovery of a spouse's adultery or a premeditated act of violence on the adulterers. Sarah's actions do not fit either scenario. The killing is not impulsive, because Sarah has known about the affair for some time, and for a planned act of revenge, it is oddly timed, because Sarah kills Bob after the affair is over, Kristina has left the country, and Bob has returned home. The seemingly illogical timing is the main complication for Marsh in regard to the revenge theory. From his perspective, Bob's return means that Sarah has gotten what she wanted—an end to the affair and her marriage back—and that her life is good again. Because Marsh cannot reconcile these points with the murder, he must try to come up with another explanation to make sense of Sarah's actions. George, too, questions the revenge theory because it does not fit with his insights about Sarah's relationship with Bob or with his assessment of the welcoming kitchen crime scene. Yet like Marsh, he struggles to find a satisfying alternative motive.

In their quest for answers, Marsh and George consider another common explanation for criminal behavior: madness. Speaking to the possibility that Sarah might not have been in her right mind when she stabbed Bob, Marsh wonders if Sarah "might be off her trolley?"[46] Similarly, George observes that Sarah seems disconnected from reality after committing the crime. Although she admits to having done it, she looks "like she didn't know what she'd done."[47] In this description, George presents readers with a traditional murder narrative in which a woman temporarily goes mad, "snaps," and kills her husband. In this type of situation, there is no doubt about who committed the crime, but this theory requires an assessment of the perpetrator's mental state—mad or malicious—in order to determine culpability and responsibility. The vague and passive excuse "something came over me" and the implication that the act was unconscious or unintentional also changes the moral assessment.[48] However banal the reason, as with adultery, describing the act as a moment of temporary madness beyond one's control or outside of one's character, "that tired old formula," disrupts the idea that the perpetrator is inherently bad or evil.[49]

In the Nash Case, the ambiguity about the nature of the crime and the circumstances surrounding Bob's death also upset a straightforward moral judgment about the responsible party. There are limited legal and narrative ways to describe the event, and George articulates three of these: murder, accident, and suicide. Each of these possible verdicts carries with it different assumptions about guilt, punishment, and justice. Murder implies intentionality, makes Sarah morally and legally responsible, and requires that she be punished for there to be justice. Although Sarah is convicted of and confesses to killing Bob, George also presents other potential scenarios as a way to unsettle readers' judgments about Sarah. One of these scenarios is that Bob's death might have been an accident. George contends that even though Sarah stabs Bob, there was no way for her to have known that the knife would strike so precisely. In this formulation, picking up the knife and aiming it toward Bob may have been intentional, but killing Bob may have been unintentional. The element of chance in this depiction of the crime lessens Sarah's level of legal and moral responsibility and suggests that a lighter sentence might be more just.

George also offers a suicide theory that shifts responsibility from Sarah to Sarah and Bob. He surmises that by returning home Bob hopes to be "brought back to life" by Sarah, but when he arrives at the house, he realizes the impossibility of that desire and that "it's not to be saved that he's come."[50] This point and George's further speculation "It took two. Something came over him as well" implies that Bob may have wanted to die and may even be complicit in his death.[51] This scenario, too, changes Sarah's level of responsibility and the appropriate punishment. Readers' different reactions to these different descriptions of and motivations for Bob's death emphasize the ways in which words matter. They change how one perceives, interprets, and assesses an event and the people involved. By making several plausible, even contradictory explanations visible through George's thoughts about language, Swift prompts readers to think critically about familiar narratives about transgression and then to understand that events and people are not as neatly or easily explained as the clichéd words and conventional stories may imply.

The end of the book nicely unsettles the moral framework about murder one more time as George makes a direct connection between his assistant, Rita, waiting for him to return to the office and Sarah waiting for Bob to come home on the fateful night. George thinks:

> Rita will be looking at her watch, waiting for my key in the street door. My God!—but no, Rita isn't the murdering type.
> None of us is.[52]

Although the scenario of a woman waiting for a man to return is the same in both cases, George feels safe, because "Rita isn't the murdering type." This sentence could imply that in spite of his defense of Sarah, she is the murdering type. However, the next line, "None of us is," upsets the simple position that people are either good or bad, murdering type or not. If "[n]one of us is" the murdering type, but murders still occur, it means that circumstance, luck, and chance can play a role in a crime rather than it happening only because of an individual's inherent badness, corruption, or immorality. In offering this possibility, Swift upsets the rigid judgments about murder and murderers and, as I will discuss below in more detail, questions a binary us/them narrative that divides people.

George's professional misconduct is another place where Swift invokes a binary moral framework about a transgressive act only to unsettle it. The relationship between language and moral judgments about transgressive acts continues to be foregrounded in the representation of George's professional misconduct; however, this example also offers a starker delineation of the personal and societal consequences of adhering to a binary way of categorizing people and judging behavior. This us or them, right or wrong, good or bad way of viewing the world relies on maintaining moral divisions between individuals and impedes empathy. "'Them,'" as Jeanette Winterson argues, "is always other—the inferior, the outsider, the outcast, the conquered, unclean, low class, foreign, strange, not one of us."[53]

George's time on the police force (before he meets Sarah) shows his adherence to this binary type of thinking. George joins the Force in order "to be on the right side of the law."[54] At that time, "before the police became the pigs, the fuzz, the filth," the moral boundaries—right and wrong—seemed clear and simple as does George's place in the world: on the right side personally, professionally, and socially.[55] The Dyson case leads to George's dismissal from the Force as he finds himself on the wrong side of the law with his suspect interrogations, the wrong side of the public's judgments about police conduct, and the wrong side of his marriage. George's new insights about language may not change the nature of his misconduct, but they reveal to himself and to readers how the words used to describe his transgressions (and transgressive acts more generally) not only shape judgments about them but also justify divisions between people. His reflections lead him to see how empathy and connecting with others offers a way to create better personal relationships that can lead to larger social change.

The Dyson case that changes George's life personally and professionally involves Ranjit Patel, who is stabbed in his store. The weapon may be the same type as the one Sarah uses to commit her act of violence, but George's opinion about the alleged perpetrator, a known criminal named Lee Dyson, differs significantly. In regard to Sarah, George can see multiple sides to her crime, which leads him to judge her less harshly, to want to help her, and to forgive her. In regard to Dyson, George's strict moral judgments prevent him from even trying to understand Dyson. Instead, George can only see Dyson as someone bad, someone on the wrong side of the law, someone morally reprehensible, and someone who needs to be brought to justice and punished. This rigid perspective and George's obsession with convicting Dyson lead to his professional disgrace, because he is ready to do whatever it takes to convict Dyson, even if it means crossing a line in terms of proper police conduct.

Based on his previous professional knowledge of Dyson, George believes that he is the person who stabbed Patel. Patel's wife, Meera, believes Dyson is guilty as well. Unfortunately, she arrives on the scene of her husband's assault, as George notes, "too late to see Dyson (if it was him)."[56] Meera and

George may be sure that Dyson is to blame, but there is no direct evidence linking him to this crime. George's parenthetical qualification also upsets readers' certainty about Dyson's guilt and complicates what justice means in this case. For the community, justice means making sure that Dyson receives fair treatment as the crime is investigated. For George, justice means putting Dyson behind bars, even if he is not guilty of this particular crime, because Dyson has committed and gotten away with other crimes, is irredeemably "bad," and should be separated from "good" society in order to keep the community safe. George makes a clear distinction between himself (good, on the right side of the law) and Dyson (bad, on the wrong side of the law); however, in his attempt to put Dyson behind bars, George commits his own transgressions. He becomes guilty of professional misconduct when he violates the 1984 PACE (Police and Criminal Evidence) Act by using coercive interview tactics to pressure Kenny into making a statement implicating Dyson and then lying to Dyson about the statement being on the record.

George's conduct in the interrogation room also complicates the investigation. After Kenny withdraws his statement that puts Dyson at the crime scene, claiming that it was not true and that George coerced him into incriminating Dyson through "intimidation and deceit," George seemingly admits to this transgressive act, but his confession is ambiguous.[57] "It's true," George says. "That's how the tape might show it."[58] The vague wording has two potential meanings. The first statement, "It's true," implies that George is guilty of professional misconduct by intimidating and deceiving someone he is interviewing. The second statement is about perception and is less clear in terms of George's guilt: true about what the tape might show could be different from true about what happened. Although the extent of George's misconduct here is unclear, his subsequent physical actions are not.

George assaults Kenny in the interrogation room after Kenny retracts his statement about Dyson. George then tries to explain his action using the same language Sarah does about killing Bob: "Something came over me."[59] In both George's and Sarah's cases, the vague wording seems to indicate a diminished responsibility, an unplanned act, a moment of madness. However, both are held accountable for their acts of violence. In order to save the police force's reputation in the community, George is "sacrifice[d] for the good of the Force" and fired.[60] The contemporary cultural climate in which police corruption became an important issue for activists means that social justice and police reform take precedence over convicting Dyson. Whether or not Dyson is guilty becomes immaterial. He goes free because George has intimidated and assaulted a witness, lied to a suspect, and been accused of police corruption.

Because George's misconduct is not only a police matter but also a matter of public trust, it is not enough to handle the matter internally. Craps argues that

> the police force seizes on George's transgression as an opportunity to polish its sullied image. By heaping all the blame for police malfunctioning and corruption upon him—even though, as George points out, he has never misused police powers to further his own ends or to put an innocent man behind bars—and eliminating the black sheep from the fold, the police force hopes to restore its tarnished reputation in the eyes of the public.[61]

Like the bench that shows the public that Frank and Jane had a good marriage, the police force must punish George publicly in order to indicate their professional divorce from George and to show that they represent the right side of the law.

This distancing between the good police force and the bad cop relies on defining the moral issues in binary terms. George explains, "Right and wrong. And I'd done wrong."[62] Even if the dismissal is justified, the language used to define George's conduct amplifies the magnitude of his transgression: "Corrupt. A word with no half measures: you've got the disease. . . . Not just a cop who'd overstepped the mark. I'd sinned."[63] Unlike more innocuous phrases to describe his behavior like "poor judgment," "overstepping the mark," or "breaking a few rules," "corrupt" has moral implications that justify the police force's and the public's harsh treatment of George. The disease language is another reason that George's actions are categorically condemned. George's corruption has the potential to infect everyone around him: the police force, the public, his family. In order to protect and distance themselves from the source of contamination, the people in these groups invoke a binary moral framework that positions George on one side of a moral line and them on the other.

George's wife, Rachel, is one of these people. She conflates George's professional misconduct with a personal failure—one infects the other—and draws a firm line between herself and George. In accordance with George's contention that Rachel never gives up the inflexible views about right and wrong that she learned as a child, she makes a decisive break from George legally, emotionally, and morally in order to insulate herself from what she sees as George's corrupt nature. George observes that "now she had the chance to make it all my fault. The taint *was* me. Not Mr. Right but Mr. Wrong."[64] Swift elaborates on the relationship between Rachel and George in an interview and notes that her response to George getting "kicked out of the force for improper behavior . . . is really a judgement. She is a pretty judgmental woman."[65] Rachel's judgmental and unforgiving behavior serves as a counterexample to the empathetic model Swift wants to articulate in *The Light of Day*. In presenting multiple perspectives on transgressive acts like adultery, murder, and professional misconduct, Swift's goal is to disrupt the conventional moral judgments associated with these acts and to challenge a divisive model of social relations. He encourages readers to try to understand a position other than their own and to see the world beyond an uncompromising moral framework. George's professional philosophy, "You have to put yourself . . . into their shoes," becomes a model for this method of understanding and a model for social interactions that applies not only to George's detective work but also to the book's larger message about empathy.[66]

Unlike Rachel who cannot leave behind a binary moral perspective of the world, George's views begin to shift when, influenced by Sarah, he thinks more carefully about words and their meaning. This attention to language makes him closely consider the ideas and the relationships they describe and to better appreciate their complexities. Even if George is not a perfect person or without his own rigid judgments about certain issues, he learns from his lessons about language to recognize and break down stereotypes and clichés about transgressive acts and behavior and to understand different points of view. George's openness to new perspectives and his more fluid way of looking at the world allow him to connect better with others. Swift contends that "the fundamental task of literature" is "to enable us to enter, imaginatively, experiences *other* than our own. That sounds simple, but it is no small thing. The hardest task in the world, against which consciousness stacks insuperable obstacles, is to understand what it is like to be someone else. But if we cannot even attempt that vital mental act, what hope do we have as the social, political and cultural animals we claim to be?"[67] In *The Light of Day*, George's narrative shows the imaginative act of understanding someone else's experiences in process and reveals its unifying potential.

Critics have linked George's last name, Webb, to webs of deceit, but I contend that George also creates a connective web for readers through his reflections on language and on the past. Even more importantly, he advocates for another type of web—a social net—that connects and protects people. George describes the ideal model for social relations as having someone who can save you and not judge you in moral terms. As he observes: "Whether he's [God's] up there or not, and whether he's got a net, I don't know. But I think it's how it ought to be just among us. There ought to be at least one other person who won't let us slip through the net. . . . No matter what we do, no matter how bad."[68] The relationship that George describes is based not on right or wrong or justice but on understanding, compassion, and protection. Like the Chistlehurst Caves that serve the important function of a natural shelter when there is trouble in the world, George suggests that people should serve as a natural shelter for one another, which is only possible if they can connect. Showing the growth in George's view of the world from his days on the police force, George even extends this model of human connection, safety, and forgiveness to Dyson. George may not be able to function as Dyson's safety net, but he believes someone should fulfill this role. "There ought even to be someone for Dyson," he now recognizes.[69] By revealing the process through which George comes to a new understanding of the world and his place in it, Swift illustrates the vital role literature plays in generating an empathetic environment that is conducive to creating social change.

NOTES

1. Graham Swift, quoted in Fiona Tolan, "Graham Swift," in *Writers Talk: Conversations with Contemporary British Novelists*, ed. Philip Tew, Fiona Tolan, and Leigh Wilson (London: Continuum, 2008), 127.

2. Mara Reisman, "Integrating Fantasy and Reality in Jeanette Winterson's *Oranges Are Not the Only Fruit*," *Rocky Mountain Review* 65, no. 1 (2011): 11.

3. In *12 Bytes: How We Got Here, Where We Might Go Next*, Jeanette Winterson addresses the global consequences of a binary worldview. "Humans love separations," she argues, "we like to separate ourselves from other humans, usually in hierarchies, and we separate ourselves from the rest of biology by believing in our superiority. The upshot is that the planet is in peril" (Winterson, *12 Bytes*, 6). Winterson suggests that one way to alleviate the global and environmental threats that humans currently face is to change the way that people think about themselves in relation to others. "Breaking the binary as the dominant narrative is an urgent business," she contends (6). "We can't move into the next phase of our human evolutionary journey and bring the binary with us" (232). It is in this evolutionary context that Winterson considers what computer science and Artificial Intelligence can offer humans: connectivity. Connectivity, she believes, has the potential to "end the delusion of separate silos of value and existence" and to change the world (6). In *The Light of Day*, Swift engages with some of these same issues of human connectivity, binary worldviews, and narrative.

4. Graham Swift, *The Light of Day* (New York: Vintage Books, 2004), 109.

5. Ibid.

6. Graham Swift, "The Challenge of Becoming Another Person," interview by Heike Hartung, *Anglistik: International Journal of English Studies* 16, no. 1 (2005): 143. Nick Bentley sees this dilemma about telling the truth represented in Swift's novel *Waterland* as well, and the example he provides nicely addresses Swift's lack of prescriptiveness about moral and ethical issues. Bentley argues: "Tom's compunction to reveal family secrets is set in contrast with his father, Henry Crick's desire to keep things hidden, as seen in his attempts to stop Dick learning to read. What appears initially to be an embarrassment on Henry's part towards Dick's lack of mental capacities, turns out to be an act of love as he wishes to protect Dick from the truth about his birth. . . . In one sense, Henry's attempts to keep things hidden emerge here

as the wiser response. But this challenges the whole nature of Tom's belief in the need to explain, to uncover and to bring to light. The morality of Tom's enlightenment imperative is complex, as the revelation does not produce happiness but leads only to despair and death. In effect, then, the novel dramatizes the moral dilemma with respect to the existence of unpleasant truths: how far should one uncover a secret (however immoral) when it is clear that its disclosure will cause harm to those it concerns. The text presents this ethical conundrum without guiding the reader towards an answer and in its ending remains open on this issue" (Bentley, *Contemporary British Fiction*, 139–40).

7. Swift, *Light of Day*, 133.

8. Criticism of the novel has focused on the depth of meaning conveyed by Swift's deceptively simple words and clichés. For more on how language and clichés work in *The Light of Day*, see Craps; Andrew James; Lee; Malcolm; and Tollance.

9. Swift, *Light of Day*, 133. The word "corrupt" also has a physical impact on George. Catherine Pesso-Miquel argues that "when George Webb pays a visit to Bob's grave, he plays with language as a means of countering the overwhelming bitterness of his emotions. He contemplates his own fate as a dishonoured cop accused of corruption, and he can feel in his soul the disgusting black mess of decay, because 'corrupt' 'is a strangely physical word' (Swift 2003, 134); thus the two meanings of the word become fused, the moral connotations being expressed through a physical image" (Pesso-Miquel, "No 'screaming and shrieking in the wind'").

10. Swift, *Light of Day*, 162.

11. Ibid., 208.

12. Ibid., 163.

13. Ibid.

14. Ibid.

15. Ibid., 164.

16. Peter Widdowson, "*The Light of Day*," in *Graham Swift* (Devon: Northcote House Publishers, 2006), 102.

17. Swift, *Light of Day*, 111.

18. Graham Swift, interview by John Crane, *Cimarron Review* 84 (1988): 12 (original emphasis).

19. Swift, *Light of Day*, 7.

20. Pascale Tollance, "'You Cross a Line': Reticence and Excess in Graham Swift's *The Light of Day*," in *Voices and Silence in the Contemporary Novel in English*, ed. Vanessa Guignery (Newcastle upon Tyne: Cambridge Scholars Press, 2009), 68.

21. Swift, *Light of Day*, 320.

22. Ibid., 57.

23. Ibid. Agnes Woolley persuasively argues that the language George uses throughout the book to describe possible roles for Kristina only offers her clichéd, "pre-defined role[s]; she could be a 'lost soul' or a 'marriage-buster' (p. 57), a 'refugee' or a 'woman about town' (p. 170)" (Woolley, "Something blurred in her?," 454). In the context of disrupting the conventional adultery narrative, another way to

interpret the multiplicity of roles in this list (even if they are clichés) is as a departure from a singular role for the mistress in an adultery narrative.

24. Swift, *Light of Day*, 41.
25. Tollance, "'You Cross a Line,'" 66.
26. Swift, *Light of Day*, 104.
27. Ibid., 76.
28. Ibid., 78.
29. Ibid.
30. Swift, interview by Hartung, 143. For a good discussion of the politics of hospitality in *The Light of Day* and the precarious status of asylum seekers and refugees, see Woolley. Engaging with Woolley's ideas, Sara Upstone addresses how the issues of empathy and hospitality represented in *The Light of Day* extend to contemporary politics. Upstone argues: "Woolley reads Kristina's incursions into the text . . . as capturing the liminal status of the refugee who destabilises the familiar and whose 'persistent presence renders her the threshold of the possibility for the imagination of otherness' (46). Swift's novel is set in the mid-1990s, yet it speaks equally to twenty-first century concerns with the presence of a transformed migrant population from Eastern Europe" (Upstone, *Rethinking Race and Identity*, 132).
31. Swift, *Light of Day*, 91.
32. Although Sarah and Bob secretly root for different sides to win the war, both seek a political solution to their personal problems. Sarah explains to George that she is pleased and relieved when the Croatians start gaining ground against the Serbians, because it may save her marriage. George may be tacitly sympathetic to Sarah's point of view, but Peter Widdowson points out the ethical problem with Sarah's feelings, describing her position as "entirely selfish" and George's response as woefully inadequate: "George makes no comment, but the appropriate response to Sarah's questions [about whether it is wrong to feel relief and joy about this shift in the war] surely is: yes, absolutely 'appalling', absolutely 'terrible'—how can safe citizens of Wimbledon hold such callously self-serving and inhumane views" (Widdowson, "*The Light of Day*," 98). The same judgment can apply to Bob who, in contrast to Sarah, wants the war to continue so that his relationship with Kristina can continue.
33. Swift, *Light of Day*, 100.
34. Ibid., 215.
35. Ibid., 216.
36. Ibid., 223.
37. Ibid.
38. Ibid., 216.
39. Ibid., 221.
40. Ibid., 222.
41. Regina Barreca, "Metaphor-into-Narrative: Being 'Very Careful with Words' in Texts by Women Writers," in *Untamed and Unabashed: Essays on Women and Humor in British Literature* (Detroit: Wayne State University Press, 1994), 163.
42. Swift, *Light of Day*, 226.
43. Tollance, "'You Cross a Line,'" 66.
44. Barreca, "Metaphor-into-Narrative," 165.

45. Stef Craps, "Adieu: Stepping into *The Light of Day*," in *Trauma and Ethics in the Novels of Graham Swift: No Short-Cuts to Salvation* (Eastbourne: Sussex Academic Press, 2005), 176. Craps effectively illustrates this point with the example of the phrase "holding her hand." He observes: "George expresses his regret that he cannot be with Sarah to '[hold] her hand' (155)—that is, to comfort her—while she relives the moment of the murder exactly two years after the event. The phrase 'holding her hand' crops up again a couple of sentences later, as George reflects that he was not with her either two years earlier: 'But I can't be with her when it happens. Holding her hand' (155). Its meaning, however, has changed. The words no longer denote a gesture of consolation, but rather refer to George's wish that he could have restrained Sarah—or, perhaps, the exact opposite: that he could have assisted her in planting the kitchen knife in her husband's heart" (Craps, "Adieu," 176–77). Anthony Quinn also comments on the ambiguous meaning of "holding her hand," noting that "There is a lovely shiver of ambiguity in that last phrase, suggesting both an act of reassurance and an act of restraint" (Quinn, "Nobody's Perfect").

46. Swift, *Light of Day*, 173.
47. Ibid.
48. Ibid., 299.
49. Ibid., 77.
50. Ibid., 303.
51. Ibid.
52. Ibid., 311.
53. Jeanette Winterson, *12 Bytes: How We Got Here, Where We Might Go Next* (New York: Grove Press, 2021), 232.
54. Swift, *Light of Day*, 174.
55. Ibid., 175.
56. Ibid., 148.
57. Ibid., 158.
58. Ibid.
59. Ibid., 160.
60. Ibid., 180.
61. Craps, "Adieu," 169.
62. Swift, *Light of Day*, 122.
63. Ibid., 180.
64. Ibid., 181 (original emphasis).
65. Graham Swift, interview by Robert Birnbaum, *Identity Theory*, July 2, 2003.
66. Swift, *Light of Day*, 79.
67. Graham Swift, "Throwing Off Our Inhibitions," *The Times*, March 5, 1988, 20 (original emphasis).
68. Swift, *Light of Day*, 182.
69. Ibid.

Chapter Four

Negotiating Identity and Building Community in Andrea Levy's *Small Island*

Early in the twentieth century, Virginia Woolf argued that in order to create something new, one needed to "[s]et fire to the old hypocrisies."[1] This incendiary approach has been the focus of many contemporary British writers, including Andrea Levy whose *Small Island* (2004) sets fire to a unified perspective on history, colonial relationships, and social relations. With its present day setting of 1948, Levy depicts diverse perspectives on immigration and British identity as she documents the complex relationship between Britain and its colonies in the postwar period and in the decades leading up to the war. In particular, *Small Island* addresses the mixed reception received by the Windrush generation who came to England after World War II for work and educational opportunities and to help with the reconstruction effort. These individuals believed that their British citizenship would make them welcome and that their colonial education would ease the transition into a new place.[2] As Levy explains in "This Is My England," "Britain was the country that all Jamaican children learned about at school. They sang God Save The King and Rule Britannia. They believed Britain was a green and pleasant land—if not the centre of the world, then certainly the centre of a great and important Empire that spanned the globe, linking all sorts of countries into a family of nations."[3] The expectation that they were not "travelling to a foreign place . . . [but to] the centre of [their] country" represented the belief of many who came to Britain from its colonies in the late 1940s.[4]

Some who came to England in the postwar period also had fought for Britain during World War II. Others were encouraged by the government's recruitment schemes to come and help rebuild the country. Maria Helena Lima explains that "[a]s British citizens holding British passports, West Indians were actively recruited to work, through advertisements placed in West Indian newspapers by London Transport, the British Hotels and Restaurants

Association, the NHS, and similar organizations."[5] Despite the important contribution to the nation made by these workers and the continued need for labor, scarce resources and a stagnating postwar economy meant that many immigrants were met with hostility and intolerance.[6] Lack of adequate housing was also a pervasive national problem. Mike Phillips and Trevor Phillips point out that "while there was a massive shortage of labour in Britain, which fueled migration, there was also a massive shortage of housing which was causing social conflicts even before the migrants arrived."[7] Although the government initially urged workers to come to England and the "*Economic Survey for 1947* stated clearly that 'foreign labour can make a useful contribution to our needs,'" as early as 1949, the government began discussing "the possibility of instituting control of coloured immigration" as a way to address some of the nation's social problems.[8] Tony Kushner makes the important point that in these policy discussions, race rather than racism was foregrounded as the source of social conflict. As a result, "the solutions considered to this 'problem' were to stop black immigration rather than to combat white racism."[9] In *Small Island*, Levy addresses the intricacies of these social and political issues and creates a model for social relations that is predicated on engagement and empathy.

For Levy, the possibility of "wider social transformation" begins with individuals meeting and learning to understand one another, what Sara Upstone describes as a "politics of encounter."[10] In *Small Island*, Levy creates a space for communication by revealing the historical, cultural, and class factors that shape each of *Small Island*'s main characters: the Jamaican-born Gilbert and Hortense and the English-born Queenie and Bernard. She also shows how the environments in which these characters grow up and live—England and Jamaica, 1948 and before—influence their identities, beliefs, and relationships. By giving each character the chance to narrate his or her story, Levy portrays the complexities of their worldviews and treats with understanding her characters' flaws and prejudices.[11] In an interview with Blake Morrison, Levy explains the ethical purpose of this narrative strategy. "You can't get rid of something unless you truly look at it in the face and try to understand it," she says. "That's not to say that I'm sympathetic [to racism] . . . but I do see how it can come about."[12] For Levy, "it's important to see how it can come about," because understanding the origins of and the historical and cultural circumstances that contribute to a person's beliefs is a crucial step for facilitating a productive dialogue with others about views that are divisive and harmful and for thinking critically about one's own views.[13]

In this chapter, I look at how the social and moral complexities that Levy depicts in *Small Island* are reflected and mediated through food and domestic activities. I argue that Levy's representation of the characters' relationships to food and domestic space illustrates their positions on class, race, gender, and national identity; shows how they negotiate their place in a changing world; and provides a way to challenge entrenched views about how the world works.[14] The first part of this chapter addresses each of the main characters' relationships to food and to the nation in the specific historical and cultural contexts of early to mid-twentieth-century England and Jamaica. These associations and environments set up the practical and ideological meanings of food that define the characters' worldviews and affect their relationships with others. In *Food, Consumption and the Body in Contemporary Women's Fiction*, Sarah Sceats argues that "food and eating are essential to self-identity and are instrumental in the definition of family, class, ethnicity."[15] "Food," she observes, "is an essentially social signifier, a bearer of interpersonal and cultural meanings."[16] In *Small Island*, food and eating function in this symbolic way as the characters introduce and express themselves through references to food. The second part of this chapter examines how food serves as an indication of cultural and political conflicts and as a method of communication and negotiation between individuals.

Levy opens the novel with a description of the 1924–1925 British Empire Exhibition at Wembley and uses this event to set up the political, cultural, and national issues addressed in the rest of the novel. The Empire Exhibition showcased Britain's power and achievements, emphasized its productive colonial relationships, and satisfied the public's interest in exotic people and places. The event was intended to foster economic development and cultural understanding, and the Exhibition guide reflects these goals: "To stimulate trade, strengthen bonds that bind the Mother Country to her Sister States and Daughters, to bring into close contact the one with each other, to enable all who owe allegiance to the British flag to meet on common ground and learn to know each other."[17] Levy's prologue stresses that one way the inhabitants of the British Empire were supposed to learn about each other was through their national products, particularly food.

The food products described at the Empire Exhibition include the coffee of Jamaica, the sugar of Barbados, the chocolate of Grenada and Africa, the yellow butter of Canada (made into a life-size model of the Prince of Wales), the apples of Australia, and the tea of Ceylon. Food in this context comes to stand for the nation. This relationship between food and national identity acts both as a distinguishing marker between people and cultures and as a site of connection under Britain's imperial position. King George V stressed this latter idea when he described the British Empire as "a family of nations" that relies on "fraternal cooperation."[18] The Empire Marketing Board also emphasized this productive and collaborative relationship. Peter Bishop notes that "between 1926 and 1933, an image was cultivated of an egalitarian, multi-racial Empire brought into health, harmony and common purpose through agriculture, plus the exchange and consumption of healthy foods. Posters showed the unique blend of exotic landscapes, wholesome foodstuffs and quiet imperial order."[19]

The Empire may be set up ideologically as a place of connection and egalitarianism, but the architecture of the Empire Exhibition enforced divisions: nations were housed separately and not all of their representative citizens and products were immediately comprehensible to their British family. This physical split and ideological dissonance accord with Corinne Duboin's contention that despite its inclusive intentions: "The exhibition's main goal was indeed the celebration of Empire trade, rather than the apparent humanist promotion of cultural diversity."[20] In *Small Island*, Levy offers an example of this lack of cultural understanding when Queenie's mother tells Queenie not to ask the women in the Indian Pavilion what the red dot on their forehead is for "in case the dots meant they were ill."[21] Levy also emphasizes how the power dynamics of the Empire were replicated at the Exhibition. A hierarchy with Britain on top and her colonies below is suggested by Queenie's description of the Exhibition "hous[ing] every country we British *owned*."[22] Attending the Exhibition gave visitors the ability to participate even more directly in this national ownership. Duboin argues that "visiting the interstitial space of each pavilion enables Queenie's family to perform (or re-enact) the colonization process, to explore and appropriate inaccessible distant overseas territories."[23]

This ownership and appropriation extended to a nation's products. Despite not being grown or produced in Britain, some colonial products became "owned" by the British not only commercially but also culturally. Tea, for example, was appropriated as a quintessentially English drink that came to represent the nation. Stuart Hall points out that although "[n]ot a single tea plantation exists within the United Kingdom. This is the symbolization of English identity—I mean, what does anybody in the world know about an English person except that they can't get through the day without a cup of tea."[24] Queenie's mother is one of the people who needs a regular cup of tea, and the smell of tea from Ceylon makes her want "a cuppa and a sit-down."[25] Levy's depiction of Queenie's mother's desire for tea works in two ways: it emphasizes the colonial aspect of English tea by reminding readers where this beverage comes from and it shows the process through which this product from Ceylon is co-opted by the English and reframed and naturalized as a representation of English comfort and tradition.

Reflecting its place at the center of English life, tea is one of the ubiquitous products in the novel and has a central place in the lives of all of the characters. It represents their national views and signifies the state of their personal relationships. Although it can connect characters through the act of hospitality, tea also can symbolize personal, social, and national tensions and divisions. Revealing the different relationship each character has with tea and other food products and the multiple and shifting meanings of these products is an integral part of Levy's strategy for destabilizing a fixed way of looking at the world. The characters' relationships to food may reveal the national and class positions they were born into that influence their social expectations, but with the exception of Bernard, the characters' beliefs and relationships can change as they learn more about themselves and others through their cultural and culinary experiences.

Three important events in Queenie's childhood and adolescence shape her identity; her beliefs about class, race, and nation; and her subsequent relationships. The first is her visit to the British Empire Exhibition, the second is her life on the farm, and the third is her work at her aunt's London sweet shop. Each of these places and experiences is linked to food and food production and contributes to Queenie's understanding of her place in the world.

At the British Empire Exhibition, one of the most memorable parts for Queenie is seeing an African man who looks like he is "carved from melting chocolate."[26] Queenie's imagery naturalizes Africa and its resources as something to be consumed: visually by the visitors at the Empire Exhibition, economically through imports, and personally through the edible-looking chocolate man. Queenie's young chaperone, Graham, adds another level of consumption when he teasingly suggests that Queenie should kiss the African man. Overhearing this exchange, the man offers a handshake as a more appropriate first greeting, thereby dispelling the colonial myths perpetuated by Exhibition spectators like Graham that nonwhite colonial subjects are uncivilized, primitive, and cannot understand or speak English.

Queenie's further descriptions of the man's features—skin "[b]lacker than . . . sooty cork," brown lips "bulged with air like bicycle tyres," hair "wooly as a black shorn sheep," and nostrils "big as train tunnels"—also reflect her English point of reference in which Africa is someplace exotic and foreign.[27] Although Queenie tries to make sense of the encounter and the man by framing his appearance and identity in terms of what she already knows—soot, bicycle tires, sheep, and trains—Alicia E. Ellis argues that her words also represent "the kind of ethnographic language associated with colonial discourses."[28] Levy's depiction of Queenie's limited perspective on the world, which is influenced by her class position, her nationality, her life on the farm, and her child's point of view, prompts readers to consider Queenie's position critically but empathetically so that they can learn from this moment. Levy explains this literary and political strategy: "I'm writing a piece of fiction and I try to make you engage in it in an emotional way. This is how she saw it:

she's a young girl from the Midlands, has never seen anyone black in her life, she sees somebody and that is what comes into her head; and what I want is for the reader then to think, to make their own . . . 'What's this, why does she think like this; what is it that makes a girl like this feel like that about another human being.'"[29] Levy hopes that this active engagement with the novel not only will allow readers to understand what has shaped Queenie's views but also will encourage them to consider their own responses to people and situations that are new to them.

For the young Queenie, a move toward greater personal and cultural understanding is difficult because of her environment and the blinkered views of those around her. Although Queenie is merely curious about this African man, her father assumes that Queenie will be disturbed by the encounter and tries to assuage her fears. Using imperialist rhetoric, he suggests that because the African man spoke English, he has "learned to be civilized."[30] In addition, he contends that the man was "likely a potentate."[31] Through these markers of civility and status, Queenie's father legitimizes the encounter: the African man is a proper, civilized subject of the British Empire. Queenie's father then reminds Queenie of her colonial power through a trip on the scenic railway. This ride takes them "up into the heavens" and allows Queenie to literally and symbolically believe her father's contention: "You've got the whole world at your feet, lass."[32] Rather than the African man looking down at Queenie as he does when they first meet, her father positions Queenie as the one in control, the one who can look down on others. His words inscribe Queenie's imperial position in which she has power because she is white and was born in England.

Queenie's family's relative class position also gives her power. Queenie is a butcher's daughter, and her parents own a pig and poultry farm. As a result, Queenie's early ideas about class are tied to food and food production. Queenie's description of the place being "our farm" denotes pride and ownership similar to the British Empire's pride and ownership of all of its colonies.[33] Queenie's family is not wealthy—essentially it is a working-class household—but they are involved in the production of goods, and they have more resources than the farm workers or the destitute miners who are part of the community. Unemployment was high during the interwar years, and the plight of the miners and their families in the 1920s was particularly bleak due to a diminishing export market, pit closures, and strikes that resulted in lost wages and lost jobs.

Food is one indication of Queenie's more privileged position in the community. She explains that the hungry miners' children would follow her around the playground asking if she had brought a meat pie for her dinner. Rather than being compassionate and sharing her food, Queenie taunts these children by showing them the "brown, crusty pastry, the pink jellied meat" and then ostentatiously eating the pie in front of them.[34] Queenie also tries to prevent her brother from sharing his food and hits Harry when he gives some of his pie to Wilfred, whose father was killed in a pit accident. Harry's explanation that Wilfred was hungry does little to satisfy Queenie. During World War II, Queenie's views will shift, and her position on the refugees as people who need help will echo Harry's argument about the miners' needs. However, as a child, she remains fixed in her feeling of class superiority, which makes her heedless of the needs and feelings of others.

Queenie's imperious reactions can partially be explained by the contradictory lessons she learns from her parents' behavior. On the one hand, even though the miners buy the cheaper eggs rather than the fertilized ones and try to hatch them, which Queenie deems stealing, her father still gives them food when they cannot pay. On the other hand, he does not allow them to continue cheating him and instructs Queenie to prick the eggs with a pin to prevent hatching. Similarly inconsistent, Queenie's mother insists that Queenie make soup to feed the unemployed men and their families who are hungry. However, she does not care enough to learn the names of the young women who help around the farm. They are "*only* miners' daughters" so she calls everyone "Girl."[35] Queenie's father also dismisses the importance of names, renaming the farmworker Graham as Jim, because it is easier to remember. Even though Queenie's parents help the miners and farm workers and expect Queenie to do the same, these examples show that they also do not treat them as quite human. As a result, Queenie does not see the miners or farm workers as individuals either and resents even more that she has to work in the kitchen to help them instead of going to dances in pretty dresses.

Queenie also refuses on principle to date any of the miners' children. As she mercenarily puts it: "Any boy I was going to walk out with would have to court me in a collar and tie . . . and a wage packet about him."[36] Queenie may not be a lady, but she aspires to that status and insists she is at least "a cut above the miners' children."[37] She believes her father's words at the Empire Exhibition about having the world at her feet and has high aspirations: higher than dating or marrying a miner's son and higher than living and working on a farm.

The person who rescues Queenie from the muck of the farm and who gives her the opportunity to become more of a lady is Aunt Dorothy, her mother's sister who lives in London. Aunt Dorothy runs a sweet shop that she inherited from her late husband, and her London life seems to be a better match for Queenie's social and sartorial aspirations. Queenie gets her own bedroom, new clothes, and lessons in elocution and deportment, all of which are designed to raise Queenie's social status. The lessons emphasize the relationship between language, etiquette, and class, and are one way that Levy shows how class distinctions are created and naturalized. Aunt Dorothy's etiquette-driven behavior is another.

Aunt Dorothy shows her sophistication through her delicacy about food. She claims to have a refined enough palate to differentiate between the pink and white parts of the coconut ice, which she cuts into neat pieces and serves on china. These mannerisms and Aunt Dorothy's lifestyle are superficial signs of success and status, and in those ways Aunt Dorothy's clean sweet shop is more refined than a bloody butcher's shop. Yet by revealing the parallels between Aunt Dorothy and Queenie's mother, Levy problematizes the created distinctions that distance people from one another. Even if Aunt Dorothy believes she is a cut above her sister, her sweet shop life is not significantly different from her sister's farm life. Both women sell food products at a shop in order to make a living, and both rely on the labor of others to support their social position. In both shops, too, class is connected to consumption.

Refinement has a double meaning in this section of the text. It refers to Aunt Dorothy's behavior and social status, but it also refers to the refined sugar that makes the licorice and humbugs sold at the shop. This linguistic connection links Aunt Dorothy's privilege to British colonialism. The sugar may be refined in England and transformed into English sweets; however, the product still comes from one of Britain's colonies. Through her depictions of the Empire Exhibition and Aunt Dorothy's sweet shop, Levy makes visible the relationship between food, imperialism, and English identity that the young Queenie assumes is natural.[38]

Extending the sugar symbolism from Aunt Dorothy's sweet shop, sugar comes to represent a name, a product, a nation, and a colonial relationship when Hortense meets a woman at the docks who is looking for her (imported) new nanny, Sugar. Seeing all Jamaicans as potentially Sugar, this woman approaches Hortense. The assumption that Hortense might be Sugar because Sugar is "one of you" naturalizes Hortense's position in the colonial hierarchy: as labor to be used for the benefit of the English and as a product to be consumed.[39] However, by seeing herself as equal in the power structure, Hortense refuses this assigned position and questions this established hierarchy.

Hortense may not grow up in England, but she, too, is a product of Empire, and there are many parallels between Queenie's and Hortense's childhood and adolescent experiences that similarly shape their identities, social and class expectations, and personal relationships. One of these is their shared feelings of superiority and sophistication. The young Queenie believes she has the world at her feet because of her relative class position, ladylike ambitions, and Englishness. Hortense believes she has the world at her feet because of her father and uncle's social position, her education, and her honey-colored skin. In regard to the latter, Hortense's views about status and power derive from the color and class hierarchy in Jamaica "inherited from the slave regimes in which skin colour and class were intertwined and indistinguishable."[40] Under this social system, what Levy describes as a "pigmentocracy,"[41] in which skin colors "were elaborately classified (mulatto, quadroon, octoroon and so on) as a divide-and-rule tactic by the British plantocracy," Hortense is taught to believe that having lighter skin means that she is of "a higher class than any darker-skinned person."[42] As a result, Hortense links her honey coloring to golden opportunities for her life.

Like Queenie who goes to live with her Aunt Dorothy, Hortense is sent to live with her father's cousin and his family so that she has a chance at a more privileged life. In this family, as in Queenie's, class and income are connected to food. As a grocery wholesaler, Mr. Philip earns his living through food, and his well-fed appearance is one indication of his success. His social influence is another. He is not the law, but community members respect his opinions and ask him to settle disputes.

Mr. Philip also wields power at home, and his authority is most evident at mealtimes. Miss Ma serves the family in an order that reflects and reinforces the household hierarchy. She serves Mr. Philip first, then the children, then herself. At the table, Mr. Philip does not allow anyone else to speak, and proper behavior is enforced. Mr. Philip also offers a long grace and prayer each evening at dinner. Hortense's gender, social, and class perspectives develop from these meals that simultaneously teach "English manners and Christian discipline."[43] The meals in this household reflect Sceats's argument that "ideology permeates food and eating practices almost invisibly, through family and social structures which perpetuate particular patterns.... [Eating] is a major means of self-definition, as well as an important channel for the transmission of culture."[44] In *Small Island*, meals both perpetuate a social and family structure and reflect the instability of these structures. The series of dinners in the Philip household that are depicted in the book reveal changes in the established family dynamic and in the consciousnesses of individual characters.

The second family dinner that Hortense describes occurs after Michael has spent some time at a boarding school. According to Miss Ma, he comes back a man, which implies that Michael has gained more social power and hints at a shift in the family structure. At this dinner, everyone sits in his or her usual place at the table; however, nothing is as usual. Throughout the meal, Michael implicitly and explicitly upsets Mr. Philip's unquestioned authority. Michael's comment that he has missed Miss Jewel's cooking is the first indication that something is different. Mr. Philip is shocked that someone other than himself has spoken at the table. From this moment on, Michael's subversive behavior intensifies. During Mr. Philip's after-dinner sermon, Michael not only interrupts him but also challenges Mr. Philip's religious teachings by offering scientific theories about the earth's rotation and about evolution. Miss Ma tries to smooth things over by hushing Michael, but Michael is persistent, and his questions to Mr. Philip disrupt the meal and the family power structure. That Michael's verbal challenges lessen Mr. Philip's power can be seen in Hortense's description of a physically diminished Mr. Philip sitting at the table. He is "no longer a mountain only a man, stunted and fat and incapable of instilling fear."[45] Once Mr. Philip loses his absolute authority, he never regains this status.

The dinner after the family and community learn about Michael and Mrs. Ryder's affair shows an even more dramatic change in the household dynamics and in Mr. Philip's power. The family is in complete ruins, and the meal reflects this disarray. Mr. Philip refuses to eat, his hands shake, and the water glass he holds wobbles and spills. Even more significantly, Mr. Philip does not speak, does not say grace, and does not hold the Bible, all of which were earlier symbols of his patriarchal authority.

The household is further dismantled when Michael leaves home to join the RAF, and Hortense is sent to school in Kingston. Hortense bitterly notes that her guardians barely registered her departure. She feels no more important to them than a fattened chicken that they feast on before throwing out the carcass. Hortense's comparison of herself to livestock highlights not only the link between food and identity but also the careless consumption of others by those in power, which earlier is linked to the Empire Exhibition. Here, this issue of power is represented at a family level rather than at a national level, but the problems with structures and institutions that rely on inequalities and disempowering some in order to maintain an individual's or a nation's control remain the same.

Although Hortense feels powerless at home, she regains her feeling of importance at school, where she gets a colonial education that makes her feel that she has a place in the powerful British Empire. Her education also influences her social expectations. Hortense receives instruction in British culture, British literature, and the English language. Her lessons also include etiquette and cooking. In her domestic science class, Hortense is taught to make fairy cakes. With their yellow coloring, the fairy cakes represent golden opportunities, and Hortense's mastery in making them reinforces her belief that she will fit effortlessly into a golden life in England.

Hortense may gain a sense of self-worth from her education, but the lessons about language, manners, and etiquette add to the class prejudices she already possesses. The connection between the two is highlighted in her judgments about the Andersons with whom she lodges. The family is recommended to Hortense by the wife of the headmaster at the Half Way Tree Parish School, and because of the headmaster's position and because his wife has had tea with a member of the royal household—both markers of status and sophistication in Hortense's opinion—she believes the recommendation ensures that the Anderson family will be respectable and refined. The Andersons might be respectable, but Hortense considers them to be coarse and vulgar. She makes these behavior-based class judgments because of the family's food etiquette: at the table, the daughter-in-law talks with food in her mouth, describes in detail the birth of her sons, and fusses over the children, while Rosa Anderson indelicately eats her chicken. Hortense associates these examples of dining informality with lower-class, undesirable people, and her descriptions of the family's manners convey deep disgust. Hortense expects that her peers like Celia, whom she invites to dinner, will share her opinions. However, rather than finding the family to be disgusting or unpleasant, Celia likes them, and they like her. Celia believes that Hortense's disconnection from and inability to appreciate the Andersons comes from her lack of understanding about them, and her conciliatory advice to Hortense is to "take the time to know" them.[46] This suggestion represents Levy's larger message that understanding is crucial to bridging gaps between individuals and to creating better personal, political, and social relationships.

In this moment, Hortense's inability to heed Celia's wise words and to set aside her class judgments—she continues to believe that she is a cut above the Andersons—prevent her from recognizing the Andersons' kindness, which includes hosting a wedding party for her and Gilbert. At the party, there is food, music, and dancing, but all Hortense notices are the family's poor manners and gluttonous behavior. The thought that living in England will raise her status high enough that she no longer will have to associate with people like the Andersons helps Hortense make it through an evening of their low-class company. However, her beliefs and behavior also distance her from a supportive community.

Hortense's disdain extends to the woman she stays with in Kingston just before her departure for England. This woman cooks Hortense a comforting meal of rice, peas, fried chicken, and green banana and tries to prepare Hortense for England by telling her about rationing and the cold. She also gives Hortense a handmade blanket to bring with her. However, because this woman earns her living by letting rooms and because her table manners do not meet Hortense's exacting standards, Hortense looks down on her and does not recognize the importance of the woman's kindness until later when the blanket brings warmth, color, and comfort to Hortense in grey, unwelcoming England. Hortense also dismisses the wisdom in the woman's account of

England, because she feels confident in her own knowledge about English life. She believes that, in contrast to her life in Jamaica, England will offer her a community that better fits her social aspirations and that the transition to her new home will be effortless. She envisions England as a place of manners, politeness, and refinement where her upbringing and education will ensure her a warm welcome. Even if the climate in England turns out to be cold, Hortense believes that her discomfort will be mitigated by friendly neighbors, hot tea, and bright color like the daffodils in Wordsworth's poem.

Hortense's fantasy of England also includes "a big house with a bell at the front door," which she imaginatively populates with a husband who fixes things and with precise details about the rooms, the furniture, and the food she will cook.[47] In regard to the latter, Hortense plans to change the meals she cooks and eats to fit fully into her English environment. When she arrives in England, Hortense seems close to fulfilling her fantasy; however, her pleasure quickly recedes as she realizes that even if the house where she will live with Gilbert is one of the tallest she has ever seen, it is dilapidated and in disrepair: window panes are missing, she cannot hear the doorbell ring, and there is dog shit on the front steps. The gloomy room Gilbert has rented also lacks color and charm, and there is not a proper kitchen in which to make her English meals.

Hortense's arrival does not have the welcome politeness she has imagined either. Unlike Gilbert and his friend Winston, who excitedly hope that her trunk holds guava, mango, rum, and yam—food and drink that signify home, comfort, and happiness—Queenie hopes that Hortense is not bringing "anything into the house that will smell."[48] If, as Sceats contends, "the acceptability of particular foods and what they signify are part of cultural identity," Queenie's comment implies an exclusion of Hortense based on cultural difference.[49] For Queenie, Jamaican food and, by extension, this woman from Jamaica signify foreignness. Even if Queenie is unaware of the full meaning of her words, her statement represents the underlying racism of questions like "Why are you here?" "When are you going back to your own country?" "Why is your food funny?"[50] It also serves as an example of Sonya Andermahr's argument that "[w]hile she [Queenie] rejects overtly racist attitudes . . . she does exhibit a racial bias, which is never really challenged over the course of the novel."[51] As Andermahr suggests, Queenie's opinions may not be as extreme as Mr. Todd's or Bernard's, both of whom overtly believe that black immigrants are ruining the country and do not have a right to call England home; however, her words about the content of Hortense's trunk imply that she is not immune to these types of exclusionary views.

Hortense is astonished that her accent also marks her as an outsider. Although she is proud of her language skills, Hortense is not easily understood when she arrives in England. Determined to establish a respected place in English society, Hortense begins listening to the BBC in order "to learn to speak in the English manner."[52] She seeks the kind of improvement that the BBC's Director-General, John Reith, aimed for in his programming. Peter Clarke observes that Reith "dedicated his life to the improvement of public taste through a carefully regulated regime of programmes, with just enough concessions to variety, entertainment and popular music to stave off mutiny by the listening public."[53] Clarke also notes that "[t]he careful elocution of the BBC announcers was all part of Reith's master plan for 'improvement': helping to establish one variant of upper-middle-class London accent as 'standard English.'"[54] Like Queenie's childhood elocution lessons, Hortense's BBC lessons are intended to raise her social status. The BBC programs also add to Hortense's cultural knowledge. When she first arrives, Hortense is surprised to discover that she does not know as much about English customs and postwar life as she believes.

These issues of language and culture are foregrounded when Queenie takes Hortense shopping. Whether it is due to shortages, miscommunication, or both, when Hortense wants to buy three wash basins, one for vegetables, one for cups and plates, and one for washing, the shopkeeper at the hardware store only gives her one. The grocer also does not seem to understand Hortense's request for condensed milk and bread, so she must resort to pointing to what she wants. When her product desires are understood, Hortense is horrified to witness the grocer picking up the bread with his bare hands. Queenie believes Hortense's reaction is due to a linguistic miscommunication, but what Hortense does not understand is why the grocer handles the bread with dirty hands and gives it to her unwrapped. She sees his action as akin to licking the bread before giving it to her. Hortense may be confident in her knowledge about English life, but she is shocked by many aspects of it. Her questioning refrain to Gilbert "Is this the way the English live?" applies not only to their rundown room but also to cultural and social issues.[55]

Hortense also learns on this shopping trip that her honey-colored skin does not confer the same status in England that it does in Jamaica. Before their walk, Queenie assures Hortense: "It doesn't worry me to be seen out with darkies."[56] Because Hortense ties her identity to her profession and believes that, as a teacher, she has more social status than Queenie who earns her living by renting rooms, Hortense does not understand why Queenie would even think to worry about being seen with her. She also is perplexed that with her light, golden complexion others would view her as dark-skinned. Further emphasizing that in England others see Hortense differently than she sees herself, on their walk home, a youth taunts Hortense and throws a bread roll, which misses Hortense but hits Queenie. Queenie displaces her anger at the youth onto Hortense and advises her that it would be good manners to step off the pavement if an English person wishes to pass. This advice is the same Mr. Todd has earlier conveyed to Queenie about how her "coloured" lodgers should act, advice that at the time makes Queenie bristle with indignation. Although Queenie has told Hortense that, unlike most people, she does not mind being seen in public with her, Queenie's repetition of Mr. Todd's words shows how easily racist attitudes can be perpetuated.

Gilbert is another character who is surprised by the racism he experiences in the Mother Country and in countries like the United States that are its allies. Like Queenie and Hortense, Gilbert begins his narrative by situating his personal identity and relationship with new places in regard to food. His perspective on British and American food and culture comes from his wartime experiences. He finds the boiled and mushy British food provided by the RAF to be torturous and wonders how the British could build empires when they feed their armies such bad, bland food. He also is relieved that the British do not impose their culinary conventions on their colonies and prevent people in those countries from frying and spicing their food. Although the reader later sees Gilbert enjoying English foods like fish and chips, he never reconciles himself to boiled food, and after the war, boiled, mushy potatoes prompt one of the first fights between Hortense and Gilbert. In the present moment, overcooked vegetables, "grey and limp on the plate," make Gilbert regret joining the RAF.[57]

In contrast to the distasteful English food that Gilbert encounters in the RAF, he enjoys delicious and abundant food while he is training in the United States. Breakfast consists of eggs, cereal, bacon, sausage, potatoes, toast, fried tomatoes, and fruit. Making this feast even better, Gilbert is given as much as he can eat. Gilbert initially conflates the wonderful food in America with the nation, believing that "America is Paradise."[58] Temporarily at least, good food trumps all other concerns including segregation. Soon, however, Gilbert's gastronomic delight is tempered by his experience of American racism and discrimination. A white American officer explains to the West Indian troops that the problem with black American soldiers is that "if his belly's full he won't work."[59] In addition, although the West Indian troops are assured that in the camp they will be treated like white Americans rather than black Americans, Gilbert's RAF unit is told that they will be confined to the camp during their stay. Gilbert may find American food to be far superior to British food, but it is not good enough to make up for these offensive and discriminatory attitudes and practices, and soon Gilbert is glad to leave America behind and go to England, even if it means a return to tasteless boiled food.

Gilbert's social experiences in England, however, are mixed. His war service is appreciated by many members of the community, but he and his unit are figures of curiosity when they go into town. In addition, the English may not practice segregation, but they do not prohibit it on the American bases or in some of the towns the Americans frequent on leave. When Gilbert visits an American base in England to pick up Spitfire parts, his interactions there are not much different than in the United States. The food he is offered is still good and abundant, but why Gilbert is fed remains problematic. The officers do not want to work with someone black, so they put him off with food, using the same kind of rationale as the officer in America: "*They* always want something to eat."[60] How Gilbert is fed also reflects the segregation on the base. The Americans cannot send Gilbert to the dining hall, so they bring him food. The food he eats may be delicious, but it makes him a little ill, and his nausea can be attributed both to the rich food and to the racism.

On his way back from the base, Gilbert picks up two black American soldiers, Levi and Jon, who are unsurprised by Gilbert's treatment at the base. They also describe to Gilbert the more subtle British racism they have encountered. Levi tells Gilbert that when he and others from his unit are invited to an English lady's house for tea, the hospitality seems to represent different treatment than they receive in the United States. However, they discover that there are limits to this friendliness and inclusion. The English lady may talk to them, ask questions, and politely pretend not to notice Jon spilling his tea because he is nervous, but when Jon smiles at the white servant who is helping him steady the cup of tea he is holding and she smiles back, the soldiers are quickly made to leave. Levi and Jon also tell Gilbert about the segregation that takes place in some of the towns where they go on leave. Although Lincoln is the closet town for their recreation, they are headed to Nottingham because this week Lincoln is a white-GIs-only town while Nottingham is for black GIs.

Gilbert may see himself as positioned differently from Levi and Jon because he is a British citizen, but his experiences in England often make him feel like an outsider in the country that should be home. For example, his encounters with people both on the bases and in the towns reveal to him how little most English know about its colonies and the people who live in them. Gilbert expects that because every West Indian is taught about British culture, history, geography, and industry, British people will have a similar range of knowledge about their colonies. However, even though they rely on colonial products like sugar, cocoa, tea, and coffee and on colonial troops during the war, the English people he meets do not even know where Jamaica is located. The Mother Country's seeming disregard for the people who live in its colonies makes him happy to return home when he finally is demobilized. He has had enough of the cold, the lack of welcome, the bland and boiled food, and even the tea. In regard to the latter, Gilbert may have some good associations with tea as a symbol of hospitality, particularly in regard to his friendship with Queenie, but it also is linked to American and British racism, British colonialism, and Arthur's senseless death. Gilbert's return to Jamaica offers a reprieve from the unsatisfying aspects of his time in England. However, after the bee business venture with his cousin Elwood fails, Gilbert decides to return to England, because even with its social problems, it offers him more economic opportunities than Jamaica. Gilbert returns to England knowing more about the challenges of life there, but the transition remains a difficult one because his desire to settle in England comes into direct conflict with those who hold conservative nationalist views about English identity, citizenship, and immigration.[61]

An aptly named Bernard Bligh represents this insular nationalist position, and his descriptions of food show that he makes moral judgments based on nationality. For Bernard, English food and traditionally used domestic space represent stability, and his English diet and identity are intimately connected to home, family, and purity. Morally good associations for Bernard are foods that represent classic English fare and activities associated with hearth and home such as Queenie in the kitchen or tea with his mother. These types of associations are solidified, Peter Bishop argues, in times of uncertainty when people "look back nostalgically to an imagined past when food was supposed to be more wholesome, natural and pure, to when the family meal stood firmly at the heart of all that was stable, enduring, reliable and of moral value."[62] The other side of this food-morality equation is that "[a]t times of racial fear and hostility food . . . carries ambivalent or hostile significations. 'Filthy foreign food' scares; calls to patriotic eating."[63] In contrast to his belief in the goodness of all things English and in accordance with Bishop's point about the hostile significations of foreign food, Bernard links unwholesome food to foreign people and places, which he sees as a threat to himself, his family, his community, and his country.

Bernard's fear of and intolerance for foreignness are exacerbated by World War II and his wartime service. He associates contaminated, bad food with the places to which he is sent during the war. In Bombay, for example, among the wares being sold are oranges and cakes. There, neither of these products is the delicious treat that it would be in England. Bernard explains: "We'd been warned about their oranges. Boiled in filthy water to make them big."[64] The cakes, too, are spoiled, "[g]audy as Christmas and speckled with black—not raisins but flies."[65] In another example of physical, moral, and gastronomic corruption, Bernard reveals that the fish the British troops are offered are rumoured to come from the Hooghly river, which is full of "rancid rotting bodies."[66] In these instances, the surface of the food may appear fine but, from

Bernard's perspective, the product and, by extension the places they come from and the people who live there are unsound and corrupt.

Further emphasizing Bernard's xenophobia, he links the non-English people that he encounters to undesirable foods. Ashok, for example, has "breath foetid with garlic" and the "Char-wallahs" sell "urns of foul tea."[67] The foul Indian tea contrasts with the "jolly good cuppa" that, to Bernard, symbolizes home, goodness, and stability.[68] Bernard's depiction of the prison in Calcutta uses this same set of associations in order to represent his English nationalism. Unlike the comforts of home, the prison floor is hard, and the sweat-soaked mattress he sleeps on feels mushy like "a biscuit dunked in tea."[69] Bernard's unpalatable images employ the things he knows, like tea and biscuits, to articulate the hardship of his current situation and to emphasize its difference from his happy English life.

The foods that Queenie associates with Bernard further reveal his character. They also accurately depict their early relationship and its evolution. Using Aunt Dorothy's sweet shop and the family farm as her points of reference, Queenie observes that Bernard's hair is "shiny as liquorice," and when she talks to him for the first time, he "blushe[s] as pink as bacon."[70] Although Bernard's nervousness around Queenie reveals his attraction to her, Queenie's mild and familiar food-based descriptions of Bernard suggest that the relationship begins neutrally for her. She may be curious about the man who comes to the shop each day for *The Times* and some sweets, but she does not feel the passion and excitement that she imagines are part of a romantic relationship. Like Hortense's discontented refrain to Gilbert "Is this it?" about their living situation, Queenie repeatedly asks her Aunt Dorothy "Is this it?" about her courtship with Bernard.

Physical contact with Bernard lacks romance for her as well. She notes that when she kisses Bernard, it feels like she is "kissing a chicken's beak."[71] Rather than a peck on the lips, Queenie desires a more sensual kiss that "taste[s] of nectar," but she never achieves this level of bliss with Bernard.[72] Recognizing her dissatisfaction, Queenie tries to end the relationship; however, Bernard seems so sad when she suggests it that she allows the courtship to continue. Yet when he proposes, her first thought is an inauspicious "blinking heck."[73] Queenie's reaction emphasizes her continued uncertainty about the relationship, but when her Aunt Dorothy dies, Queenie is forced to put aside her reservations about Bernard and their compatibility. Queenie's options are limited: she can go home to the farm or she can marry Bernard. Because a life on the farm is what she wants least in the world, Queenie chooses a life with Bernard. However, even in her grief, Queenie is not consoled by him. While they wait for the ambulance to take her aunt away, Bernard makes Queenie a cup of tea with sugar. Her description of the sweet tea as "foul" (a word that echoes Bernard's depiction of the tea he has in India) shows that their relationship fails even at the basic level of sympathy and comfort. Later when her father-in-law, Arthur, offers Queenie the same liquid consolation after she is injured by a bomb, Queenie's appreciation of the lovely, warm sweet tea shows that the issue with the tea Bernard gives her after her aunt's death is not the tea but their incompatible relationship.[74]

Unfortunately, getting married to Bernard does not change Queenie's feelings for him. Bernard remains unstimulating company for her, and he continues to lack physical and sexual appeal. Still using food to represent her feelings, Queenie describes Bernard's breath as unappealingly smelling like "tobacco mixed with whiffs of digesting potatoes."[75] She also notes that when they have sex, the corners of his mouth fill with spit "white as breadcrumbs" and his penis is alternately "slippery as a greasy sausage" or dry like tree bark.[76] Queenie's distaste for Bernard becomes even clearer when, as I will discuss, she uses the same foods to describe her lover, Michael Roberts, but makes the imagery appetizing and sensual.

Tea is the first indication that Queenie feels differently about Michael than she does about Bernard. Although tea signifies difficulties and incompatibilities in Queenie and Bernard's marriage, it represents a budding romance between Queenie and Michael, who, along with two other RAF officers stay with Queenie when they are in London. Queenie's strong physical attraction to Michael is shown through the problems she has making tea the morning after he arrives. She fails in her offer of tea because she is so preoccupied by his presence that she forgets the word "tea." She then forgets to boil the water and pours cold water into the teapot. Because wartime shortages mean she cannot waste the precious tea leaves, she attempts to remake the pot, but she remains too agitated to light a match. Even Michael's help lighting the stove does not alleviate Queenie's problems, because she then forgets to put new water in the kettle, and it starts to burn. In a final representation of her flustered state, she knocks the strainer off the draining board and gets tea leaves on her leg. Emphasizing their shared attraction, food and flirtation mix while Michael appreciatively examines her tea-splattered leg and her body.

That evening, rather than going out with his friends, Michael brings Queenie and Arthur ham, chocolate, and an orange. Michael's offerings represent a welcome contribution to the civilian wartime household, but Queenie also recognizes that the gifts are "his war-time weapons of seduction."[77] The effectiveness of these weapons can be seen in Queenie's food-based description of Michael's erotic appeal. Michael's lips are attractively "plump like sausages," which contrasts sharply with her description of Bernard's unappealing "greasy sausage."[78] With Michael, food and sex also combine in a sensual way. Queenie describes the pleasure she feels when Michael "lap[s] between her legs like a cat with cream."[79] As this image reveals, the sex between Queenie and Michael is undeniably better than between Queenie and Bernard. Queenie's full attention to her partner during sex emphasizes this point as well. Mrs. Bligh, she admits, "usually worked out what she could make for dinner" while she had sex with her husband.[80] With Michael, Queenie focuses on their mutual sexual satisfaction. There is no need to plan dinner, because they are each other's meals.

This erotic connection continues on a later visit as well. Michael looks at Queenie as he would a "delicious dish to be savoured," and they savor each other for three nights as both their desires and their bodies are fed.[81] Their feast of bread and jam in bed, during which they playfully lick the leftover jam from each other's lips and "wriggl[e] about to get rid of the crumbs," represents another food-based example of the different relationship Queenie has with Michael.[82] The crumbs here are romantic unlike the image of the breadcrumb-like spit that accumulates in the corner of Bernard's mouth when they have sex.

When Bernard finally returns after the war, their lack of romantic connection continues despite Queenie's hope that he might have changed from his time away and become more heroic and more attractive. Unfortunately for her, Bernard's eating habits quickly show that his character has remained the same. Rather than taking his tea "hot like a man," Bernard is still the fretful, timid man who blows on his tea before drinking it so that it does not burn his mouth.[83] For Queenie, this action signifies Bernard's lack of masculinity, and his other habits of overly stirring the tea, tapping his spoon, and slurping his drink instantly irritate her. None of these behaviors bode well for the renewal of their marital relationship. Queenie may use tea to welcome Bernard home, but she also uses it to mitigate the discomfort of his return and to avoid talking about anything important. "With every awkward silence," she explains, "I'd offered him tea."[84] The copious amount of tea that Queenie serves and that Bernard drinks signals the tension between the couple. It also indicates Bernard's dismay over the changes that have taken place in the household while he was away. In his absence, Queenie has taken in lodgers to make ends meet and has even rented the room that used to be his mother's. Bernard, who finds any change to be disconcerting, is particularly upset by this repurposed space, because his mother's room represents a happier, more stable time when he nostalgically remembers being able to enjoy tea and muffins in front of the fire. From Bernard's perspective, he comes home not to the house or to the country of his memory but to its decaying shell.

Bernard tries to minimize the changes he perceives by re-creating past comforts, notably through food preparation. The morning after his return, he makes breakfast for Queenie and uses his mother's silver toast rack to bring her "[t]riangles neatly laid in a row."[85] The toast rack's familial history and the toast's orderly placement in the rack suggests to Bernard a time when everything was neat and proper or at least can be remembered as such. Yet despite his desire to remain in the past, Bernard cannot ignore that the war has permanently changed the country. Bernard's nationalist views, however, remain largely unchanged. If anything, they have become more entrenched. Rachel Carroll points out that "his encounters with non-white British subjects serve not to broaden but to narrow his understanding of Britishness; he returns from a war fought against fascism convinced of the necessity for racial segregation."[86] In accordance with this position, Bernard believes that their nonwhite lodgers make the neighborhood less respectable and, more generally, that immigrants detract from England's national identity.

That Queenie does not feel the same way about the house's familial past, England's national identity, or Bernard's ideas about Englishness is suggested by her physical reaction to the toast he serves her. She may appreciate Bernard's gesture of making breakfast, but she finds his oppressive attitudes hard to swallow. When he asks about the lodgers and starts voicing Mr. Todd's opinions about "coloureds swamping the place," the bite of toast sticks in her throat.[87] In this moment, Queenie recognizes that Bernard's presence and beliefs are the trouble rather than the toast.

Unlike the other characters, Bernard does not learn from his experiences. Emily Johansen astutely observes that "[i]n almost every scenario, his actions and responses reveal that his view of the world is fundamentally naïve at best; he holds a worldview that is shaped primarily by his refusal to engage actively and intelligently with what he sees. He encounters the world, but he either cannot learn from it or learns something fundamentally misguided from nearly every experience."[88] Even as Levy wants readers to understand the origins of Bernard's view of the world, she problematizes his inability to adapt and even more so his refusal to make an effort to understand or to engage with perspectives other than his own.

Although sharing a similarly necessitous start and an unromantic beginning, Hortense and Gilbert's relationship offers a different model of adaptation, cooperation, and support than Queenie and Bernard's. Hortense's and Gilbert's ability to change their views based on what they learn from new experiences eventually allows them to understand and to appreciate each other's different perspectives and beliefs. This engagement, Levi suggests, leads to better marital stability for the couple and provides a solid foundation on which to build a more functional home in England and to develop a stronger community.

Hortense and Gilbert meet by accident when Hortense mistakes Gilbert for her cousin, Michael. It is not love at first sight for either party. Hortense's first impression of Gilbert is that he is uncouth. Gilbert's first reaction to Hortense is amusement at the pawpaw on her legs and feet. Based on this first encounter with Hortense, Gilbert gives her the nickname Miss Mucky Foot. As they get to know one another, this nickname alternately signals his affection for and exasperation with Hortense. In regard to the latter, Gilbert often finds Hortense's high-class attitudes difficult to understand and to deal with. The nickname, which links her identity to a moment when she is not immaculate, represents one way that Gilbert subtly shows Hortense that her value is not predicated on distinguishing and distancing herself from others and serves as a challenge to Hortense's haughtiness and classist views.

Hortense and Gilbert's second meeting occurs when Celia, who has been dating Gilbert, introduces the two only to discover that they have met. Gilbert uses this opportunity to tease Hortense again about her pawpaw-splattered foot. He also teases her when he invites Celia to go with him to England and jokingly describes the difference between the life of food shortages in Jamaica, where Hortense will be, and the leisurely life of England, where he and Celia will be. The allure of an idealized England of refined tea drinking and visits to historic landmarks is too great for Hortense. She sabotages Celia's plans to go by telling Gilbert about Celia's mad mother and reminding Celia of her obligation to care for her.

When Celia goes silent with rage, an embarrassed Gilbert tries to alleviate the tension by buying the two women some ice cream. Gilbert's action and Hortense's response nicely reveal their characters and how they relate to one another in difficult circumstances: Gilbert uses food to try to make a situation better; Hortense is dissatisfied with his solution despite the effort. Her observation that Gilbert "disappeared before I could tell him that I was not fond of that icy cold stuff" emphasizes that she has her own opinions and cannot easily be appeased.[89] It also shows that Gilbert's assumptions about what Hortense might like are wrong. These dynamics exemplify their early relationship and are played out many times during their marriage, especially when Hortense first arrives in England.

Hortense's discontent with Gilbert and her disillusionment about England are portrayed through her dismay about their living space and their arguments about food. The small and dilapidated room that Gilbert rents from Queenie does not match Hortense's grand expectations of life in England. She cannot believe that Gilbert has brought her from Jamaica "just for this."[90] Even though Gilbert has attempted to fix up the room for her arrival, it remains messy and confined. In this limited space where a single room must be used for multiple purposes—cooking, dining, relaxing, and sleeping—none of these activities can be done well or comfortably.

Despite this spatial disadvantage, Gilbert tries to make Hortense happy, and tea plays a central role in his efforts. He puts a chair near the heater as he prepares to welcome her with a hot cup of tea. However, like the failed attempt to smooth things over with ice cream, Gilbert's tea making is not a success and does not satisfy Hortense. Instead, it leaves both characters frustrated and upset. Among other problems, the milk has gone bad, the cups are dirty, the water takes too long to boil, and Gilbert burns himself on the kettle. These irritations are only part of the tea preparation going dramatically wrong. Nervous because of Hortense's obvious displeasure about the room, Gilbert empties the chamber pot into the sink before he realizes that the tea cups are still in the basin. He had intended to wash them, but did not. He had intended to empty the chamber pot in the downstairs bathroom, but did not. Hortense is livid with disgust. "You live like an animal," she declares.[91] Hortense's rebuke after the disastrous tea making finally provokes Gilbert to speak directly. He tells her they are lucky to even have this room in which to live.

Gilbert may know that they are fortunate to have a place to live, but Hortense does not yet understand that the war has limited their housing options. Many houses were bombed during the war and were either completely destroyed or uninhabitable, and reconstruction efforts were slow and difficult due to labor shortages and a scarcity of resources. Racism made finding a place to live more challenging as well. Levy recounts that when her father tried to find housing in England in the late 1940s, he "faced incredible hostility when looking for somewhere to live because of the colour of his skin. . . . [T]he signs in the windows read 'no niggers, no dogs, no Irish.'"[92] Gilbert's difficulty finding a room to rent reflects the problems faced by many who came to England after the war. However, his explanation to Hortense about the ordinariness of their postwar living situation does little to reconcile her to the conditions of her new life.

The next morning, Gilbert makes another attempt to cheer up Hortense by bringing her a cup of tea before he goes to work. The cups may now be clean, but Hortense remains unimpressed with Gilbert and with her new home. It is so dark and grey out that Hortense imagines even the English birds need to be roused with cups of tea. When Gilbert tentatively asks if Hortense will make dinner that night and suggests chips, Hortense agrees to cook, but lack of space makes dinner preparation difficult. Because he is cold, Gilbert sits in front of the fireplace when he returns from work; however, there is not room enough for him to sit there and for Hortense to cook comfortably. His legs are in the way, so Hortense must contort herself to make the meal. Frustrated by their difficult living situation, Hortense tries to impose order and civility on her new space and on Gilbert when she asks him to sit at the table to eat. The relationship between class and eating etiquette is foregrounded in Hortense's insistence that the table is the "proper" place to have dinner and in Gilbert's response to "Miss High-class" that she can eat where she likes but he is cold and is not moving.[93] In this moment, neither Hortense nor Gilbert is willing to consider the merits of the other's position. Their inability to communicate effectively and empathetically creates a tense beginning to their marital life.

Hortense's cooking adds to this tension. The meal she prepares ends up being just as unsuccessful as Gilbert's tea making. Even if Hortense is educated about English cooking and confident in her abilities, practically she is inept. The eggs and chips Hortense makes for dinner are a disaster. Cynthia James's argument about Hortense's linguistic experiences in England apply to her cooking as well. James argues that

> [t]he parody of Hortense lies in the laughable way in which her secure notions of cultured language are undermined. It lies in her pride that she can speak English with the best, and "better" English than most English persons. . . . In the West Indies where using what is considered high English confers a superior identity, Hortense's "recognition" is assured. However, in London she lacks familiarity with the cultural idiomatic load of British English and so does not belong.[94]

In regard to cooking, Hortense may be recognized in Jamaica for her aptitude with fairy cakes and be proud of this achievement, but she is unfamiliar with the culinary equivalent of idiomatic British English, quintessential English foods like chips. Because Hortense has already haughtily informed Gilbert that she knows how to cook from her domestic science class, she is unwilling to admit to Gilbert that she does not know what a chip is or how to cook it. As a result, Hortense must ask Queenie for information about chips. Queenie explains that "a chip is a potato cut up small," but what Hortense does not know, and Queenie likely assumes is self-evident, is that chips are fried not boiled.[95]

Already upset by his day at work and the racism he encounters daily, Gilbert misdirects his frustration at the meal. "This is not chips," Gilbert complains when he sees what Hortense has made, and he remains unappeased when Hortense tells him he should be thankful for the food the Lord provides.[96] The reader, however, knows that Gilbert will not be thankful for any food that is boiled. Making his mood even worse, Gilbert burns his finger on the hot potatoes. After bad-temperedly accusing Hortense of not being able to cook, Gilbert tries to diffuse the strained situation by offering to show Hortense how to make chips, but she stubbornly refuses. Her pride will not allow her to admit that her cooking skills leave something to be desired.

The rest of the meal is even worse. Because Queenie has told Hortense that "the English like to serve chip with egg," and Hortense wants to prove her aptitude in all things English, Hortense decides to make this meal.[97] She knows from her domestic science class how to prepare a four-minute egg "like the English do."[98] She also has been taught that the proper etiquette for eating the egg is to slice the top with a knife rather than to tap it with a spoon, and she is curious to see what Gilbert does with the egg. As she expects, Gilbert fails this test by shattering the shell with his spoon. Hortense may not be surprised by Gilbert eating the egg wrong, but, like Gilbert, she is surprised by the content: the egg has gone bad and smells terrible.

The addition of a rotten egg to a rotten day angers Gilbert, and he throws his plate on the floor and storms out of the room. He cannot appreciate that Hortense has tried to make him a nice meal, which meant she had to swallow her pride and ask Queenie for help, and he does not notice that she has tried to make their space nicer by cleaning and tidying the room.[99] Gilbert is insensitive to these efforts, because his experiences in England have made his dreams of becoming a lawyer, getting a good job, and having a comfortable place to live seem out of reach. He does not even feel welcome in the Mother Country.

Food may be the catalyst for Gilbert's outburst, but it also has the power to fix the situation. While he is out walking, a woman offers a visibly upset Gilbert a cough sweet to warm him up, touches his arm, smiles, and reminds him of the importance of home. Gilbert is grateful for the woman's compassion. "A simple gesture, a friendly word, a touch, a sticky sweet rescued me," he explains.[100] Gilbert's response to the woman's simple act of human kindness reveals how making the effort to connect with another person can have a broader personal and social impact.

Because of this nice encounter, Gilbert is able to make his own gesture of kindness. He brings two portions of fish and chips back to Hortense. As he puts their meal on a plate, Gilbert tells Hortense that the English eat fish and chips straight from the newspaper. He notes: "I knew this high-class woman would not be able to keep her face solemn in the presence of such barbarity."[101] This scene demonstrates that Gilbert is beginning to comprehend Hortense's "high-class" ways, and this understanding and acceptance are key to making the relationship work. Gilbert next offers Hortense a chip, which she eats eagerly. Hortense is delighted by her first taste of prepared English food and the introduction to English culture that it symbolizes. Having satisfied Hortense's appetite for food, friendship, and Englishness, Gilbert takes the opportunity to tell her more about England and English life—the good and the bad parts—in the hope that this knowledge will ease the transition into her new home.

Hortense and Gilbert reconcile over this meal, but that does not mean that Hortense's cooking improves or that their living situation becomes substantially easier. Both points are emphasized when Kenneth tries to invite himself to dinner. Hortense does not like Kenneth or want him in her home. However, rather than being direct, Hortense shows her discontent through domestic activity. Demonstrating an increased knowledge about his wife's character, Gilbert understands that Hortense banging pots as she cooks means that Kenneth's presence is upsetting her. Kenneth, however, is either oblivious to Hortense's dislike or hungry and continues to try and wrangle a dinner invitation. He attempts to win her over with a smile and a compliment, but his tactics do not work. Too disdainful to reply, Hortense gives Kenneth a withering look. Kenneth may be undaunted by Hortense's fierce stare, but he changes his mind about staying for dinner when he looks more closely at the food she is preparing. He then quickly excuses himself by pretending to have a previous engagement. That hungry Kenneth makes an excuse not to stay for free food reveals the continued dreadfulness of Hortense's cooking.

That Gilbert stays even though he knows the bad quality of the food is a testament to his character and his commitment to the relationship. He does admit that when Hortense gives him a plate of the unappealing food, he is tempted to follow Kenneth's lead; however, Gilbert does not go. He even tries to be gracious about the unrecognizable food. "Lovely," he tells her as he crunches on grains of rice that should be soft.[102] Gilbert's effort to eat the nearly inedible meal diffuses the potentially fraught situation. Yet even Gilbert's good manners do not entirely satisfy Hortense. She does not scold him for ingratitude, but she cannot stop herself from complaining about their room again and telling Gilbert that she does not think that it befits her position as a teacher. Gilbert is as awed by Hortense's continued haughtiness as he is by her ability not to notice how bad the food is. Somehow, she manages to eat it with grace. Even if Hortense is disappointed by her living situation, her ability to maintain her class-conscious manners shows that her dreams of England are still largely intact.

The meal precipitates Hortense's attempt to get a teaching job and her subsequent realization that England is not the place of golden opportunities that she has imagined. Gilbert accompanies Hortense to the education authority office for contradictory reasons: to gloat when she fails to get a teaching job and to protect her from the disappointment of rejection. When he sees how upset she is after being told that she is not qualified to teach in England, his better nature takes over, and he focuses on protecting Hortense and cheering her up.[103] As part of this effort, Gilbert takes Hortense to see the sights of London and buys her tea and cake in a café, an echo of the idealized England of sipping tea and visiting the statue of Nelson he earlier described to Hortense and Celia.

This tea represents a significant and lasting change in Gilbert and Hortense's relationship. At the beginning of the meal when Hortense expresses her concern that tea will spoil Gilbert's appetite for her food, Gilbert holds back his teasing. He may think: "I do hope so," but he does not say the words out loud.[104] By the end of their meal, Gilbert can voice his real feelings, and their relationship is stronger for it. The change begins when Hortense finally lets down her guard and she and Gilbert have their first discussion about their dreams and disappointments. This openness contrasts with the tea that Queenie and Bernard have when he returns home. During that tea, Queenie and Bernard hide their true feelings by sipping tea rather than talking. At the tea shop, tea facilitates communication between Hortense and Gilbert.

The tea shop scene also offers a model for how a willingness to understand and to engage with another person's perspective and beliefs can create personal and social change. While she stirs her tea, Hortense tells Gilbert that London has not matched her dream of the place. Her distress and disillusionment about life in England are clear as she cries into her tea, and her sadness infuses the English beverage. Hortense's openness and vulnerability prompt a confession from Gilbert, who shares his lost dream of becoming a lawyer.

Building on these revelations, Gilbert and Hortense try to figure out new dreams and goals to make up for their former ones. Gilbert asks Hortense what she can do besides teach, and she tells him that she can sew. Gilbert pursues this assertion: "'Of course' [you can sew] like you can cook? Or is it 'of course' because you can actually sew?"[105] Hortense may not get angry at Gilbert's questions, but she still insists that she can cook. The two debate Hortense's claim, but it is done without rancor:

> "My teacher, Miss Plumtree said my cake was the best outside the tea-shops of southern England."
> "Your teacher taste it?"
> "Of course."
> "And still she say it better than one she eat in a tea-shop."
> "Yes."
> "She tell you where this tea-shop is, because we must be sure not to go there."[106]

Gilbert's teasing and Hortense's lack of defensiveness show progress. This meal allows the couple to renegotiate their relationship as it moves from one of economic and social necessity to one of real connection in which both characters recognize each other's flaws, value, and humanity. If in Levy's novels, food often signifies problems in communication, it also can unite people. Hortense and Gilbert's new connection allows them to better face adversity and the challenges of living in England, because they can support one another.

The need for a support system based on community is also evident when Gilbert and three Caribbean men greet each other at the tea shop. Even though they do not know one another, Gilbert explains to Hortense that he feels a bond with them because "they are from home."[107] When they are leaving the tea shop, another Caribbean man greets the couple. It may take Hortense a considerable amount of time to learn the importance of connecting with others rather than holding herself apart because she believes she is superior, but Gilbert's kindness to Hortense and his explanation of the communal association he has with the men from home results in an important change in her character. She is nice rather than disdainful to the Caribbean man outside the tea shop, which contrasts with her treatment of Kenneth, the Andersons, and the woman she spends the night with in Kingston. Instead of ignoring this man, Hortense looks past his dirtiness and answers him politely. Her action signifies an engagement with those around her rather than a judgment about their status and is a step toward building a better home in England.

Despite the difficulties and setbacks Gilbert and Hortense have faced, the end of the book offers the possibility of a real home for them where their relationship and new dreams can continue to grow. The house that Winston gives them the opportunity to fix up, manage, and live in, and the inspection of the place symbolize a way forward for the couple as they start to talk things through and to make decisions together. Gilbert thinks the new place is nice, but he knows from past experience and from his knowledge of Hortense's character that convincing her of the house's potential might be a challenge. When Hortense inspects the place, her reaction to what she sees shows that her expectations and her relationship with Gilbert have radically changed. She begins with the same question "Just this?" but the question represents a desire for information instead of a discontented judgment.[108]

In fact, Hortense approves of the new place, believes it can be fixed up, and is delighted that there is more than just one room for them. Their new flat will have the space and separate rooms that Hortense expected at Queenie's house but that were not there: two bedrooms, a kitchen with a sink and stove, and a bathroom of its own. There also will be a doorbell that works. Whereas Hortense and Gilbert could never make their current room into something livable because of the house's history, Bernard's presence, and Bernard's inability to adapt to a changing world, their new place offers a more functional domestic space and an opportunity to make a home in England. No longer stifled by unrealistic expectations and able to communicate with one another, their dreams of England can be revised, remade, and flourish. That their relationship becomes stronger in this moment is shown in two distinct places: when Hortense finally lets Gilbert into their bed and when she compares him to her noble and intelligent father—her highest praise—after Gilbert speaks his mind to Bernard, who continues to see only differences between himself and nonwhite British like Hortense and Gilbert. Andermahr argues that "Bernard's dyed-in-the-wool colonial attitudes contrast strikingly with Gilbert's complex and empathetic response to the other man's disillusionment."[109] Gilbert's ability to "understand the complex and multidirectional ways in which their stories are intertwined" represents the larger lesson about British history that Levy wants readers to learn.[110]

The final scene, which fittingly takes place over tea, shows the shifts in the relationships between the characters and the places where divisions remain. Queenie and Gilbert's relationship has been built around the hospitality of tea, and although Queenie tries to show renewed hospitality to him and to Hortense before the couple leaves for their new home, she is thwarted by Bernard's racism and intolerance. Queenie may force Bernard into grudging politeness when she tells him to get the tea for their guests, but his inhospitality and resentment toward Gilbert and Hortense show in his service of it. He sets down the tray roughly on the table, spills the milk, and refuses to serve them. Although the other characters have changed from their experiences, this scene emphasizes that Bernard is unable and unwilling to change his views.

Despite Bernard remaining stuck in his prejudicial beliefs, Levy hopes that her readers can develop the empathy that he cannot. Hortense and Gilbert represent a model for this type of change. They can move forward in their relationship and in their life because rather than judging people based on a limited perspective of the world, they embrace Celia's earlier advice to Hortense about getting to know people. This suggestion "to take the time to know" exemplifies Levy's broader argument that understanding—or even wanting to understand—is crucial to bridging gaps between individuals and to building stronger, more diverse communities.

NOTES

1. Virginia Woolf, *Three Guineas* (New York: Harcourt Brace Jovanovich, 1966), 36.
2. "The British Nationality Act of 1948 confirmed the right of entry to Britain for the citizens of Empire, who were deemed British subjects," but as Dominic Head points out, these legal rights were diminished in subsequent legislation (Head, *Cambridge Introduction to British Fiction*, 163). Following a series of Immigration Acts in the 1960s and 1970s that restricted immigration, the British Nationality Act of 1981 "sought further to erode the automatic right of British citizenship for people of the former British colonies, to be British one had to prove one's descent from an ancestor born in Britain (being born in Britain oneself was now insufficient)" (180). The 2022 Nationality and Borders Act is the most recent legislation to address British national-

ity. It amends some of the 1981 laws restricting the transmission of British citizenship and opens up more pathways for acquiring it.

3. Andrea Levy, "This Is My England," *The Guardian*, February 19, 2000.

4. Ibid.

5. Maria Helena Lima, "'Pivoting the Centre': The Fiction of Andrea Levy," in *Write Black, Write British: From Post Colonial to Black British Literature*, ed. Kadija George (London: Hansib Publications, 2005), 59.

6. Sonya Andermahr argues that "[a]n identical dynamic has been at play in recent years in British society in the context of austerity and Brexit through the 'hostile environment' towards immigrants fostered by Theresa May, first as Home Secretary (2010–16) and then as Prime Minister (2016–19) until her government's forced climbdown on the policy in 2018" (Andermahr, "Decolonizing Cultural Memory," 568). By making connections between these time periods, Andermahr shows how *Small Island* can serve as a model for addressing divisions in contemporary society.

7. Mike Phillips and Trevor Phillips, *Windrush: The Irresistible Rise of Multi-Racial Britain* (London: HarperCollins, 1998), 129.

8. Tony Kushner, "Immigration and 'Race Relations' in Postwar British Society," in *20th Century Britain: Economic, Social, and Cultural Change*, ed. Paul Johnson (New York: Longman, 1994), 413, 414.

9. Ibid., 414.

10. Sara Upstone, *Rethinking Race and Identity in Contemporary British Fiction* (New York: Routledge, 2020), 17.

11. Rachel Carroll notes that the 2009 BBC adaptation of *Small Island* makes "two significant changes" to the novel's narrative structure: "the first concerns the omission of one of the four narrative voices which make up the narrative structure of the novel and the second concerns the introduction of a prominent voiceover whose function is equivalent to that of an omniscient narrator" (Carroll, "*Small Island*, Small Screen," 73). In regard to the former, Carroll argues: "The omission of Bernard's narrative perspective from the 2009 BBC adaptation has the effect not only of removing a wider colonial context but also of diminishing the extent to which racist attitudes are given expression by its white British protagonists" (74).

12. Andrea Levy, interview by Blake Morrison, *Women: A Cultural Review* 20, no. 3 (2009): 332.

13. Ibid.

14. For more on the relationship between food, identity, and nation, see Githire. For a good discussion of the relationship between home and identity in Levy's novels, see Pready. Sarah Brophy also examines the meaning of home in *Small Island* in order to make an argument about how "cross-racial encounters" in this space function (Brophy, "Entangled Genealogies," 115).

15. Sarah Sceats, *Food, Consumption and the Body in Contemporary Women's Fiction* (Cambridge: Cambridge University Press, 2000), 1.

16. Ibid., 125.

17. Corinne Duboin, "Contested Identities: Migrant Stories and Liminal Selves in Andrea Levy's *Small Island*," *Obsidian III* 12, no. 1 (2011): 26.

18. King George V, quoted in Anne Clendinning, "On the British Empire Exhibition, 1924–25," in *BRANCH: Britain, Representation and Nineteenth-Century History*, ed. Dino Franco Felluga (Extension of *Romanticism and Victorianism on the Net*, 2012).

19. Peter Bishop, "Constable Country: Diet, Landscape and National Identity," *Landscape Research* 16, no. 2 (1991): 35.

20. Duboin, "Contested Identities," 7.

21. Andrea Levy, *Small Island* (New York: Picador, 2004), 4.

22. Ibid., 3 (emphasis added).

23. Duboin, "Contested Identities," 4.

24. Stuart Hall, "Old and New Identities, Old and New Ethnicities," in *Culture, Globalization, and the World-System: Contemporary Conditions for the Representation of Identity*, ed. Anthony D. King (Minneapolis: University of Minnesota Press, 1997), 49.

25. Levy, *Small Island*, 4.

26. Ibid., 5.

27. Ibid.

28. Alicia E. Ellis, "Identity as Cultural Production in Andrea Levy's *Small Island*," *EnterText: An Interactive Interdisciplinary E-Journal for Cultural and Historical Studies and Creative Work* 9 (2012): 77.

29. Andrea Levy, quoted in Bruce Woodcock, "Small Island, Crossing Cultures," *Wasafiri* 23, no. 2 (2008): 55.

30. Levy, *Small Island*, 6.

31. Ibid.

32. Ibid.

33. Ibid., 201.

34. Ibid., 200.

35. Ibid., 199 (emphasis added).

36. Ibid., 203.

37. Ibid., 200.

38. For more on the history of sugar, see Burnett; Mintz; Morgan; Sheller; Walvin; and Panayi.

39. Levy, *Small Island*, 12.

40. Phillips and Phillips, *Windrush*, 15.

41. Andrea Levy, quoted in Susan Alice Fischer, "'Andrea Levy in Conversation with Susan Alice Fischer' (2005 and 2012)," in *Andrea Levy*, ed. Jeannette Baxter, David James, and Lawrence Scott (London: Bloomsbury, 2014), 135.

42. Andrea Levy, "Back to My Own Country," in *Six Stories and an Essay* (London: Tinder Press, 2014), 14, 7.

43. Levy, *Small Island*, 51.

44. Sceats, *Food, Consumption, and the Body*, 125.

45. Levy, *Small Island*, 41.

46. Ibid., 73.

47. Ibid., 9.

48. Ibid., 16.

49. Sceats, *Food, Consumption, and the Body*, 125.

50. Levy, "Back," 8.

51. Sonya Andermahr, "Decolonizing Cultural Memory in Andrea Levy's *Small Island*," *Journal of Postcolonial Writing* 55, no. 4 (2019): 565.

52. Levy, *Small Island*, 372.

53. Peter Clarke, *Hope and Glory: Britain 1900–2000* (New York: Penguin Press, 2004), 117.

54. Ibid.

55. Levy, *Small Island*, 18.

56. Ibid., 191.

57. Ibid., 106.

58. Ibid.

59. Ibid., 110.

60. Ibid., 126 (emphasis added).

61. Levy's critique of these views in *Small Island* applies not only to the postwar period but also to narrow and xenophobic expressions of British nationalism in the twenty-first century.

62. Bishop, "Constable Country," 36.

63. Ibid., 32.

64. Levy, *Small Island*, 282.

65. Ibid.

66. Ibid., 309.

67. Ibid., 316, 314.

68. Ibid., 316.

69. Ibid., 330.

70. Ibid., 209, 208.

71. Ibid., 211.

72. Ibid., 212.

73. Ibid., 213.

74. During the war while Bernard is away fighting, Queenie's relationship with Arthur turns into a mutually beneficial domestic one. No longer oppressed by his son's presence, Arthur takes an active role in the household by queuing for food, cooking meals, and growing vegetables. Queenie describes Arthur as a magician in the garden. He skillfully grows a variety of vegetables including onions, which were a rare commodity during the war. The only items out of the garden that Queenie does not find magical are Arthur's runner beans. Queenie contends that the runner beans should be used as a weapon against Hitler, because they are so tough that his troops would be too busy chewing on them to fight. Albeit for the benefit of the Germans, Kate Colquhoun describes the National Loaf in similarly strategic terms: "Legally adulterated with chalk to bolster calcium deficiencies in the national diet, dry and grey, it was so hated that it was quickly dubbed 'Hitler's secret weapon'" (Colquhoun, "Fleeting Tortures," 340). With the exception of the ornery runner beans, Arthur's garden admirably fulfills the government's push for its citizens to grow victory gardens and allows Arthur to create palatable dishes for himself and Queenie when resources are scarce.

75. Levy, *Small Island*, 222.
76. Ibid., 215.
77. Ibid., 249.
78. Ibid., 245.
79. Ibid., 248.
80. Ibid.
81. Ibid., 408.
82. Ibid., 410.
83. Ibid., 357.
84. Ibid.
85. Ibid., 359.
86. Rachel Carroll, "*Small Island*, Small Screen: Adapting Black British Fiction," in *Andrea Levy*, ed. Jeannette Baxter, David James, and Lawrence Scott (London: Bloomsbury, 2014), 73.
87. Levy, *Small Island*, 360. Emily Johansen connects the language that Bernard uses to describe colonial immigrants to "Thatcher's infamous 1978 television interview where she observes 'that people are really rather afraid that this country might be rather swamped by people with a different culture'" (Johansen, "Muscular Multiculturalism," 389). She also contends that the same issues of "bodies, space, and living with difference" were evoked in David Cameron's 2011 speech at the Munich Security Conference where he addressed the "failure of state-sponsored multiculturalism" (383).
88. Emily Johansen, "Muscular Multiculturalism: Bodies, Space, and Living Together in Andrea Levy's *Small Island*," *Critique: Studies in Contemporary Fiction* 56 (2015): 392.
89. Levy, *Small Island*, 79.
90. Ibid., 17.
91. Ibid., 26.
92. Levy, "My England."
93. Levy, *Small Island*, 266.
94. Cynthia James. "'You'll Soon Get Used to Our Language': Language, Parody and West Indian Identity in Andrea Levy's *Small Island*," *Journal of West Indian Literature* 18, no. 2 (2010): 53, 58.
95. Levy, *Small Island*, 265.
96. Ibid., 264.
97. Ibid., 266.
98. Ibid.
99. Mirko Casagranda sees this reordering as a method of control for Hortense and argues: "Although she is disgusted by the run-down state of Queenie's house and by the way Gilbert lives in his room—at first she does not understand that since the war everybody in London has been facing similar conditions—she immediately takes control of the situation and rearranges the furniture according to her own vision. Hortense regenders Gilbert's room because it is the only space over which she can have power" (Casagranda, "How Many Women," 366).
100. Levy, *Small Island*, 270.

101. Ibid., 271.
102. Ibid., 369.
103. Sonya Andermahr examines this scene through the framework of trauma theory and argues that laughter represents a strategy of resilience in *Small Island*. Andermahr observes: "However humiliating and demoralizing Hortense's experience in the broom cupboard at the time, Levy gets her character to laugh at herself when looking back at the episode through Gilbert's gently mocking eyes. Gilbert manages to transform Hortense's sense of utter rejection into a sense of solidarity and it is at this point that love between the couple begins to grow. Through the character of Gilbert, Levy advocates a strategy of 'laughing through the tears', which helps to build resilience in the face of traumatic experience and makes it more bearable so that it can be put into narrative and become part of cultural memory" (Andermahr, "Decolonizing Cultural Memory," 562). Jeannette Baxter and David James similarly see humor in Levy's novels as "creat[ing] sites of resistance and moments of reprieve" (Baxter and James, "Introduction," 4). They further suggest that through her use of humor, Levy "moves towards articulating an ethics of empathy" (4). In an interview by Susan Alice Fischer, Levy addresses this idea as well. Seeing humor as "part of the human condition," Levy maintains that "comedy really helps to understand the tragic, and the tragic helps you understand the comedy. . . . And then you start to acknowledge the real *humanity* in people. People then stop becoming just the victim of a tragedy. They become real people, and you can understand how their lives would have evolved. They become like you and me. And that's always what I try to do" (qtd. in Fischer, "Andrea Levy in Conversation," 136, 137 [original emphasis]).
104. Levy, *Small Island*, 384.
105. Ibid., 385.
106. Ibid.
107. Ibid., 384.
108. Ibid., 417.
109. Andermahr, "Decolonizing Cultural Memory," 566.
110. Ibid.

Chapter Five

Subverting Cultural and Political Power in Jeanette Winterson's *The Daylight Gate*

A central concern in all of Jeanette Winterson's work is how power is institutionalized and legitimized through social conventions, cultural and historical narratives, and language. Winterson's novel *The Daylight Gate* (2012) continues her project of destabilizing social, political, and gender conventions. In the book, commissioned by Arrow Books, a subsidiary of Hammer, the famous producers of horror films, Winterson uses the seventeenth-century Lancashire witch trials as a lens to investigate questions of power and to examine the complex relationship between power and moral authority. The book illuminates the instability of the contemporary power structures and the problems with a political system that relies on the arbitrary use of power in order to maintain control. My focus in this chapter is on the moral implications of these shifting and unstable power hierarchies.

In *The Daylight Gate*, as she does in many of her novels, Winterson includes a careful historical and cultural context for her story. In particular, Winterson focuses on the religious climate and the social and political environment that led to the witch trials, which took place in Lancashire, England, in 1612. In the Pendle Hill witch trials, twelve men and women were accused of witchcraft. Of these, one died in prison, ten were hanged, and one was sent to the pillory. Winterson's book documents the circumstances leading up to the trials and their aftermath. Some of the key figures who influenced or were directly involved in the trials included the monarch King James VI and I, who was interested in witchcraft and wrote a treatise on it; the court clerk Thomas Potts, who wrote a popular transcript of the trial; Roger Nowell, the local magistrate; the Chattox and Demdike families, who were rival healers and who were among those accused of witchcraft; Alice Nutter, a Catholic woman of means and relative social power, who also was accused of witchcraft; and Jennet Device, a member of the Demdike family, who was the only person in her immediate family to survive the witch trials and whose testimony condemned others to death. A separate trial in Lancashire involved three women from Samlesbury, Jane Southworth, Jennet Bierley, and Ellen Bierley, who also were accused of witchcraft and held at Lancaster Castle. They were acquitted when the accusation proved to be part of a Catholic conspiracy. This trial and the Pendle Hill witch trials "combined the two big threats to Jacobean order in Lancashire, witchery and popery."[1]

The first part of this chapter addresses the national and cultural climate that prompted the witch trials. Then I address how this environment affected those living in the small town of Lancashire. In particular, I look at Jennet Device, Alice Nutter, and Jane Southworth, women from different social classes and religious backgrounds, each of whom was affected, albeit differently, by the atmosphere of fear and suspicion that developed during King James's reign. Jennet temporarily gained power and thrived, Alice lost power and her life, and Jane suffered but was vindicated. These women also represent two different moral philosophies. Jennet's self-serving philosophy contrasts with the philosophy of Alice and Jane, who believe in self-sacrifice if it leads to greater good for the community. I argue that Winterson speculates on and describes the motivations and thoughts of these historical figures in order to develop an argument about moral authority. Even though those who hold economic, social, and political power often insist that they have moral power as well because it helps them maintain their privileged place in the social hierarchy, Winterson shows that moral authority is not inherently linked to institutional power but comes from being a socially responsible and compassionate individual.

As the reigning monarch during the early seventeenth century, King James shaped national politics and was at the apex of the power structure. Already the King of Scotland, James VI succeeded Elizabeth I in 1603 to become the King of England and the King of Ireland.[2] It was, as historian Pauline Croft notes, "the first time the King of England, the King of Scotland, the King of Ireland and the ruler of the principality of Wales were one and the same monarch."[3] As such, James held enormous power, and he would rule over this United Kingdom until his death in 1625. James claimed power through divine right and believed that "kings are not only God's lieutenants on earth, but even by God himself they are called gods."[4] As his words suggest, James set himself against the other big institutional power at the time, the Church, and maintained that the Church's authority should be subordinate to the King's.

Intent on protecting his authority, James used legal means to suppress the power of anyone who threatened him. In the early seventeenth century, he believed that Catholics and witches posed a particular danger to himself, to the nation, and to the social order. Although James was Protestant, many in

England expected him to be more tolerant of Catholics than Elizabeth and to restore some of their legal rights. However, James continued the nation's religious move to Protestantism, which began when Henry VIII split from the Roman Catholic Church in 1532.

One result of this continuing religious shift was that beliefs that previously had been institutionalized and desirable were no longer morally or legally sound. Even so, some Catholics refused to compromise their religious convictions. John A. Clayton contextualizes this resistance to the national faith by explaining that

> the generation born before the Reformation had been raised within a strong Catholic culture, as had their priests. It would be impossible for strongly held beliefs to be subjugated within a single generation and it is no surprise, therefore, that pockets of Catholic 'resistance' existed at the time of the 1612 Pendle Witch Trials amongst certain gentry families and also amongst ordinary people. ... The older generation such as Demdike and Chattox, were instilled with the Catholic doctrines as many generations of their forefathers had been.[5]

In *The Daylight Gate*, Alice Nutter makes the same point about religious tradition when she reminds Roger Nowell that "every family in England [was Catholic] till King Henry left the Church of Rome. The Church of England is not yet a hundred years old and you wonder that many still follow the old religion?"[6] For the most part, the Catholic beliefs and practices that Alice defends and the pockets of resistance that Clayton describes were simply Catholics continuing to practice their chosen religion.

However, there also was some active and violent resistance to the imposition of these new religious expectations, which included attempts to overthrow the King. The most notable of these plots was the 1605 Gunpowder Plot in which a group of Catholics tried to kill King James by blowing up Parliament. In the years leading up to the Lancashire witch trials, there also were rumors of other Catholic plots: the "'*Bye Plot*' of 1603 was a conspiracy to kidnap the king and force him to repeal anti-Catholic legislation whilst the '*Main Plot*' was an alleged plan by Catholic clergy and nobles to remove the king and replace him with his cousin, the Catholic Arabella Stuart."[7] These threats to James's security and attempts to undermine his power made him even less tolerant of Catholics. He imposed a number of laws trying to rid the country of Catholics and their influence. In 1604, he "order[ed] all priests out of the realm" and "reversed his repeal of recusancy fines ... [which] became payable immediately with arrears."[8] In Lancashire, the local official charged with enforcing these laws was Roger Nowell. He also would play an important role in the 1612 witch trials. In *The Daylight Gate*, Winterson pays particular attention to the power that Nowell wields in the prosecution of Catholics, who violated the law through their worship, and witches, who violated social custom. She also highlights James's influence on local politics in relation to these two groups.

Even before the Catholic plots against James, a group of witches in North Berwick "attempt[ed] to destroy the king" by summoning storms while he was at sea.[9] The plot failed, and the trials of these witches, Croft notes, "launched a period of prosecutions with two peaks in 1590-1 and 1597" during which "at least 70 and perhaps more than 100 witches were tortured, tried and executed."[10] The number of witch trials in this time period and James's involvement with them indicate the threat he felt from witches. These trials also had far-reaching effects as James's desire to eradicate witches from his kingdom influenced the 1612 Lancashire witch trials.

Even though James did not attend the Lancashire witch trials, his beliefs about witchcraft, the laws about witchcraft that he enacted, and his writings about the subject impacted the outcome of these legal proceedings. By the early seventeenth century, James's sentiments about witchcraft were well known, and his 1597 book, *Daemonologie*, had introduced Continental ideas about witchcraft to England that would be important to the trial. The legal changes subsequent to the book's publication also played a vital role in the Lancashire witch trials, because they broadened the acts defined as witchcraft and increased the penalties for those convicted of witchcraft. Under the earlier witchcraft laws of 1563, "the penalty for damage caused to persons or their property by witchcraft was one year's imprisonment and being pilloried for six hours once in every quarter of that year for the first offence. For any subsequent infraction, an offender faced the death sentence."[11] The Witchcraft Act of 1604, which replaced this earlier set of laws, expanded the charges that were considered witchcraft and made more of these charges punishable by death, even for first time offenders. In "The Pilot's Thumb: *Macbeth* and the Jesuits," Richard Wilson describes some of the capital offenses defined in this new Act: it "specifically decreed death for those who 'take up any dead man, woman, or child out of his, her, or their grave, or any other place where the dead body resteth—or the skin, bone, or any other part of the dead person—to be employed or used in any manner of witchcraft, sorcery, charm, or enchantment.'"[12] Under the new law, conjuring spirits, demonic compacts, and using witchcraft to harm another also carried a death sentence for the first offense. These were among the charges brought against the accused at the Lancashire trials.

In *The Wonderfull Discoverie of Witches in the Countie of Lancashire*, the court clerk Thomas Potts documents these charges in his account of the Pendle Hill and Samlesbury witch trials. Potts's book became and still is the definitive record of these trials. It is supposed to be a precise and unmediated account, but in recent years, historians have questioned Potts's reliability, exposed the crafted nature of his narrative, and revealed his political and personal motivations. By reflecting the King's agenda and incorporating points from *Daemonologie* to support his trial account, Potts hoped "to illuminate and validate his narrative of the witches of Lancashire," get James's attention, demonstrate his loyalty to the King, and advance his career.[13]

In *The Daylight Gate*, Winterson emphasizes the ways in which Potts's narrative reflects the contemporary national and cultural climate of fear and intolerance in which Catholicism and witchcraft were seen as the major social threats of the time. The beginning of the novel further contextualizes King James's intent to eliminate these threats to his person and to his kingdom. Winterson reasons: "Perhaps you could not blame him. In 1589, bringing his bride home to Scotland from Denmark, a storm had nearly drowned him. It was witchcraft, he knew it."[14] Winterson also includes information about the Gunpowder Plot to account for the King's concerns for his safety. The dual threats of witchcraft and Catholicism help to explain the menace that James felt from Lancashire, which represented the loci of these social, political, and personal threats. Winterson emphasizes this point when she remarks that in addition to Lancashire being witch country, "[a]ll of the conspirators of the 1605 Gunpowder Plot fled to Lancashire. And Lancashire remained a stronghold of the Catholic faith throughout the seventeenth century."[15] These details contributed to Lancashire's reputation as a dangerous, lawless, and superstitious place and reveal why James would want to reassert his power over this part of his kingdom. He hoped to neutralize the threats against him and against the nation. In this volatile atmosphere, accusations of witchcraft flourished and provided fertile ground for the witch trials to occur.

The peddler John Law was at the center of the incident that prompted the Pendle Hill witch trials. While traveling through Lancashire, Law refused Alizon Device's request for pins. She cursed him, and he subsequently fell ill. The contemporary diagnosis was lameness brought on by witchcraft, and the visible changes in Law's appearance and the dramatic decline in his physical condition added credibility to this charge. However, a more likely explanation for these symptoms is that Law suffered a stroke caused by poor health and his dread of Alizon and her family, the Demdike clan. The Demdikes were healers, but they also were feared in the community because they could use these skills to cause harm. Healers held a contradictory position in Lancashire. Although some members of the community viewed them with trepidation, Clive Holmes explains that for the most part the community "not only tolerated the petty thefts, begging and extortion of the suspected witches, but employed them routinely both in domestic industry and in healing."[16] In the early seventeenth century, this carefully balanced social structure would be destroyed by King James's political agenda and by social and economic instability throughout Europe.

Pauline Croft connects these social and economic concerns to contemporary fears about strong, outspoken women, who were seen as dangerous and disruptive. She notes:

> Between the mid-sixteenth century to the 1660s . . . male society became obsessed by the fear of disorder. Women were increasingly seen as unruly and resentful of their proper subordination to men. This fear of females was closely linked to the steady deterioration in the economic conditions suffered by the poor, from amongst whom most of the women victims emerged. All over Europe, economic instability and increasing poverty were major ingredients of witchcraft persecutions.[17]

The economic decline that Croft describes was felt acutely in Lancashire and was a significant factor in the Pendle Hill witch trials.

These social and economic conditions also provide an important context for Winterson's exploration of moral issues. By giving a voice and a history to those considered to be disorderly and disruptive, Winterson undermines the idea that the laws and social structures legitimizing the power of men and the upper classes are fundamental and inherently moral. In *The Daylight Gate*, Christopher Southworth's musings about chance and "if" emphasize the arbitrary nature of this conventional power structure. Southworth observes:

> At every moment the chances change. If Jane [his sister who is awaiting trial for witchcraft] were with him now. If they were escaping together. If James had not come to the throne. If the Gunpowder Plot had never happened. If Elizabeth had not executed Mary. If Henry had not wanted a divorce. If the Pope had not excommunicated England. If England were a Catholic country still.
> All the history, all the facts, what were they but chances?[18]

Southworth's list of chance moments primarily focuses on the monarchy and its relationship to Catholicism. These transformative events in history, Winterson suggests, reflect the personal decisions and interests of those in power rather than a natural order or a natural justice.

Similarly, Winterson's depiction of the Lancashire witch trials reveals that power is neither immutable nor stable. Although the old power structure eventually is reestablished through the legal system, there are moments when some of the dispossessed temporarily gain power. One of the people who gains power through the trials is Jennet Device. Jennet is the granddaughter of Old Demdike, the daughter of Elizabeth Device, and the sister of James Device. At just nine years old, she is the youngest in a very poor family. At the start of Winterson's book, Jennet is the most powerless character in the text.

She is economically and socially disadvantaged, and she suffers sexual and physical abuse at the hands of her family and by members of the community.

Winterson's depiction of Jennet highlights her extreme poverty, hunger, and desperation. When Alice Nutter, on whose property the family lives, asks Jennet's mother when her daughter last ate, Elizabeth replies: "Three days ago, like the rest of us."[19] Elizabeth then articulates the social and religious rationale that sanctions her family's poverty: "The parson calls Lent a fast, for it suits the church to starve the poor. I begged from the church and the parson said that a fast did a woman good."[20] Elizabeth's words show the family's place in the community and Jennet's place in the family. Both are neglected by those who have a personal or social responsibility to care for them.

Jennet's family not only fails to keep Jennet safe but actively puts her in harm's way. With his mother's knowledge, Jennet's brother, James, regularly sells his sister for sex to Tom Peeper, who "liked his sexual conquests to be too young to fall pregnant."[21] Although Tom's sexual predilections are well known in the community, no one stops him from molesting young children. Even the Constable, Harry Hargreaves, accepts Tom's behavior because Tom has qualities that are useful to Harry. As "a spy and a sadist," he makes the Constable's job "easier."[22] The situation reveals that the legal and local power structures that should protect Jennet do not. Through multiple examples, Winterson shows that the injustices Jennet and other poor women in the community experience are institutionally sanctioned and pervasive. Silvia Antosa argues that seventeenth-century Lancashire is a world "where power is entirely held by men, who exercise their gender and class privileges through physical and mental abuse, sexual violence and religious and political persecution. All these forms of power are legitimised by both the royal and the Divine Laws, which are deemed to be preternatural and incontrovertible."[23] The social structure described by Antosa is predicated on the exploitation of the weak, like Jennet.

In *The Daylight Gate*, after Jennet's family has been charged with witchcraft and Jennet must fend for herself, her brother James and Tom Peeper try to take advantage of her vulnerable status in order to promote their self-interests. James offers to take care of Jennet as a way to escape witchcraft charges and prison. Tom offers to care for Jennet in order to take further sexual advantage of her. Compounding the impropriety of Tom's offer, Jennet's mother, Elizabeth, reveals that Tom is actually Jennet's father. Even the self-serving James is shocked and appalled. For him, there is a moral distinction between selling his sister for sex and selling his sister for sex to her father. Elizabeth, however, is unconcerned about this detail about paternity. She reasons to James: "You would have sold her to someone. . . . At least he bought her a dress now and then."[24] Elizabeth may be pragmatic, but the horror of Jennet's situation is not lost on readers. Winterson's depictions of the family dynamics and the social structure show the conditions that shape Jennet's character. She is a "miserable, underfed, and abused" child, whose difficult circumstances also make her savage, vicious, and prepared to do anything to survive.[25]

Jennet is also smart, cunning, and patient, and these skills eventually help her take revenge on those who have wronged her, including her mother, her brother, and Tom Peeper. Because she is a child, Jennet's presence is often forgotten, and she uses this social and familial invisibility to her advantage. She sits in the shadows, watches others, gathers information, and acquires knowledge. Jennet is a witness and a scavenger, and her willingness to seize any opportunity that will help her gain status or, at least, get food ultimately gives her power. In one example of her industriousness, Jennet collects teeth from the graveyard for her mother's spells and is rewarded for her efforts with a welcome piece of bread. She also provides her mother with body parts including a skull and a tongue, which her mother uses to make a spirit guide.

In spite of Jennet's valuable contributions to her mother's work, Elizabeth still neglects her daughter's needs. The spells to create an enchanted doll that will cause Roger Nowell to fall ill and to animate the spirit guide require Elizabeth to use Jennet's most loved possession, a fetus in a bottle. The spells might give the family power, but Jennet is powerless to stop her mother from using the jarred baby. All she can do is cry. "That was my toy," she says sadly.[26] "I shall have nowt to talk to now the baby is boiled."[27] A fetus may not be a proper toy, but it is all that Jennet has. It is a friend as well as a plaything, and after her mother has used it for her spells, Jennet salvages a small hand from the cauldron that she carefully hides in her dress. When all of her family are arrested and in jail, the hand and enchanted head keep Jennet company.

The head also offers Jennet guidance. It asks Jennet if she wants her imprisoned family to return and when Jennet decides she does not, it encourages her to "[m]ake sure they do not."[28] By heeding this advice, Jennet consciously chooses to put her needs and desires first. As a result, she begins to gain power over her own life and to exercise control over the fate of her family who have controlled her for so long. Jennet then lays claim to the physical household: "She went and curled up in the clean bed that belonged to Old Demdike. She had never been allowed in here."[29] Although the young Jennet has no family to care for her, her family's absence means that Jennet has more comforts: a clean bed, a sense of safety, and enough food. She also has companions, the head and the hand, which, unlike most people in her life, do not want anything from her.

Once she attains some power, Jennet refuses to relinquish it. When Tom Peeper comes to take advantage of Jennet's isolation, she asserts herself.

Tom tries to lure Jennet out of her safe space with food and kind words. "I've got a big bag of bread and cheese and apples and tarts from Roger Nowell's kitchen," he tells her, "and we'll live here safe and sound, just the two of us, Daddy and his little girl."[30] Jennet is not fooled by Tom's words, because she knows from experience the sexual danger he poses to her. Confirming her suspicions, while he tries to convince Jennet to come out of hiding, he is "undoing his breeches."[31] Although Tom is a threat, for the first time in her life, Jennet is in a position to defend herself against his advances.

Jennet uses her small size, quickness, good eyesight, and knowledge of the house to her advantage. She knows the trapdoor to the cellar is open, and when Tom begins to chase her, she leads him in that direction. Because the room is dark, Tom cannot see the danger ahead. When he lunges toward Jennet, she moves out of his reach, and he falls "through the open trapdoor into the cellar."[32] Although she knows that Tom is hurt, Jennet is not sympathetic. Instead, she actively makes sure that he cannot escape. She disconnects the ladder, closes the trapdoor, bolts it shut, and moves a heavy table over it. These precautions do nothing to stop Jennet from hearing Tom's distress, but she remains unmoved: "All night Tom Peeper shouted, and all the next day, and the days after that. . . . And then he didn't shout any more."[33] Jennet's actions may be callous, but Tom's death is the only way to ensure her safety.

Preventing her family's return to Malkin Tower also increases Jennet's safety and well-being. She achieves this outcome by testifying against the members of her family who have been arrested and charged with witchcraft. Winterson's description of the scene accords with Potts's trial record in which a small, frightened young girl testifies while standing on a table. Jennet may be young and physically weak from years of malnourishment, but her identification of those assembled at Malkin Tower on Good Friday, her description of her family's witchcraft, and her physical position above those seated in the courtroom empower her. When Jennet testifies against her brother, James, Potts takes note of her composure, arguing that "although she were but very yong, yet it was wonderfull to the Court, in so great a Presence and Audience, with what modestie, gouernement, and vnderstanding, shee deliuered this Euidence against the Prisoner at the Barre."[34]

In his account, Potts further amplifies Jennet's power by casting her testimony as a kind of divine intervention. As Clayton describes, "Potts fains surprise at the appearance of Jennet, calling her '*This unexpected witness*.'"[35] With these words, "he gives the impression that God Himself had sent the child trotting along to the court in order to carry out His work in routing out the ubiquitous devil from amongst the poor foresters."[36] While this religious sanction elevates the significance of Jennet's words for Potts, the truth of Jennet's testimony was questionable at best. Historian Frank Hird suggests that Jennet's account was not only unreliable but also coaxed and rehearsed. "The child was intelligent and cunning" he observes, "and there is an ugly suspicion that she glibly repeated a lesson she had been taught."[37] Rather than facilitating justice, Jennet's testimony served several other purposes: helping those in power eradicate what they perceived as threats to the community, allowing Jennet to exact revenge for her ill treatment, and furthering Jennet's personal gain.

In *The Daylight Gate*, Winterson suggests similar reasons for Jennet's testimony. In the courtroom, Jennet implicates the people who have wronged her physically (her brother and mother), emotionally (her sisters and Chattox), and aesthetically (Mouldheels):

> Jennet looks at them. Her brother who sold her. Her mother who neglected her. Her sisters who ignored her. Chattox who frightened her. Mouldheels who stank.
> She names them one by one and condemns them one by one.[38]

Winterson's inclusion of Jennet's motives and the description of Jennet calmly condemning each person to death implies that her testimony is a deliberate act of retribution by a very young girl.

Historical accounts of the trial consistently emphasize that the evidence about the Good Friday meeting of witches, which formed the foundation of the prosecution, "was based solely upon the testimony of a child of nine."[39] Attaching such importance to the testimony of one so young was unprecedented at the time and played an important role in legitimizing the testimony of children in other cases. Jennet's testimony would even influence the Salem witch trials in colonial Massachusetts that took place later in the seventeenth century. Frances Cronin observes:

> There had been earlier cases of children being witnesses in witch trials, but the law stated those under 14 were not credible witnesses because they could not be sworn under oath. Jennet's testimony changed all that. . . . Thomas Potts' writings and Jennet's evidence were included in a reference handbook for magistrates, *The Country Justice*.
> The book was used by all magistrates, including those in the colonies in America, and led them to seek the testimony of children in trials of witchcraft.[40]

In an effort to eliminate the threat of witches, King James had been an early advocate for a change to contemporary trial practices. In *Daemonologie*, he proposed that under exceptional conditions, children and witches should be allowed to give evidence in court. He writes: "In my opinion, since in a mater of treason against the Prince, barnes or wiues, or neuer so diffamed persons, may of our law serue for sufficient witnesses and proofes. I think surely that by a far greater reason, such witnesses may be sufficient in high treason against God: For who but Witches can be prooues, and so witness of the doing of Witches."[41] The Pendle Hill witch trials fit James's definition of extraordinary circumstances, and the Judge's conviction that Jennet's evidence was credible validated James's claim about the importance of allowing unconventional witnesses to testify when there is a threat to the nation. Jennet's legal influence also shows that under the right historical circumstances, the least powerful figure can become, at least temporarily, one of the most powerful. Jennet may not gain social status from her court testimony, but she does gain personal power and power over the lives of family and community members who she believes have wronged her.

Although Jennet's actions are understandable, Winterson does not idealize her new power. Author Fay Weldon's argument in *Before the War* that the powerless are not inherently good people also holds true for Jennet. "Because people are victims does not mean they are necessarily nice," the narrator of that novel observes, "on the contrary, they tend to learn the same tricks as their oppressors."[42] Jennet is a perfect example of the formerly oppressed gaining power and then behaving badly. She and her family may experience social and economic injustice, and Jennet may be a victim of her family, her community, and the society in which she lives, but that does not automatically give her the moral high ground.[43] Given the chance and under the right set of cultural circumstances, she also makes other people victims and generates her power at their expense. In the Pendle Hill witch trials, her testimony leads to the death of her grandmother, who dies in prison while awaiting trial, and the execution of ten people, including her mother, her brother, and Alice Nutter.

The same historical circumstances and political climate that temporarily empower Jennet disempower others such as Alice Nutter and Jane Southworth. Both Alice and Jane were accused of witchcraft, the former by Jennet, the latter by another young woman, and fell victim to a cultural environment in which these types of accusations were often more powerful than the truth. By emphasizing Alice's and Jane's moral integrity in times of crisis, Winterson presents these characters as counterexamples to Jennet and her misuse of power.

Although Alice and Jane have historical counterparts, Winterson includes fictional details about them in order to develop her multifaceted argument about power, morality, and social responsibility. In regard to Jane, Winterson adds depth to her character and emphasizes her moral integrity through the decisions she makes about escaping from jail. In regard to Alice, Winterson seeks to answer the question that puzzled contemporary audiences and modern historians: why was Alice part of the group who were tried for and convicted of witchcraft? In spite of Jennet's testimony, in which she identifies

Alice as one of those assembled at Malkin Tower on Good Friday, there is little convincing evidence that Alice was a witch.

Winterson offers a range of plausible possibilities for Alice's conviction that hinge on personal, social, and political power relations. Before the trials, Alice has a high social status in the community. She owns land, has a regular source of income, is confident, helps those in need, and possesses physical beauty and strength. Alice's distinctive qualities, including her masculine attire and fearless behavior, are emphasized at the start of *The Daylight Gate* as she summons a falcon to her outstretched, leather-clad arm and feeds it a dead mouse. Many members of the community suspect that Alice has magical abilities because she can control nature and she maintains a youthful appearance year after year, but initially these suspicions do not cause problems for Alice or make her a social outcast. Winterson highlights Alice's good standing in the community by making parallels between her and Roger Nowell. Although it is more socially acceptable for Roger to wield power because he is wealthy, a man, and holds a position of authority, both he and Alice are described as attractive, active, learned, rich, powerful, and well-respected.

Alice can maintain this privileged status, because she understands the importance of social conventions and knows when to abide by them. Her horseback riding is an example of her ability to conform to customary behavior when she needs to. She rides, dresses, and acts conventionally for religious, social, and business matters. At these times, she rides side-saddle and wears an elegant riding habit. Yet when there is no good reason for Alice to adhere to these gendered social formalities, she puts her personal desires first and rides astride.

When Alice is nonconfrontational, her unconventional qualities are not problematic and are even admired by some. However, Alice is not afraid to be assertive when she needs to be. She believes that her economic and social power in the community comes with a responsibility to help those who do not have the same resources or access to power that she has. She helps the Demdikes by allowing them to live on her land and, when necessary, by speaking to the authorities on their behalf. Alice also speaks out against any injustices that she witnesses and argues against the arbitrary or improper use of power by established authorities in the community. These acts and her refusal to grant the current social structure an inherent authority represent both her moral power in the text and the moments when she becomes vulnerable to local gossip and persecution.

One example of this dual dynamic is when Alice uses her physical and social power to save Sarah Device from being beaten and killed by Tom Peeper. Sarah is among the powerless women in the text. The violence and poor treatment that Sarah endures emphasize her complete lack of social and legal power. Like Jennet, Sarah is poor, voiceless, and suffers sexual abuse that not only goes unpunished but also is implicitly condoned by the representatives of the law in the community. The physical assault by Tom that Alice interrupts begins as a rape, ostensibly in retaliation for the spell Alizon Device, one of Sarah's family members, put on John Law. Tom also sees the rape as an appropriate punishment for Sarah being a witch and a temptress. Although the local authority, Constable Harry Hargreaves, is present, he does not stop Tom from sexually assaulting Sarah. Even more egregiously, Harry facilitates the rape by holding her down. When Tom then encourages another young boy, Robert, to have sex with Sarah, Harry continues to be a passive observer. He also does nothing when Tom gets ready to slit Sarah's throat after she has bitten off Robert's tongue when he tried to kiss her. Alice arrives at this point and stops Tom from killing Sarah by riding her horse into him and knocking him over. She then challenges Tom's and the Constable's authority by deriding their behavior with her comparison of it to a mob's and by questioning their contention that, because Sarah is a witch, the assault represents a kind of justice.

Harry may yield to Alice's authority in the moment, but he is upset that she has reprimanded him, especially in front of others. After he and Tom leave the scene, Harry questions Alice's allegiance to the dangerous and despised women in the community, witches like Sarah and her family. When Tom asks Harry if he thinks that Alice is a witch, Harry equivocates but then affirms the point. The whispered rumor that Alice is a witch is nothing new, but Harry's more open articulation of hostility toward Alice is. He casts aspersions on her character and on her behavior when he provocatively says to Tom: "A woman astride and a falcon following—that's unnatural."[44] By designating Alice's behaviors as "unnatural," Harry situates Alice's unconventionality as a threat to the community. Harry's bolder comments about Alice also reflect the influence King James is beginning to have on Lancashire. James's views about witchcraft and religion made community intolerance of nonconformist behavior more acceptable and legitimized the persecution of Catholics, witches, and anyone else who was deemed a threat to local, national, or royal power.

Winterson's descriptions of James as a "Protestant, a devout man, a man who wanted no dyes or fancy stuffs" and as a "man who had two passions: to rid his new-crowned kingdom of popery and witchcraft" directly link the downturn in Alice's status to James being in power and set up James as an antagonist to Alice in economic, social, and religious terms.[45] From James's perspective and from the perspective of his authorized representatives in Lancashire, Alice embodies multiple threats to the nation and to the community: she is Catholic; possesses magical abilities; and is a powerful, outspoken, and independent woman. In this new cultural climate, Alice's Catholic beliefs and her visible and repeated challenges to local and patriarchal authority, to the social structure, and to conventional gender roles, which had been tolerated, begin to endanger her.

Alice is further affected by James's rule because of her association with John Dee, Queen Elizabeth's astrologer. Although Winterson's story about the relationship between John Dee and Alice is speculative, she fictionally makes the connection between these characters in order to show how James's ascendancy to the throne changed national and local views about magic and witchcraft. Dee had substantial power and influence when Elizabeth I was his patron; however, Stephanie Spoto notes that "with the transition from Elizabeth to James, John Dee's status as natural philosopher and 'good' magician fell into jeopardy as James had a less flexible view of witchcraft and magic."[46] The same is true of Alice's good magic, which the community reassesses after James's influence is felt in Lancashire and his beliefs and anxieties begin to affect local politics. With James as King, both Dee and Alice are redefined "dangerous" and "bad" and their magical abilities are devalued. This abrupt change in status suggests that the moral judgments about these characters are politically motivated. Yet even if the reassessment of Dee's and Alice's characters is subjective, the physical and social dangers that they face in this new power structure are very real.

In *The Daylight* Gate, Alice's position becomes particularly precarious after James takes a greater interest in Lancashire politics. Roger Nowell is the local official charged with arresting the witches in the community, and this duty eventually extends to arresting Alice. Winterson shows Nowell to be in a complicated position. Although for personal reasons he wants to curb Alice's power—she won the lawsuit he initiated against her over a parcel of land—he objects to the political pressure he receives from the King in regard to his magistrate duties. He claims that King James is a "meddler" and tells Alice, "When the King is a meddler, the rest of us must be meddlers."[47] James's "meddling" means that Nowell must enforce the local laws about religious practices and prosecute all suspected witches, which goes against his natural inclinations. Nowell's description of James's involvement also implies that the King is misusing his authority and forcing Nowell to do the same.

When the King's representative, Thomas Potts, arrives in Lancashire, he poses similar difficulties for Nowell. James's agenda gives Potts license to go after those who threaten the social order, and he pressures Nowell to find and punish all the Catholics and witches in the community. At the very least, Potts's presence means that Nowell must be seen to act. Although historians describe Nowell as actively involved in the prosecution of Catholics and witches, Winterson portrays him as a reluctant participant who complies with Potts's demands because of political pressure rather than because of his ideological beliefs. In *The Daylight Gate*, Nowell initially represents a thoughtful authority. Provided that there are no direct conflicts that he must negotiate, he is happy to let people believe what they want. This position contrasts with Potts and members of the community who are eager to punish anyone accused of breaking the law. Even when the local and national climate begins to change and community members demand that he take action, Nowell refuses to radically change his agenda. He may arrest the accused witches in an attempt to appease the community, but he also hopes that the community's zeal will dissipate before he needs to do more than that. However, his plan fails because the story about the Lancashire witches becomes known beyond the local community. As a result, outside political pressure gets in the way of Nowell's more moderate agenda, and he is forced to act decisively to alleviate the threats that others perceive.

Alice is one of these perceived threats. When Nowell is asked to arrest her for witchcraft, his private beliefs and his public responsibilities come into direct conflict. Because he does not consider Alice to be a threat to public safety, Nowell initially refuses to arrest her. However, when Potts applies more political pressure, Nowell must take her into custody. Nowell tries to turn Alice's arrest to his advantage by using it as leverage to find and prosecute Christopher Southworth, a Jesuit priest who was instrumental in the Gunpowder Plot and who is Alice's close friend. Nowell also hopes that if Alice helps him catch Southworth, Potts will allow him to drop the charges against her. With this plan in mind, Nowell offers Alice a deal: he will not pursue charges against her for witchcraft if she tells him where to find Southworth. "I have you," Nowell observes, "but I could let you go."[48] Nowell's attempt to get Alice to save herself by sacrificing Southworth shows the intricacies of power. Within this corrupt system, Alice can buy her freedom by providing information to Nowell. That the witchcraft charge against Alice can so easily be dismissed emphasizes the arbitrary nature of the allegation. The interaction also shows that when it is expedient for him, Nowell uses his legal power to manipulate people rather than to advocate for and mete out justice.

In spite of his relative power, Nowell feels constrained by this self-interested social system in which survival depends on putting one's own needs above those of others. "I am caught in this trap every bit as much as you are," he tells Alice. "There has to be a sacrifice."[49] Nowell's statement shows his awareness that everyone is implicated in and endangered by this system; however, it also reveals that he accepts the inevitability of the situation and of the power structure. In practical terms, Nowell's acquiescence to convention means that if Alice will not sacrifice Southworth, Nowell will sacrifice her in order to protect himself and his power in the community.

In contrast to Nowell whose actions perpetuate an unjust political system, Alice questions a power structure in which one's options are binary and circumscribed. Alice believes that the only way to save herself and her community is to try to change the system by refusing the available choice to sacrifice someone or to be sacrificed. Nowell gives Alice multiple opportunities to save herself by turning in Southworth, but Alice is invulnerable to coercion, because she believes that trading Southworth's life and freedom for her own would be morally wrong. Even when Nowell pairs his demand for information with the physical threat of incarceration, Alice refuses to betray Southworth, and her imprisonment and subsequent torture cannot shake her resolve. After Alice has been convicted of witchcraft and sentenced to die, Nowell tries to negotiate with her one last time. He offers Alice a chance to avoid execution, telling her, "Even now, if you would help us catch Christopher Southworth, I could," but she cuts off the offer. "I could not" she says.[50] With these three simple words, Alice differentiates her moral position from Nowell's.

Part of Alice's moral code comes from recognizing the same quality of loyalty and selflessness in Southworth. For his role in attempting to blow up Parliament, Southworth is captured and tortured. Winterson emphasizes the extent of Southworth's self-sacrifice by describing in precise detail the systematic and prolonged torture that he endures. Alice knows that in spite of suffering gruesome abuse, including castration, Southworth refused to confess the names of the others involved in the plot against the King, because it would endanger them. Like Southworth, Alice does not consider unquestioned submission to authority to be an option when other people's lives are at stake. She rejects Nowell's deal, because it would reinforce and perpetuate a corrupt political system. Through her actions, Alice advocates for a social structure in which communal needs outweigh those of the individual.

In another example of Alice's loyalty, when a poppet of Nowell is found in her study and Potts asks how it got there, Alice remains silent rather than incriminate her friend whose help she enlisted in order to retrieve the doll from Elizabeth Device. It does not matter that Alice's intention was to save Nowell from the ill effects of Elizabeth's spell, because answering Potts's question might implicate her friend in a plot to break into the prison and in witchcraft, and Alice knows that her words could be used to justify the arrests of others. Alice's silence means that she cannot defend herself, but she would rather sacrifice herself than put someone else in harm's way. She understands that in a political climate where an accusation is often enough for one to be found guilty of a crime, words can be dangerous. In contrast to Nowell and Jennet who put political interest and self-interest first, Alice is self-sacrificing rather than self-serving. She refuses to do what is safe if she does not believe it is morally right and will not knowingly harm others, even to save herself. By making these choices, she not only maintains her personal integrity but also shows the relationship between thoughtful self-sacrifice and social responsibility.

Jane Southworth shares her brother, Christopher Southworth's, and Alice Nutter's integrity, and her character adds another element to Winterson's argument about the need for individuals to be socially responsible, especially in times of crisis. Jane falls victim to the same cultural circumstances that allowed Jennet's testimony to be admitted in court and Alice to be tried for witchcraft. Like Alice, Jane is accused of witchcraft by a young girl, and despite the weak evidence against her, is arrested, indicted under the 1604 Witchcraft Act, and committed to Lancaster Castle. Along with Jennet Bierley and Ellen Bierley, Jane is charged with bewitching fourteen-year-old Grace Sowerbutts. Grace claimed that these women "met at a place called Red Bank," ate "magical food," and "[a]fter they had eaten, the three women, together with Grace, danced, each of them with one of the black things. After their dancing, she assumed that the three women had sex with three of the black things, for she herself too believed that 'the black thing that was with her, did abuse her bodie.'"[51] Collectively designated the Samlesbury witches, Jennet Bierley, Ellen Bierley, and Jane Southworth were imprisoned, tried, and eventually acquitted when Grace admitted to lying.

In her defense, Grace claimed that she was encouraged to make the accusations against these women by the Jesuit priest Christopher Southworth. Although sharing a name and profession, this historical figure is not the model for Winterson's Christopher Southworth. Winterson's character is guilty of participating in the Gunpowder Plot rather than of manipulating a young girl into making false witchcraft accusations. In the historical account of the Samlesbury witches, Grace said that Southworth "did perswade, counsel, and advise her, to deale . . . against her said Grand-mother, Aunt and *Southworths* wife."[52] Philip Almond explains that the accused women believed that "they had been incriminated by Southworth for having converted to Protestantism and left the Catholic faith."[53] The case became a prime example of a Catholic conspiracy.

The inclusion of the case in Potts's *The Wonderfull Discoverie of Witches in the Countie of Lancashire* served a religious and a political purpose. He used the case as Protestant propaganda and shaped the narrative about the Samlesbury witches to make it "about popish conspiracies against Protestants, about devious priests, innocent Anglicans and divine providence" rather than about witchcraft.[54] Almond contends that the case's placement in Potts's book—"[s]andwiched between the trials of the Pendle witches who pleaded guilty . . . and those who pleaded not guilty"—also had a political purpose.⁵⁵ Potts used the case to showcase Judge Edward Bromley's wise and just court and to "enhance Judge Bromley's image by relating how he exposed the fraudulent nature of Sowerbutts's accusations."⁵⁶ In addition, Judge Bromley's ability to see through Grace's story and to ascertain that the charges against the Samlesbury witches were false made Jennet's evidence in the Pendle Hill witch trials seem more reliable. As Potts's narrative implies, if this shrewd judge thought Jennet's testimony was credible, it must be, and, therefore, those whom she accused of witchcraft must be guilty.

Winterson uses some of the historical details of the Samlesbury case in her depiction of Jane Southworth but then adapts the story and characters to make a statement about social justice and personal loyalty. In *The Daylight Gate*, the claim that Jane is a witch remains much the same, but the accusation becomes part of a bigger plot to draw Jane's brother, Christopher, into the open so that he can be captured. Christopher knows that Jane's arrest is a trap, but he is loyal to his friends and family and committed to protecting Jane. He does not prioritize his own safety when his sister's life may be at stake. Winterson depicts Christopher's loyalty, self-sacrifice, and consideration of others (qualities that Alice and Jane also share) as admirable, because they are integral to building a supportive and united community.

The interaction between Jane and her brother at the jail also sets up a larger argument about the importance of personal and social responsibility. Although the accusations against Jane are false, she has endured abysmal conditions in jail, it is possible she will be found guilty and executed, and her brother has risked his life to help her, Jane refuses to escape with him. Like Alice, she believes she has a duty and a responsibility to stand up for the truth, to speak for and represent those who are powerless, and to act in the best interest of the community. Jane articulates this moral position when Christopher urges her to save herself and to leave with him. "If I escape with you tonight," she tells her brother, "they will claim it as witchcraft. . . . Then they have won. If they win others will suffer."⁵⁷ Jane is aware that, in the eyes of the law and from the perspective of members of the community, her escape would imply that she is guilty of witchcraft. Even more importantly, Jane knows that her escape would lead to others suffering and would reinforce the political structure that persecutes innocent people. Because she understands that her plight and the fate of others are connected, she does her part to promote change. Jane believes that her only chance to change this system is to stand up to it. She refuses to prioritize her life over the lives of others, and through this selfless act, she effectively challenges the institutions that perpetuate inequality and injustice.

In this instance, standing up for her rights and the rights of others means being put on trial (rather than circumventing the legal system and running away) in the hope that she is found not guilty, freed, and vindicated. Jane's resolve and faith are rewarded, and she eventually is acquitted after her accuser confesses to having been pressured by a Catholic priest to make allegations of witchcraft against Jane. By not compromising her beliefs, Jane ends up saving herself and others. Jane may suffer physically from her imprisonment, but she never questions her decision to stay in jail, because she understands the power of solidarity and that one's actions can profoundly affect other individuals, the community, and the nation. Like Alice, Jane is aware of her position in the larger social and political structures and realizes the power and importance of this set of social relationships. Winterson extends this argument in her most recent book, *12 Bytes: How We Got Here, Where We Might Go Next* (2021), and asserts: "It is co-operation, not competition, that will save the planet. . . . Compassion and co-operation are our best chance now."[58]

In *The Daylight Gate*, Alice and Jane serve as behavioral counterexamples to Jennet whose actions may save her but cause irreparable harm to other people. The form of selflessness that Alice and Jane represent—choosing not to cause harm to others, even in order to save themselves—ends up being the moral center of Winterson's book. Moral authority, she suggests, is not about institutional power but about empathy, compassion, and social responsibility. Alice's and Jane's actions also demonstrate the importance of individuals making conscious decisions to do what is right rather than doing what is expedient. Their power comes from recognizing that there are always choices rather than seeing the world and its power structures as inevitable, natural, and predetermined. Through these characters, Winterson shows that challenging unjust political systems and questioning the institutional structures that offer individuals only limited choices is crucial to creating social, global, and planetary change.

NOTES

1. Stephen Pumfrey, "Potts, Plots, and Politics: James I's *Daemonologie* and *The Wonderfull Discoverie of Witches*," in *Lancashire Witches: Histories and Stories*, ed. Robert Poole (Manchester: Manchester University Press, 2003), 31.

2. In 1567, at the age of thirteen months, James VI became King of Scotland.

3. Pauline Croft, *King James* (New York: Palgrave Macmillan, 2003), 3.

4. King James I, quoted in Sandra M. Gilbert and Susan Gubar, eds., *The Norton Anthology of Literature by Women*, Vol. 1 (New York: W. W. Norton & Company, 2007), 124.

5. John A. Clayton, *The Lancashire Witch Conspiracy: A History of Pendle Forest and the Pendle Witch Trials* (Barrowford: Barrowford Press, 2007), 111, 284.

6. Jeanette Winterson, *The Daylight Gate* (New York: Grove Press, 2012), 55.

7. Clayton, *Lancashire Witch Conspiracy*, 163.
8. Ibid.
9. Croft, *King James*, 26.
10. Ibid.
11. Philip C. Almond, *The Lancashire Witches: A Chronicle of Sorcery and Death on Pendle Hill* (New York: I. B. Tauris, 2017), 13–14.
12. Richard Wilson, "The Pilot's Thumb: *Macbeth* and the Jesuits," in *Lancashire Witches: Histories and Stories*, ed. Robert Poole (Manchester: Manchester University Press, 2003), 128–29.
13. Almond, *Lancashire Witches*, 8.
14. Winterson, *Daylight Gate*, 7.
15. Ibid., viii.
16. Clive Holmes, quoted in Almond, *Lancashire Witches*, 35–36.
17. Croft, *King James*, 26.
18. Winterson, *Daylight Gate*, 168–69.
19. Ibid., 31.
20. Ibid.
21. Ibid., 29.
22. Ibid., 86.
23. Silvia Antosa, "In a Queer Gothic Space and Time: Love Triangles in Jeanette Winterson's *The Daylight Gate*," *Altre Modernità* 13 (2015): 156.
24. Winterson, *Daylight Gate*, 160.
25. Ibid., 29.
26. Ibid., 120.
27. Ibid., 121.
28. Ibid., 207.
29. Ibid.
30. Ibid., 208.
31. Ibid.
32. Ibid.
33. Ibid., 209.
34. Thomas Potts, *The Wonderfull Discoverie of Witches in the Countie of Lancaster* (San Bernadino: Filiquarian Publishing, 2017), 77.
35. Clayton, *Lancashire Witch Conspiracy*, 193.
36. Ibid.
37. Frank Hird, quoted in Clayton, *Lancashire Witch Conspiracy*, 139.
38. Winterson, *Daylight Gate*, 215.
39. Hird, quoted in Clayton, *Lancashire Witch Conspiracy*, 139.
40. Frances Cronin, "The Witch Trial That Made Legal History," *BBC Magazine*, August 17, 2011.
41. King James I, *Daemonologie* (Project Gutenberg, 2008), 62.
42. Fay Weldon, *Before the War* (London: Head of Zeus, 2016), 115.
43. Claudia FitzHerbert argues that rather than depicting Jennet and her family as sympathetic because they are poor, oppressed, and abused, "Winterson presents us instead with a snarling, cursing, incest-riven coven of desperate low-lifers who think

nothing of interfering every witch [*sic*] way with a weirdly loitering corpse-robbing nine-year-old girl who turns key witness" (FitzHerbert, Review of *The Daylight Gate*).

44. Winterson, *Daylight Gate*, 17.
45. Ibid., 7.
46. Stephanie Irene Spoto, "Jacobean Witchcraft and Feminine Power," *Pacific Coast Philology* 45 (2010): 59.
47. Winterson, *Daylight Gate*, 99.
48. Ibid., 174.
49. Ibid., 175.
50. Ibid., 217.
51. Almond, *Lancashire Witches*, 123.
52. Ibid., 127.
53. Ibid., 130.
54. Ibid., 107.
55. Ibid.
56. James Sharpe, "Introduction: The Lancashire Witches in Historical Context," in *Lancashire Witches: Histories and Stories*, ed. Robert Poole (Manchester: Manchester University Press, 2003), 4.
57. Winterson, *Daylight Gate*, 166.
58. Jeanette Winterson, *12 Bytes: How We Got Here, Where We Might Go Next* (New York: Grove Press, 2021), 202, 139.

Conclusion

For a work of literature to remain relevant, Patrick McGrath argues, it needs to "illuminate some area of human experience."[1] In their novels, McGrath, Kazuo Ishiguro, Graham Swift, Andrea Levy, and Jeanette Winterson illuminate the intricacies of human experience and the complexities of morality in order to facilitate social change. The change they envision is predicated on empathy, political and personal engagement, understanding oneself in relation to other people, critical thinking, adaptability, and compassion.

Emphasizing the significance of relational identities and empathy to creating a more just world, Swift contends: "If we can imagine ourselves into the lives of others, that clearly has a moral effect. What else is morality based on than the ability to be not just a solipsistic unit but to imagine what it's like to be someone else?"[2] Swift's philosophy about writing also serves as a model for transforming personal and political relationships. "One of my articles of faith as a novelist," he explains, "is that you are suspending judgment, you are not saying that this is better than that. You're putting sympathy and compassion before moral judgment—which is not the same as saying there is no moral dimension to writing, far from it. I think there is a moral dimension, but it's a moral dimension which is governed by empathy, compassion, and a preparedness to suspend easy judgment on anyone who features in the story."[3] The authors discussed in this book approach Swift's ideas on two levels: they treat their characters nonjudgmentally and empathetically (which allows readers to better understand a diverse group of characters and points of view) and, by example, they show readers how to apply this empathetic model of social relations to their lives.

Although these authors take different approaches to their narratives, including singular and multiple first-person narrators, unreliable narrators, and third-person narration, they understand the important role that storytelling plays in the lives of their characters and in the lives of their readers. As their characters share their stories and articulate how they understand their lives and the choices they have made, they help readers carefully consider their own experiences, decisions, and beliefs. Swift observes that one of the values of telling stories is that it allows people to "com[e] to terms with this world and what we experience, what we suffer, what we undergo."[4] Reflecting this point of view in his books,

> [the] central character is usually somebody in a state of crisis, and thus the story he has to tell has about it a great deal of urgency if not necessity. It's as though the character has lost hold of experience, has suffered the shattering of some illusion perhaps, realizes he no longer can see his life in the orderly terms he might have done before. And he's in a position of having to put together the pieces, and he does so via the process of telling a story.[5]

Swift's description of his characters' reasons for telling their stories applies to the characters in Ishiguro's, McGrath's, Levy's, and Winterson's books as well. In each of their novels, the lives of the characters have been destabilized personally or politically, and their beliefs about how the world works have been challenged. As these characters reach the point where they realize that their lives or relationships did not turn out as they expected or they recognize that their position in the world has shifted due to political, national, or social changes, they tell their stories, as Swift suggests, in order to make sense of their lives in a changing world. Significantly, however, they do not all put the pieces back together in the same way, and this multiplicity adds to readers' perspectives on how people can deal with complex social and moral issues.

How the characters try to reconstruct their unsettled lives also gives readers insight into the contemporary power structures that affect the characters' lives and into the characters' positions in the social hierarchy. Characters like Bernard Bligh and Peter Cleave, who have enjoyed power because of their class, race, and gender, are invested in trying to shore up or rebuild the traditional social structures that have crumbled in the postwar era. Characters like Alice Nutter and Jane Southworth must figure out how to survive in a world where shifts in the social structure have given other people control over their social position and where their access to power is now limited. In the present moment, the only thing Alice and Jane can control is how they engage with the people who hold institutional power, and both refuse to grant authority to people, institutions, and social systems that they believe are unsound. Characters like Stevens, George Webb, Hortense Roberts, Gilbert Joseph, and Queenie Buxton have had their illusions about the world shattered and their place in it unsettled, but they turn this ideological and political instability into an opportunity to rebuild their lives in new, more productive ways. Through depictions of characters who think critically about their beliefs and their place in the world, Ishiguro, McGrath, Swift, Levy, and Winterson encourage readers to examine their beliefs, their relationships with and responsibilities to others, and their place in the social structure.

They also encourage readers to think critically about the structures themselves, particularly the social, economic, and political structures that perpetuate inequality. "Inequality is not a law of nature, like gravity," Winterson reminds her readers.[6] By revealing the ways in which language and institutional structures can create, perpetuate, and naturalize inequality, Ishiguro, McGrath, Swift, Levy, and Winterson effectively disrupt readers' beliefs that there is an intrinsic organization to traditional social structures and that the moral authority and power these structures grant certain people is inherently right. These authors approach social and moral issues differently in their work, but they reach similar conclusions about the importance of literature in challenging conventions, facilitating communication, and promoting empathy.

One of the ways that Ishiguro, McGrath, Swift, Levy, and Winterson promote greater understanding of the world and other people is to make all of their characters plausible and comprehensible to readers, even characters who are flawed, prejudiced, or transgressive. This strategic and thoughtful work fosters readers' engagement with and connection to a wide range of characters and their disparate points of view. Even if readers do not share the characters' beliefs, they are able to suspend easy moral judgments about them, because they understand what has shaped their views of the world. This contextual understanding allows readers to engage with perspectives different from their own rather than simply judging, ignoring, or dismissing them. Their willingness to participate in a kind of literary dialogue about new ideas and important issues serves as a good foundation for social and political change.

The ideas about communication, cooperation, empathy, and new ways of understanding the world that Ishiguro, McGrath, Swift, Levy, and Winterson present in their work are even more vital as social discord; violence; economic disparities; unequal access to healthcare, food, and other essential resources; and environmental problems are experienced locally, nationally, and globally. "The world is at a critical time," Winterson argues, as "wars, climate breakdown and social collapse" threaten to "throw us backwards towards basic survival and away from our future."[7] Reflecting their profound concerns about the state of the world, Winterson and Ishiguro have increasingly emphasized the connections between literature and social activism, and they have used their public roles as authors to advocate for social and political change.

In his Nobel Prize lecture, for example, Ishiguro addressed the problems of national and global instability, economic inequality, racism, and divided communities. He told his audience that recent "political events in Europe and in America" and "acts of terrorism all around the globe" have made him reflect on how divided and unstable the world has become.[8] He also discussed some of the issues and events that have led to the current state of affairs. Since the late 1980s, he observes:

> [e]normous inequalities—of wealth and opportunity—have been allowed to grow, between nations and within nations. In particular, the disastrous invasion of Iraq in 2003, and the long years of austerity policies imposed on ordinary people following the scandalous economic crash of 2008, have brought us to a present in which Far Right ideologies and tribal nationalisms proliferate. Racism in its traditional forms and in its modernised, better-marketed versions, is once again on the rise, stirring beneath our civilised streets like a buried monster awakening. For the moment we seem to lack any progressive cause to unite us. Instead, even in the wealthy democracies of the West, we're fracturing into rival camps from which to compete for resources or power.[9]

Ishiguro maintains that, with its ability to promote communication, literature can help alleviate these social, national, and political divisions.[10] As he persuasively argues: "In a time of dangerously increasing division, we must listen. Good writing and good reading will break down barriers. We may even find a new idea, a great humane vision around which to rally."[11] Winterson proposes a similar solution to these problems when she suggests that we need to "find a narrative that unites us, not one that divides us."[12]

The authors discussed in this book know that literature can play an important role in re-conceptualizing social relations and in creating political change. Without being prescriptive, they present alternative ways that institutions and social structures can be organized. As global instability and social divisions increase, the discussions in these books about dismantling hierarchical power structures, developing empathy, asking questions, fostering connections, and being compassionate seem even more timely. Through their writing, Ishiguro, McGrath, Swift, Levy, and Winterson provide models for engagement and social responsibility that contribute to the development of new narratives that encourage productive conversations about morally complex issues. Collectively, their work helps readers learn more about themselves and the world they live in; better understand other people's views and be willing to consider alternative perspectives; question the social structures that seem fixed; think critically about their own beliefs; be cognizant of their position in the world and their place in the power structure; consider how they use their power and who, it affects; realize and appreciate that everyone's lives are important and connected; and recognize their role in creating a less divided and more just world.

NOTES

1. Patrick McGrath, interview by Lindsey Crittenden, *Turnstile* 3, no. 2 (1992): 51.
2. Graham Swift, interview by Stef Craps, *Contemporary Literature* 50, no. 4 (2009): 651.
3. Ibid., 649.
4. Graham Swift, interview by John Crane, *Cimarron Review* 84 (1988): 8.
5. Ibid.
6. Jeanette Winterson, "We Need to Build a New Left: Labour Means Nothing Today," *The Guardian*, June 24, 2016.
7. Jeanette Winterson, *12 Bytes: How We Got Here, Where We Might Go Next* (New York: Grove Press, 2021), 139.
8. Kazuo Ishiguro, "My Twentieth Century Evening and Other Small Breakthroughs: The Nobel Lecture" (London: Faber & Faber, 2017), 31, 32.
9. Ibid., 32–33.
10. Kazuo Ishiguro reiterates this point in a 2021 interview in which he observes that one of the important functions of literature is its ability to help "human beings communicate with each other" (Ishiguro, interview by Mary Laura Philpott). He also emphasizes the importance of communication in his most recent novels, *The Buried Giant* (2015) and *Klara and the Sun* (2021).
11. Ishiguro, "My Twentieth Century Evening," 36.
12. Winterson, "We Need to Build a New Left."

Bibliography

Almond, Philip C. *The Lancashire Witches: A Chronicle of Sorcery and Death on Pendle Hill*. New York: I. B. Tauris, 2017.

Andermahr, Sonya. "Decolonizing Cultural Memory in Andrea Levy's *Small Island*." *Journal of Postcolonial Writing* 55, no. 4 (2019): 555–69.

Antor, Heinz. "Unreliable Narration and (Dis-)Orientation in the Postmodern Neo-Gothic Novel: Reflections on Patrick McGrath's *The Grotesque* (1989)." *Miscelánea: A Journal of English and American Studies* 24 (2001): 11–38.

Antosa, Silvia. "In a Queer Gothic Space and Time: Love Triangles in Jeanette Winterson's *The Daylight Gate*." *Altre Modernità* 13 (2015): 152–67.

Association of Jewish Refugees. Accessed May 12, 2021. http://www.ajr.org.uk/documents/cb_4_arrival_in_gb.pdf.

Bareis, J. Alexander. "Ethics, The Diachronization of Narratology, and the Margins of Unreliable Narration." In *Narrative Ethics*, edited by Jakob Lothe and Jeremy Hawthorn, 41–55. Amsterdam: Rodopi, 2013.

Barreca, Regina. "Metaphor-into-Narrative: Being 'Very Careful with Words' in Texts by Women Writers." In *Untamed and Unabashed: Essays on Women and Humor in British Literature*, 162–72. Detroit: Wayne State University Press, 1994.

Baxter, Jeannette, and David James. "Introduction: Towards Serious Work." In *Andrea Levy*, edited by Jeannette Baxter, David James, and Lawrence Scott, 1–8. London: Bloomsbury Publishing, 2014.

Beedham, Matthew. "*The Remains of the Day* 3: Interdisciplinary Approaches." In *The Novels of Kazuo Ishiguro: A Reader's Guide to Essential Criticism*, 84–101. New York: Palgrave Macmillan, 2010.

Bentley, Nick. *Contemporary British Fiction*. Edinburgh: Edinburgh University Press, 2008.

Berberich, Christine. "Kazuo Ishiguro's *The Remains of the Day*: Working Through England's Traumatic Past as a Critique of Thatcherism." In *Kazuo Ishiguro: New Critical Visions of the Novels*, edited by Sebastian Groes and Barry Lewis, 118–30. New York: Palgrave Macmillan, 2011.

Berguno, George. "A Phenomenological Analysis of Existential Conscience in James Ivory's (1993) *The Remains of the Day*." *Existential Analysis* 25, no. 1 (2014): 91–102.

Bill Moyers on Faith and Reason: Jeanette Winterson. Films Media Group, 2006. *Films on Demand*, April 25, 2010. http://digital.films.com/play/7X8FJ5.

Bishop, Peter. "Constable Country: Diet, Landscape and National Identity." *Landscape Research* 16, no. 2 (1991): 31–36.

Black, D. A. *Broadmoor Interacts: Criminal Insanity Revisited*. London: Barry Rose Law Publishers Limited, 2003.

"Blind Loyalty, Hollow Honor: England's Fatal Flaw." In *The Remains of the Day*. 1993; Culver City, CA: Columbia Tristar Home Entertainment, 2001. DVD.

Booth, Wayne C. *The Rhetoric of Fiction*. Chicago: The University of Chicago Press, 1961.

Bowlby, John. "Some Causes of Mental Ill-health." In *Child Care and the Growth of Love*, 11–17. Melbourne: Penguin Press, 1953.

Brophy, Sarah. "Entangled Genealogies: White Femininity on the Threshold of Change in Andrea Levy's *Small Island*." *Contemporary Women's Writing* 4, no. 2 (2010): 114–33.

Burnett, John. "Tea: The Cup That Cheers." In *Liquid Pleasures: A Social History of Drinks in Modern Britain*, 49–69. New York: Routledge, 1999.

Carroll, Rachel. "*Small Island*, Small Screen: Adapting Black British Fiction." In *Andrea Levy*, edited by Jeannette Baxter, David James, and Lawrence Scott, 65–77. London: Bloomsbury Publishing, 2014.

Casagranda, Mirko. "How Many Women Were on the *Empire Windrush*? Regendering Black British Culture in Andrea Levy's *Small Island*." *Textus* 23 (2010): 355–70.

Chamberlain, Stewart. *The Foundations of the Nineteenth Century*. Volume 1. London: Ballantyne and Company, 1911.

Childs, Peter. "Kazuo Ishiguro: Remain in Dreams." In *Contemporary Novelists: British Fiction since 1970*, 123–40. New York: Palgrave Macmillan, 2005.

Clarke, Peter. *Hope and Glory: Britain 1900–2000*. 2nd ed. New York: Penguin Press, 2004.

Clayton, John A. *The Lancashire Witch Conspiracy: A History of Pendle Forest and the Pendle Witch Trials*. 2nd ed. Barrowford: Barrowford Press, 2007.

Clendinning, Anne. "On the British Empire Exhibition, 1924–25." *BRANCH: Britain, Representation and Nineteenth-Century History*, edited by Dino Franco Felluga. Extension of *Romanticism and Victorianism on the Net*. Access: November 8, 2021. http://www.branchcollective.org/?ps_articles=anne-clendinning-on-the-british-empire-exhibition-1924-25. Published August 2012.

Cohen, Jeffrey. "Tracing the Developments of the Mental Health Act Commission and Its Predecessors." In *Understanding Treatment without Consent: An Analysis of the Work of the Mental Health Act Commission*, written by Ian Shaw, Hugh Middleton, and Jeffrey Cohen, 13–40. London: Ashgate, 2008.

Colquhoun, Kate. "Fleeting Tortures and Discontented Domesticity: Waste the Food Help the Hun." In *Taste: The Story of Britain through Its Cooking*, 323–44. London: Bloomsbury Publishing, 2011.

Cooper, Lydia R. "Novelistic Practice and Ethical Philosophy in Kazuo Ishiguro's *The Remains of the Day* and *Never Let Me Go*." In *Kazuo Ishiguro: New Critical Visions of the Novels*, edited by Sebastian Groes and Barry Lewis, 106–17. New York: Palgrave Macmillan, 2011.

Craps, Stef. "Adieu: Stepping into *The Light of Day*." In *Trauma and Ethics in the Novels of Graham Swift: No Short-Cuts to Salvation*, 166–81. Eastbourne: Sussex Academic Press, 2005.

Croft, Pauline. *King James*. New York: Palgrave Macmillan, 2003.

Cronin, Frances. "The Witch Trial That Made Legal History." *BBC Magazine*, August 17, 2011. http://www.bbc.com/news/magazine-14490790.

Dell, Susanne, and Graham Robertson. *Sentenced to Hospital: Offenders in Broadmoor*. New York: Oxford University Press, 1988.

Doane, Janice, and Devon Hodges. *From Klein to Kristeva: Psychoanalytic Feminism and the Search for the 'Good Enough' Mother*. Ann Arbor: The University of Michigan Press, 1995.

Duboin, Corinne. "Contested Identities: Migrant Stories and Liminal Selves in Andrea Levy's *Small Island*." *Obsidian III* 12, no. 1 (2011): 14–33.

Eaglestone, Robert, ed. *Brexit and Literature: Critical and Cultural Responses*. New York: Routledge, 2018.

Ellis, Alicia E. "Identity as Cultural Production in Andrea Levy's *Small Island*." *EnterText: An Interactive Interdisciplinary E-Journal for Cultural and Historical Studies and Creative Work* 9 (2012): 69–83.

Everitt, Dulcie. *BrexLit: The Problem of Englishness in Pre- and Post-Brexit Referendum Literature*. Washington: Zero Books, 2021.

Falco, Magali. "Patrick McGrath's Case Histories or the Ruin(s) of Psychoanalysis." *Anglophonia: French Journal of English Studies* 15 (2004): 95–103.

Ferguson, Christine. "Dr. McGrath's Disease: Radical Pathology in Patrick McGrath's Neo-Gothicism." In *Spectral Readings: Towards a Gothic Geography*, edited by Glennis Byron and David Punter, 233–43. New York: Palgrave Macmillan, 1999.

Fischer, Susan Alice. "'Andrea Levy in Conversation with Susan Alice Fischer' (2005 and 2012)." In *Andrea Levy*, edited by Jeannette Baxter, David James, and Lawrence Scott, 121–38. London: Bloomsbury Publishing, 2014.

FitzHerbert, Claudia. Review of *The Daylight Gate*, by Jeanette Winterson. *The Spectator*, August 18, 2012.

Foucault, Michel. "The Birth of the Asylum." In *Madness and Civilization: A History of Insanity in the Age of Reason*, 241–78. New York: Vintage, 1973.

Freeman, Nicholas. "Patrick McGrath." In *Dictionary of Literary Biography: British Novelists since 1960 Fourth Series*, edited by Merritt Moseley, 146–51. Detroit: Gale Group, 2001.

Gilbert, Sandra M., and Susan Gubar, eds. *The Norton Anthology of Literature by Women*, Volume 1. New York: W. W. Norton & Company, 2007.

Githire, Njeri. "The Empire Bites Back: Food Politics and the Making of a Nation in Andrea Levy's Works." *Callaloo* 33, no. 3 (2010): 857–73.

Greene, Gayle. "Mad Housewives and Closed Circles." In *Changing the Story: Feminist Fiction and the Tradition*, 58–85. Bloomington: Indiana University Press, 1991.
Haffenden, John. "Angela Carter." In *Novelists in Interview*, 76–96. New York: Methuen, 1985.
Hall, Stuart. "Old and New Identities, Old and New Ethnicities." In *Culture, Globalization, and the World-System: Contemporary Conditions for the Representation of Identity*, edited by Anthony D. King, 41–68. Minneapolis: University of Minnesota Press, 1997.
Hansen, Per Krough. "Reconsidering the Unreliable Narrator." *Semiotica* 165, no.1/4 (2007): 227–46.
Head, Dominic. *The Cambridge Introduction to Modern British Fiction, 1950–2000*. New York: Cambridge University Press, 2003.
Horton, Emily. "'A Genuine Old-Fashioned English Butler': Nationalism and Conservative Politics in *The Remains of the Day*." *American, British, and Canadian Studies* 31 (2018): 11–26.
Ingersoll, Earl G. "Desire, the Gaze and Suture in the Novel and the Film: *The Remains of the Day*." *Studies in the Humanities* 28, no. 1–2 (June–December 2001): 31+.
Ishiguro, Kazuo. "'I'm Sorry I Can't Say More': An Interview with Kazuo Ishiguro." Interview by Sean Matthews. In *Kazuo Ishiguro*, edited by Sean Matthews and Sebastian Groes, 114–25. New York: Continuum Books, 2009.
———. Interview by Gregory Mason. *Contemporary Literature* 30, no. 3 (1989): 335–47.
———. Interview by Brian W. Shaffer. *Contemporary Literature* 42, no. 1 (2001): 1–14.
———. Interview by Graham Swift. *BOMB* 29 (Fall 1989): 22–23.
———. "Kazuo Ishiguro: 'Some Awful Things Have Happened in the Last Year . . . But These Are Not Uninteresting Times.'" Interview by Mary Laura Philpott. *The Washington Post*, June 22, 2021.
———. "My Twentieth Century Evening and Other Small Breakthroughs: The Nobel Lecture." London: Faber & Faber, 2017.
———. *The Remains of the Day*. New York: Vintage, 1993.
Ivory, James, dir. *The Remains of the Day*. 1993; Culver City, CA: Columbia Tristar Home Entertainment, 2001. DVD.
James, Andrew. "Language Matters: An Investigation into Cliché in *The Light of Day*." *Connotations* 22, no. 2 (2012/2013): 214–34.
James, Cynthia. "'You'll Soon Get Used to Our Language': Language, Parody and West Indian Identity in Andrea Levy's *Small Island*." *Journal of West Indian Literature* 18, no. 2 (2010): 45–64.
James, David. "The Immediacy of *Small Island*." In *Andrea Levy*, edited by Jeannette Baxter, David James, and Lawrence Scott, 53–64. London: Bloomsbury Publishing, 2014.
Jeffers, Jennifer M. "Heritage and Nostalgia: What Remains of *The Remains of the Day*." In *Britain Colonized: Hollywood's Appropriation of British Literature*, 41–75. New York: Palgrave Macmillan, 2011.

Johansen, Emily. "Muscular Multiculturalism: Bodies, Space, and Living Together in Andrea Levy's *Small Island*." *Critique: Studies in Contemporary Fiction* 56 (2015): 383–98.

King James I. *Daemonologie*. Printed by Robert Walde-graue, Printer to the Kings Majestie, 1597. Project Gutenberg, 2008.

Kushner, Tony. "Immigration and 'Race Relations' in Postwar British Society." In *20th Century Britain: Economic, Social and Cultural Change*, edited by Paul Johnson, 411–26. New York: Longman, 1994.

Lang, James M. "Public Memory, Private History: Kazuo Ishiguro's *The Remains of the Day*." *Clio* 29, no. 2 (2000): 143–65.

Lee, Hermione. "Someone to Watch Over You." Review of *The Light of Day*, by Graham Swift. *The Guardian*, March 8, 2003.

Levy, Andrea. "Back to My Own Country." In *Six Stories and an Essay*, 3–19. London: Tinder Press, 2014.

———. Interview by Blake Morrison. *Women: A Cultural Review* 20, no. 3 (2009): 325–38.

———. Interview by Charles Henry Rowell. *Callaloo* 38, no. 2 (2015): 257–81.

———. *Small Island*. New York: Picador, 2004.

———. "This Is My England." *The Guardian*, February 19, 2000.

Lewis, Mitchell R. "The Gothic Gaze: The Politics of Gender in Patrick McGrath's *Asylum*." *Anglistik & Englischunterricht* 69 (2007): 159–74.

Lima, Maria Helena. "'Pivoting the Centre': The Fiction of Andrea Levy." In *Write Black, Write British: From Post Colonial to Black British Literature*, edited by Kadija George, 56–85. London: Hansib Publications, 2005.

Lodge, David. "The Unreliable Narrator (*Kazuo Ishiguro*)." In *The Art of Fiction: Illustrated from Classic and Modern Texts*, 154–57. New York: Penguin Press, 1994.

London, Louise. *Whitehall and the Jews, 1933–1948: British Immigration Policy, Jewish Refugees and the Holocaust*. Cambridge: Cambridge University Press, 2000.

Long, Robert Emmet. "England." In *James Ivory in Conversation: How Merchant Ivory Makes Its Movies*, 197–23. Berkeley: University of California Press, 2005.

"Love and Loyalty: The Making of *The Remains of the Day*." In *The Remains of the Day*. 1993; Culver City, CA: Columbia Tristar Home Entertainment, 2001. DVD.

Lowe, Gordon. *Escape from Broadmoor: The Trials and Strangulations of John Thomas Straffen*. Gloucestershire: The History Press, 2013.

Machinal, Hélène. "'The Turn of the Screw' in McGrath's *Asylum*." In *Patrick McGrath: Directions and Transgressions*, edited by Jocelyn Dupont, 65–79. Newcastle upon Tyne: Cambridge Scholars Press, 2012.

Malcolm, David. "The Narrow Way: *The Light of Day* (2003)." In *Understanding Graham Swift*, 187–214. Columbia: University of South Carolina Press, 2003.

Marwick, Arthur. *The Penguin Social History of Britain: British Society since 1945*. 3rd ed. New York: Penguin Press, 1996.

McGrath, Patrick. *Asylum*. New York: Vintage Books, 1998.

———. "A Childhood in Broadmoor Hospital." *Granta* 29 (1989): 155–62.

———. "In Pursuit of Sublime Terror." Interview by Suzie MacKenzie. *The Guardian*, September 2, 2005.

———. "Interview by Lindsey Crittenden." *Turnstile* 3, no. 2 (1992): 27–51.
———. "Interview by Gilles Menegaldo." *Creative Voices* (1998): 109–27.
———. "Problem of Drawing from Psychiatry for a Fiction Writer." *Psychiatric Bulletin* 26 (2002): 140–43.
Mintz, Sidney W. *Sweetness and Power: The Place of Sugar in Modern History*. New York: Penguin Press, 1986.
Moncrieff, Joanna. "The Politics of a New Mental Health Act." *The British Journal of Psychiatry* 183 (2003): 8–9.
Morgan, Kenneth. "The Sugar Trade." In *Bristol and the Atlantic Trade in the Eighteenth Century*, 184–218. Cambridge: Cambridge University Press, 1993.
Nünning, Angsar. "Reconceptualizing Unreliable Narration: Synthesizing Cognitive and Rhetorical Approaches." In *A Companion to Narrative Theory*, edited by James Phelan and Peter J. Rabinowitz, 89–107. Malden, MA: Blackwell Publishing, 2005.
Nünning, Vera. "Unreliable Narration and the Historical Variability of Values and Norms: *The Vicar of Wakefield* as a Test Case of a Cultural-Historical Narratology." *Style* 38, no. 2 (2004): 236–52.
Panayi, Panikos. "Changes in British Eating Habits." In *Spicing Up Britain: The Multicultural History of British Food*, 95–122. London: Reaktion Books, 2008.
Parkes, Adam. *Kazuo Ishiguro's* The Remains of the Day*: A Reader's Guide*. New York: Continuum, 2001.
Partridge, Ralph. *Broadmoor: A History of Criminal Lunacy and Its Problems*. London: Chatto & Windus, 1953.
Pesso-Miquel, Catherine. "No 'screaming and shrieking in the wind': The Playfulness of Reticence in Graham Swift's *Last Orders*, *The Light of Day*, and *Tomorrow*." Études britanniques contemporaines 41 (2011). https://doi.org/10.4000/ebc.2350.
Phelan, James, and Mary Patricia Martin. "The Lessons of 'Weymouth': Homodiegesis, Unreliability, Ethics, and *The Remains of the Day*." In *Narratologies: New Perspectives on Narrative Analysis*, edited by David Herman, 88–109. Columbus: Ohio State University Press, 1999.
Phillips, Mike, and Trevor Phillips. *Windrush: The Irresistible Rise of Multi-Racial Britain*. London: HarperCollins, 1998.
Potts, Thomas. *The Wonderfull Discoverie of Witches in the Countie of Lancaster*. 1613. San Bernadino: Filiquarian Publishing, LLC, 2017.
Pready, Jo. "The Familiar Made Strange: The Relationship between the Home and Identity in Andrea Levy's Fiction." *EnterText: An Interactive Interdisciplinary E-Journal for Cultural and Historical Studies and Creative Work* 9 (2012): 14–30.
Pumfrey, Stephen. "Potts, Plots and Politics: James I's *Daemonologie* and *The Wonderfull Discoverie of Witches*." In *Lancashire Witches: Histories and Stories*, edited by Robert Poole, 22–41. Manchester: Manchester University Press, 2003.
Quinn, Anthony. "Nobody's Perfect." Review of *The Light of Day*, by Graham Swift. *New York Times*, May 4, 2003.
Reisman, Mara. "Complicating a Feminist Reading of Fay Weldon's Fiction." In *Fay Weldon, Feminism, and British Culture: Challenging Cultural and Literary Conventions*, 45–72. New York: Lexington Books, 2018.

———. "Integrating Fantasy and Reality in Jeanette Winterson's *Oranges Are Not the Only Fruit*." *Rocky Mountain Review* 65, no. 1 (2011): 11–35.

———. "The Shifting Moral Ground in Fay Weldon's Fiction." *Women's Studies* 40, no. 5 (2011): 645–71.

Rowbotham, Sheila. *A Century of Women: The History of Women in Britain and the United States*. New York: Viking Press, 1997.

Russell, Richard Rankin. "Monsters of Anti-Semitism in Ishiguro's Rural English Landscape: Re-reading *The Remains of the Day* as Ethical Fantasy Novel." *Critique: Studies in Contemporary Fiction* 61, no. 4 (2020): 440–52.

Sceats, Sarah. *Food, Consumption and the Body in Contemporary Women's Fiction*. Cambridge: Cambridge University Press, 2000.

Scull, Andrew. *Social Order/Mental Disorder: Anglo-American Psychiatry in Historical Perspective*. Oakland: University of California Press, 1989.

Sharpe, James. "Introduction: The Lancashire Witches in Historical Context." In *Lancashire Witches: Histories and Stories*, edited by Robert Poole, 1–18. Manchester: Manchester University Press, 2003.

Shaw, Ian. "A Short History of Mental Health." In *Understanding Treatment without Consent: The Changing Role of the Mental Health Act Commission*, written by Ian Shaw, Hugh Middleton, and Jeffrey Cohen, 3–11. London: Ashgate, 2008.

Shaw, Kristian. *Brexlit: British Literature and the European Project*. New York: Bloomsbury Academic, 2021.

Sheller, Mimi. "Tasting the Tropics: From Sweet Tooth to Banana Wars." In *Consuming the Caribbean: From Arawaks to Zombies*, 71–104. London: Routledge, 2003.

Showalter, Elaine. *The Female Malady: Women, Madness, and English Culture, 1830–1980*. New York: Penguin Press, 1987.

Spoto, Stephanie Irene. "Jacobean Witchcraft and Feminine Power." *Pacific Coast Philology* 45 (2010): 53–70.

Stackelberg, Roderick, and Sally A. Vinkle, eds. *The Nazi Germany Sourcebook: An Anthology of Texts*. New York: Routledge, 2002.

Stam, Robert. "Introduction: The Theory and Practice of Adaptation." In *Literature and Film: A Guide to the Theory and Practice of Film Adaptation*, edited by Robert Stam and Alessandra Raengo, 1–52. Malden, MA: Blackwell Publishing, 2005.

Stoker, Bram. *Dracula*. Ontario: Broadview Press, 2000.

Su, John J. "Refiguring National Character: The Remains of the British Estate Novel." *Modern Fiction Studies* 48, no. 3 (2002): 552–80.

Sutherland, John. "Why Hasn't Mr. Stevens Heard of the Suez Crisis?" In *Where Was Rebecca Shot?: Curiosities, Puzzles, and Conundrums in Modern Fiction*, 185–89. London: Weidenfeld and Nicolson, 1998.

Swift, Graham. "The Challenge of Becoming Another Person." Interview by Heike Hartung. *Anglistik: International Journal of English Studies* 16, no. 1 (2005): 139–46.

———. Interview by Catherine Bernard. *Contemporary Literature* 38, no. 2 (1997): 217–31.

———. Interview by Robert Birnbaum. *Identity Theory*, July 2, 2003.

———. Interview by John Crane. *Cimarron Review* 84 (1988): 7–15.

———. Interview by Stef Craps. *Contemporary Literature* 50, no. 4 (2009): 637–61.
———. *The Light of Day*. New York: Vintage Books, 2004.
———. "Throwing Off Our Inhibitions." *The Times*, March 5, 1988.
———. *Waterland*. New York: Vintage Books, 1992.
Teverson, Andrew. "Acts of Reading in Kazuo Ishiguro's *The Remains of the Day*." *Q/W/E/R/T/Y: Arts, Littératures & Civilisations du Monde Anglophone* 9 (1999): 251–58.
Tolan, Fiona. "Graham Swift." In *Writers Talk: Conversations with Contemporary British Novelists*, edited by Philip Tew, Fiona Tolan, and Leigh Wilson, 125–41. London: Continuum, 2008.
Tollance, Pascale. "'You Cross a Line': Reticence and Excess in Graham Swift's *The Light of Day*." In *Voices and Silence in the Contemporary Novel in English*, edited by Vanessa Guignery, 63–73. Newcastle upon Tyne: Cambridge Scholars Press, 2009.
Upstone, Sara. *Rethinking Race and Identity in Contemporary British Fiction*. New York: Routledge, 2020.
Wachtel, Eleanor. "Kazuo Ishiguro." In *More Writers & Company: New Conversations with CBC Radio's Eleanor Wachtel*, 17–35. Toronto: Knopf Canada, 1996.
Walkowitz, Rebecca L. "Ishiguro's Floating Worlds." *ELH* 68, no. 4 (2001): 1049–76.
Wall, Kathleen. "*The Remains of the Day* and Its Challenges to Theories of Unreliable Narration." *The Journal of Narrative Technique* 24, no. 1 (1994): 18–42.
Walvin, James. *Fruits of Empire: Exotic Produce and British Trade, 1660–1800*. London: Palgrave Macmillan, 1997.
Weldon, Fay. *Before the War*. London: Head of Zeus, 2016.
Wheelright, Julie. "No Hiding Place." Review of *Asylum*, by Patrick McGrath. *New Statesman* 125, September 13, 1996.
Widdowson, Peter. "*The Light of Day*." In *Graham Swift*, 92–107. Devon: Northcote House Publishers Ltd., 2006.
Wilson, Richard. "The Pilot's Thumb: *Macbeth* and the Jesuits." In *Lancashire Witches: Histories and Stories*, edited by Robert Poole, 126–45. Manchester: Manchester University Press, 2003.
Winterson, Jeanette. *12 Bytes: How We Got Here, Where We Might Go Next*. New York: Grove Press, 2021.
———. *The Daylight Gate*. New York: Grove Press, 2012.
———. "Interview by Eleanor Wachtel." *Malahat Review* 118 (1997): 61–73.
———. "We Need to Build a New Left: Labour Means Nothing Today." *The Guardian*, June 24, 2016.
Wong, Cynthia F. "Kazuo Ishiguro's *The Remains of the Day*." In *A Companion to the British and Irish Novel 1945–2000*, edited by Brian W. Shaffer, 493–503. Malden, MA: Blackwell Publishing, 2005.
Woodcock, Bruce. "Small Island, Crossing Cultures." *Wasafiri* 23, no. 2 (2008): 50–55.
Woolf, Virginia. *Three Guineas*. New York: Harcourt Brace Jovanovich, 1966.
Woolley, Agnes. "'Something blurred in her?': Imagining Hospitality in Graham Swift's *The Light of Day*." *Textual Practice* 26, no. 3 (2012): 449–65.

Zerweck, Bruno. "Historicizing Unreliable Narration: Unreliability and Cultural Discourse in Narrative Fiction." *Style* 35, no. 1 (2001): 151–78.

Zlosnik, Sue. *Patrick McGrath*. Cardiff: University of Wales Press, 2011.

Index

Almond, Philip, 145–46
America, 108–9
Andermahr, Sonya: on British history, 122; on laughter, 127n103; on racial bias, 106; on societal divisions, 123n6
Antor, Heinz, 46, 71n100
Antosa, Silvia, 135
architecture: of British Empire Exhibition, 98; of Broadmoor Lunatic Asylum, 49, 51; morality in, 49, 52
Asylum (McGrath), 1; binaries in, 50; character names in, 69n35; control in, 47, 50–51, 60–61, 63–64, 66; disorientation in, 63; doctors' power in, 48; gender and power in, 45; gender roles in, 55–56; judgments shifting in, 50, 60; marriages in, 53–55; paternalism in, 6–7, 45, 51, 65; time period in, 47–48, 53–54; transgression in, 45–46, 54–55, 58; unreliable narrator in, 6–7, 45–47, 60–63, 66–67; values in, 6. *See also* Broadmoor Lunatic Asylum; women
asylums: control in, 49–50; family and, 50, 52; hierarchies in, 6, 45; history of, 48
Atkinson, Rob, 40n46

Bareis, J. Alexander, 67n1
Barreca, Regina, 84
Baxter, Jeannette, 127n103
Beedham, Matthew, 40n46
Before the War (Weldon), 139
Bentham, Jeremy, 68n22
Bentley, Nick, 91n6
Berberich, Christine: on appeasement, 34; on culpability, 24–25; on cultural context, 40n39; on politics, 13
Berguno, George, 43n106
Bernard, Catherine, 3
Bierley, Ellen, 130, 145
Bierley, Jennet, 130, 145
"The Birth of the Asylum" (Foucault), 52
Bishop, Peter, 97–98, 110
Booth, Wayne C., 46, 62, 67n1
Bowlby, John, 58
Brexit, 2, 38n7, 123n6
British Empire Exhibition: architecture of, 98; connection through, 97–98; food at, 97; power dynamics in, 98
British Nationality Act (1948), 122n2
British Nationality Act (1981), 122n2
Broadmoor Lunatic Asylum, 6, 45; architecture of, 49, 51; hierarchy in, 50–52, 68n22; history of, 48, 69n35; power structure at, 49–50; women at, 60

Bromley, Edward, 146
Brophy, Sarah, 123n14
The Buried Giant (Ishiguro), 38n7, 155n10
Bye Plot, 131

Cameron, David, 126n87
Carroll, Rachel, 114, 123n11
Carter, Angela, 3
Casagranda, Mirko, 126n99
Catholics: as danger, 130, 133; Gunpowder Plot by, 131, 133–34, 143, 145; in Lancashire, 133; Nutter as, 129, 141; persecution of, 141–42; plots by, 131–32; witnesses pressured by, 147
Chamberlain, Neville, 36
Chattox family, 129, 131, 138
Child Care and the Growth of Love (Bowlby), 58
Childs, Peter, 17, 24
Clarke, Peter, 107
Clayton, John A., 131
Colquhoun, Kate, 125
Cooper, Lydia R., 24, 41n57
Craps, Stef: on ambiguity, 84, 94n45; on misconduct, 89
Criminal Lunatics Act (1860), 48
Croft, Pauline: on James VI, 130; on witch trials, 132; on women, 134
Cronin, Frances, 138
curiosity: in *The Remains of the Day*, 3, 6, 34–35, 38; in *Waterland*, 3–4

Daemonologie (James VI and I): Potts referencing, 133; witch trials influenced by, 132; on witnesses, 138–39
The Daylight Gate (Winterson), 1; context of, 129, 134; family dynamics in, 135–36; morality in, 8–9, 129–30; power in, 8, 129. *See also* Catholics; James VI and I; Nutter, Alice; witch trials
Dee, John, 142

Demdike family, 129, 131, 133
Device, Alizon, 133
Device, Elizabeth: neglect by, 134–35; spells by, 136, 144
Device, James, 134–35
Device, Jennet, 129–30; abuse of, 135–36; character of, 136, 148n43; as dispossessed, 134–35; power of, 136–37, 139; testimony by, 137–39
Device, Sarah, 140–41
Dickman, Cyril, 43n88
discrimination: in America, 108; antisemitism, 22–25, 28–29; against Muslims, 4, 10n11
Duboin, Corinne, 98

Elizabeth I (Queen): astrologer for, 142; Catholics tolerated by, 131; impact of, 134; James VI succeeding of, 130
Ellis, Alicia E., 99
empathy: in *The Light of Day*, 7, 90–91, 93n30; Swift on, 7, 151; transgression and, 74

Falco, Magali, 62
Ferguson, Christine, 68n23
Fischer, Susan Alice, 127n103
FitzHerbert, Claudia, 148n43
The Floating World (Ishiguro), 38
food, 8, 96; in America, 108; appropriation of, 98; at Empire Exhibition, 97; etiquette around, 105, 117; fairy cakes, 104, 117; flirtation and, 112; as gift, 118; identity and, 97, 104, 106, 108, 110; ideology permeating, 103; morality and, 110–11; National Loaf, 125n74; as peace offering, 115–16; power dynamics with, 103–4; pride and, 117–18; privilege and, 100–101, 103; racism and, 106; refinement and, 102; segregation and, 108–9; sex and, 112–13; as simile, 111–13; sugar, 102; tea, 98–99, 109–13, 116,

119–20, 122; victory gardens for, 125n74; xenophobia and, 110–11
Food, Consumption and the Body in Contemporary Women's Fiction (Sceats), 97, 103
Ford, Ford Madox, 46–47
Foucault, Michel, 52

gender: inequality in, 55; power and, 6–7, 45, 52–53, 56; roles in, 53–57; time period influencing, 47; visibility in, 56–57. *See also* women
George V (King), 97
The Good Soldier (Ford), 46–47
The Grotesque (McGrath): transgression in, 71n100; unreliable narrator in, 46, 61
guilt, 4
Gunpowder Plot: impact of, 134; against James VI, 131; Lancashire as locus of, 133; Southworth, C., in, 143, 145

Hall, Stuart, 98
Hargreaves, Harry, 135, 141
Head, Dominic, 122n2
Hird, Frank, 137–38
Holmes, Clive, 133
Hopkins, Anthony, 29
Horton, Emily, 41n51, 44n115

imagination: morality and, 3; race and, 96
immigration, 8; to England, 95–96, 122n2; speeches about, 126n87. *See also* refugees
inequality, 2; in gender roles, 55; Ishiguro on, 153–54; of power, 47–48; Winterson on, 153
Ingersoll, Earl G., 18, 20
Ishiguro, Kazuo: *The Buried Giant* by, 38n7, 155n10; on communication, 155n10; on *The Floating World*, 38; on Hitler, 33; on individuals' desire to contribute, 38n1; on inequalities, 153–54; Mason interview with, 5; on social and moral issues, 1–3, 5; on Stevens, 44n114; Swift interview with, 11. *See also The Remains of the Day*

James, Cynthia, 117
James, David, 127n103
James VI and I (King): *Daemonologie* by, 132–33, 138–39; as King of Scotland, 130, 147n2; as meddler, 142; Nutter affected by, 141–42; plots against, 131–33; politics shaped by, 129–30; power of, 130; for Protestantism, 130–31; witch trials and, 132. *See also Daemonologie*
Jeffers, Jennifer, 42n80
Jews: antisemitism against, 22–25, 28–29; as refugees, 26, 42n58; in *The Remains of the Day*, 12, 22–32, 41n50
Johansen, Emily, 114, 126n87

Kushner, Tony, 96

Lancashire witch trials, 8; background of, 129–30, 133; economic factors in, 134; James VI impacting, 132; power in, 134–35; witness testimony at, 137–39. *See also* Device, Jennet
Lang, James, 21
Law, John, 133
Levy, Andrea: on humor, 127n103; on narrative strategy, 96, 99–100; on racism, 116; on readers, 4; on social and moral issues, 1–3; "This is My England" by, 95; on truth and reconciliation, 4–5. *See also Small Island*
Lewis, Mitchell R., 56
The Light of Day (Swift), 1; adultery in, 74–82, 92n23; binary thinking in, 75, 87–89, 91n3; concessions and sacrifices in, 81–82; "corrupt" in, 89, 92n9; empathy in, 7, 90–91, 93n30; justice in, 82, 88; linguistic strategies

in, 74, 84, 92n8, 94n45; madness in, 85; murder in, 82–86; oppositional language in, 73, 75; passive and active language in, 80–81; presumptions in, 76–77; professional misconduct in, 86–89; transgression in, 7, 73–74, 78–79, 86–89; webs in, 90–91; word play in, 83–84
Lima, Maria Helena, 95–96
Long, Robert Emmet, 40n39

Machinal, Hélène, 68n22
Main Plot, 131
marriages: adultery in, 74–82, 92n23; in *Asylum*, 53–55; gender roles in, 53–57; judgment in, 54–55; power and, 52–53, 64
Martin, Mary Patricia, 46
Mason, Gregory, 5
May, Theresa, 123n6
McGrath, Patrick: on character names, 69n35; childhood of, 48; *The Grotesque* by, 46, 61, 71n100; on novels, 151; on social and moral issues, 1–3; *Trauma* by, 61; unreliable narrator used by, 5, 62–63. *See also Asylum*
Mental Health Act (1959), 47–48
Mental Health Act (1983), 47–48
mental illness, 1, 6–7; contradistinction in, 68n23; labeling of, 64; legislation about, 47–48; madness, 64, 69n44, 85; morality in, 48–49, 57
Moncrieff, Joanna, 47–48
morality: in architecture, 49, 52; in *The Daylight Gate*, 8–9, 129–30; disease language about, 89; food and, 110–11; imagination and, 3; Ishiguro on, 1–3, 5; in language, 73; Levy on, 1–3; McGrath on, 1–3; in mental illness, 48–49, 57; of Nutter, 139, 143–44; power and, 5; in *The Remains of the Day*, 15; societal influences on, 50, 61; of Southworth, J., 139; Swift on, 1–3, 5; truth and, 75; Winterson on, 1–3; about women, 53; writing as function of, 73. *See also* transgression
Muslims, 4, 10n11

Nationality and Borders Act (2022), 122n2
noblesse oblige, 17
Nowell, Roger, 129; arrests by, 142–43; Catholics prosecuted by, 131–32; negotiations by, 144; power of, 140; spell against, 136
Nünning, Ansgar, 67n1
Nünning, Vera, 46, 67n1
Nuremberg trials, 24, 41n50
Nutter, Alice, 129–30, 135; character of, 139–40; as dangerous, 142; James VI impacting, 141–42; moral integrity of, 139, 143–44; power of, 140; on religion, 131; as self-sacrificing, 144–45; as unnatural, 141

Parkes, Adam, 40n33, 41n50
Peeper, Tom: as child molester, 135, 141; physical assault by, 140–41; revenge on, 136–37
Pendle Hill witch trials. *See* Lancashire witch trials
Pesso-Miquel, Catherine, 92n9
Phelan, James, 46
Phillips, Mike, 96
Phillips, Trevor, 96
Philpott, Mary Laura, 38n1
"The Pilot's Thumb" (Wilson), 132
Potts, Thomas, 129; *Daemonologie* referenced by, 133; as King's representative, 142–43; Nutter questioned by, 144. *See also The Wonderfull Discoverie of Witches in the Countie of Lancashire*
power: at Broadmoor, 49–50; butler as metaphor in, 23–24; in *The Daylight Gate*, 8, 129; of Device, Jennet, 136–37, 139; of doctors, 48, 52, 63–65; in Empire Exhibition, 98; food and,

103–4; gender and, 6–7, 45, 52–53, 56; hierarchy in, 50–52; of James VI, 130; in Lancashire witch trials, 134–35; marriages and, 52–53, 64; morality and, 5; naturalized inequalities of, 47–48; of Nowell, 140; of Nutter, 140; paternalism in, 6–7, 45, 51, 65; in race and class, 100; in *Small Island*, 100, 104; social responsibilities and, 23–24; women lacking, 52–53, 56, 64–65

Quinn, Anthony, 94n45

racism, 8; in America, 108; in England, 109; food and, 106; housing and, 116; Levy on, 116; segregation and, 109; skin color and, 102–3, 107; in *Small Island*, 106–9, 116; tea and, 110. *See also* discrimination; xenophobia
referendum, EU (2016): Muslims and, 10n11; social disintegration and dispossession in, 2, 9n1, 38n7. *See also* Brexit
refugees: asylum status for, 80–81, 93n30; Jewish, 26, 42n58. *See also* immigration
Reith, John, 107
The Remains of the Day (Ishiguro), 1; adaptability in, 12–13; allegations in, 22; antisemitism in, 22–25, 28–29; Benn in, 12, 27–28, 33, 42n78; Cardinal, D., in, 14; Cardinal, R., in, 3, 6, 18–19, 21, 30, 33–37; class in, 13, 17, 23, 29; Conference in, 12, 13–21; contentment in, 27, 42n58; cosmopolitanism in, 44n115; covert behavior in, 17; cultural context in, 40n39; curiosity in, 3, 6, 34–35, 38; democracy in, 30–31; disparate views in, 16; fair play ethic in, 16–17; fascism in, 22, 24, 26–27; film adaptation of, 5–6, 12, 18–21, 25–32, 35–36; Geoffrey in, 12, 26–27; German voice in, 14–15, 20; idealism in, 15; ideological process in, 33; Jewish housemaid dismissal in, 12, 22–32, 41n50; Kenton in, 23–30, 32–33, 40n46, 42n60; Lewis in, 16–21, 36–37, 40n33; listening in, 15–16; loyalty in, 23–25; memory in, 36–37; moral complexities in, 15; neutral language in, 24–25, 32, 41n57; passive acquiescence in, 34–35, 40n46, 41nn50–51, 43n106; personal responsibility in, 28–29; politics and professionalism in, 27–28; post-Conference meeting in, 12, 33; pre-Conference meeting in, 12, 17–19; professionalism in, 16–17, 32; reinterpretation in, 11–12, 21; skepticism in, 20–21; social responsibility in, 11, 23–24; structural disruption in, 22–23; trap in, 20; universal metaphors in, 12–13; values in, 5–6
The Rhetoric of Fiction (Booth), 46, 62, 67n1
Rowbotham, Sheila, 54
Russell, Richard Rankin, 41n51

Salem witch trials, 138
Samlesbury witch trials, 132, 145–46
Sceats, Sarah, 97, 103, 106
Scull, Andrew, 49–50
Shaffer, Brian W., 44n114
Shaw, Kristian, 2; on Ishiguro, 38n7; on Muslims, 10n11
Showalter, Elaine, 64
Small Island (Levy), 1; accent in, 106–7; active engagement with, 99–100; adaptation in, 114, 118–22; BBC adaptation of, 123n11; class in, 100–103, 105, 118–19; control in, 126n99; created distinctions in, 102; cultural understanding lacking in, 98, 100, 107; Empire Exhibition in, 97, 99; fantasy in, 105–6; hierarchy in, 102–4; household dynamics

in, 103–4; identity in, 7–8, 99, 107; incendiary approach in, 95; judgments in, 104–5, 114; laughter in, 127n103; narrative strategy of, 96; pigmentocracy in, 103; power in, 100, 104; racism in, 106–9, 116; refinement in, 102; support system in, 121; tea in, 98–99, 109–13, 116, 119–20, 122; understanding in, 105, 122; xenophobia in, 110–11, 125n61. *See also* food

social responsibility, 1; power and, 23–24; reading increasing, 4; in *The Remains of the Day*, 11

Southworth, Christopher: on chances, 134; as historical figure, 145; integrity of, 144, 146; trap for, 143

Southworth, Jane, 130; acquittal of, 147; integrity of, 145–46; moral integrity of, 139

Sowerbutts, Grace, 145–46

Spoto, Stephanie, 142

Stackelberg, Roderick, 28

Stam, Robert, 18

Stoker, Bram, 66, 72n117

Straffen, John, 69n35

Stuart, Arabella, 131

Su, John J., 29–30, 42n78

Sutherland, John, 44n110

Swift, Graham: Bernard interview with, 3; on empathy, 7, 151; Ishiguro interview with, 11; on literary strategy, 3; on motives, 152; on novels, 77–78, 90; on social and moral issues, 1–3, 5; on writing, 73. *See also The Light of Day*; *Waterland*

Teverson, Andrew, 32–33

"This is My England" (Levy), 95

Tollance, Pascale, 78–79, 84

transgression: ambiguity in, 79–80, 84–86; in *Asylum*, 45–46, 54–55, 58; as banal, 78, 85; empathy and, 74; in *The Grotesque*, 71n100; interpretations of, 78–79; in *The Light of Day*, 7, 73–74, 78–79, 86–89; purpose of, 71n100

Trauma (McGrath), 61

Tuke, Samuel, 52

12 Bytes (Winterson), 147

unreliable narrator: in *Asylum*, 6–7, 45–47, 60–63, 66–67; credibility in, 61–62; definitions of, 46, 67n1; in *The Good Soldier*, 46–47; in *The Grotesque*, 46, 61, 71n100

Upstone, Sara, 93n30, 96

values: in *Asylum*, 6; in *The Remains of the Day*, 5–6. *See also* morality

Vinkle, Sally A., 28

Wachtel, Eleanor, 2, 9n1

Walkowitz, Rebecca L., 41n57

Wall, Kathleen, 22–23, 25

Waterland (Swift): curiosity in, 3–4; truth in, 91n6

Weldon, Fay, 10n5, 139

Wheelright, Julie, 53

Widdowson, Peter, 77, 93n32

Wilson, Richard, 132

Winnicott, Donald, 58

Winterson, Jeanette, 87; on art, 9; on binary thinking, 91n3; on EU referendum, 9n1; on false choices, 7; on inequality, 153; on power, 5; on social and moral issues, 1–3; on societal disintegration, 2; *12 Bytes* by, 147; on unity, 154; Wachtel interview with, 2, 9n1. *See also The Daylight Gate*

Witchcraft Act (1604), 132

witch trials: child witnesses in, 137–38; economic concerns and, 134; figures in, 129–30; James VI and, 132; laws impacting, 132; religion and, 131; Salem, 138; Samlesbury, 132, 145–46. *See also* Lancashire witch trials

women: behavioral expectations for, 64, 71n103; at Broadmoor Lunatic

Asylum, 60; fear of, 134; judgment of, 54–55, 57, 59–60, 66; madness of, 64, 69n44, 85; morality about, 53; as mother, 56, 58–60, 66, 70n77; as objects, 64–65; power lacking for, 52–53, 56, 64–65; purification of, 66–67, 72n117; roles of, 53–56; visibility of, 55–57, 59. *See also* witch trials

The Wonderfull Discoverie of Witches in the Countie of Lancashire (Potts): as definitive, 132; on Device, Jennet, 137–38; reliability of, 133; Samlesbury witch trial in, 145–46

Wong, Cynthia, 15, 38

Woolf, Virginia, 95

Woolley, Agnes, 92n23, 93n30

xenophobia, 110–11, 125n61

York Retreat, 52

Zerweck, Bruno, 67n1

Zlosnik, Sue, 54

About the Author

Mara E. Reisman is a professor of British literature and women's literature at Northern Arizona University. She is the author of *Fay Weldon, Feminism, and British Culture: Challenging Cultural and Literary Conventions* (2018).

www.ingramcontent.com/pod-product-compliance
Lightning Source LLC
Chambersburg PA
CBHW061448300426
44114CB00014B/1895